MW01705453

Volume I

SOCIAL PSYCHOLOGY

Shelley E. Taylor, University of California, Los Angeles

Letitia Anne Peplau, University of California, Los Angeles

David O. Sears, University of California, Los Angeles

Custom Edition for Stratford Career Institute

Taken From:
Social Psychology, Eleventh Edition
By Shelley E. Taylor, Letitia Anne Peplau, David O. Sears

PEARSON Custom Publishing

PEARSON Prentice Hall

Cover Art: *Color Conscience III*, by Christina Lanzl.

Taken from:

Social Psychology, Eleventh Edition
by Shelley E. Taylor, Letitia Anne Peplau, and David O. Sears

Published by Prentice-Hall, Inc.
Upper Saddle River, New Jersey 07458

This special edition published in cooperation with Pearson Custom Publishing.

Printed in the United States of America

10 9 8 7 6 5 4 3 2 1

Please visit our web site at www.pearsoncustom.com

ISBN 0-536-72977-8

BA 997087

LF

PEARSON CUSTOM PUBLISHING
75 Arlington Street, Suite 300, Boston, MA 02116
A Pearson Education Company

BRIEF CONTENTS

CONTENTS

Social Psychology

VOLUME 1

In the News

Cell Phone Etiquette

Modern technology can be a blessing and a curse. The invention of the cell phone has unquestionably made it easier to keep in touch with family and to conduct business. A tourist riding a bus in New York City can now use her long-distance cell phone to tell her husband in Nigeria about her sight-seeing adventures. During the armed robbery of a store, a clerk hiding in a back room can use his cell phone to call the police. But the ringing of cell phones has also become a public nuisance, interrupting college lectures, distracting moviegoers, and even intruding into the most solemn occasions.

Mourners at a recent funeral service were shocked by a particularly egregious breach of cell phone etiquette. No sooner had the rabbi begun to chant the traditional prayer to begin the service when a cell phone sounded. One of the men carrying the body used his free hand to reach into his pocket, take out his cell phone, and begin a conversation. A stunned mourner later remembered, "I was astonished. I gave him a hard glance that said, 'If you don't get off the phone, I'm digging a . . . grave to bury you in.' He terminated the call" (Lobdell, 2001, p. B1). At a happier occasion, a recent bride and groom found their wedding interrupted not once but three times by the ringing of a phone belonging to the priest officiating at the ceremony. "I felt so bad," explained the bride. "It was quite a culture clash—the ancient rites of marriage and someone fumbling with a cell phone" (Lobdell, 2001, p. B8).

Those who suffer at the hands of thoughtless cell phone owners are now trying to create new rules for cell phone etiquette. Some professors have added a warning about cell phone use during class to their course syllabi. At theaters and concerts, there are public reminders to turn off cell phones and pagers. Signs at churches and synagogues remind the faithful about the obligation to turn off phones. A major wireless phone company, Sprint PCS, recently hired the founder of the Protocol School in Palm Beach, Florida to help create basic rules for cell phone courtesy. One suggestion: When you must carry a phone, set it to vibrate rather than ring, and sit near an exit.

For social psychologists, efforts to develop rules of etiquette for the use of cell phones illustrate a very basic aspect of social life: how groups and communities strive to influence the behavior of their members by creating rules for acceptable conduct.

CHAPTER 1

THEORIES AND METHODS IN SOCIAL PSYCHOLOGY

Focus of This Chapter

- The Social Psychological Approach
- Historical Roots of Social Psychology
- Theories in Social Psychology
- Research Methods in Social Psychology
- Research Ethics
- Cultural Highlight: America's Diverse Population
- Research Closeup: Meta-Analysis in Social Psychology

Social psychologists use scientific methods to study how we perceive people and social events, how we influence others, and the nature of human relationships. In reading this book, you will learn that some social psychologists study perceptions and attitudes: how people view themselves and each other, how they interpret people's behavior, and how their attitudes form and change. Other social psychologists focus on interactions among people, including friendship and altruism, prejudice and aggression, and conformity and power. Social psychologists also study how people act in groups and how groups affect their members. We can define **social psychology** as the scientific study of how people think about, influence, and relate to others. Social psychological principles help us understand a variety of important issues, including ways to promote healthier lifestyles, the influence of the media on public attitudes, and strategies for resolving international conflict.

The Social Psychological Approach

Of course, many scholarly fields study social behavior. What is unique about social psychology is its approach. The social psychological approach differs from disciplines that study large-scale societal processes and from those that focus on the individual. Let's compare these three approaches or levels of analysis using the specific example of violent crime in big cities.

The societal level of analysis is used by sociologists, economists, political scientists, and other social scientists. These scholars attempt to understand general patterns of social behavior, such as homicide rates, voting behavior, or consumer spending. According to this viewpoint, social behavior can be explained by such forces as economic hard times, class conflicts, clashes between competing ethnic groups, regional crop failures, governmental policies, or technological change. The goal of societal analysis is to identify links between broad social forces and general patterns of social behavior. To study violence in urban areas, social scientists might identify relationships between rates of violent crime and such factors as poverty, immigration, or the industrialization of a society.

The individual level of analysis is typically used by clinical and personality psychologists, who explain behavior in terms of a person's unique life history and psychological characteristics. According to this viewpoint, personality traits and motives can explain why individuals behave as they do, and why two people may react quite differently to the same situation. Emphasis is given to individual differences in childhood experiences, in ability and motivation, and in personality or psychological adjustment. The individual approach explains violent crime in terms of the unique histories and characteristics of the criminal. For example, of all the bank tellers in Chicago, why does one individual go berserk and shoot five of his coworkers? To understand such behavior, the psychologist using the individual approach would consider the personality and background of the person: Was the bank teller depressed or suffering from paranoid delusions or using drugs? What kind of life had the bank teller led? For example, was he physically abused as a child?

Social psychologists adopt a different level of analysis: the interpersonal level. Social psychologists typically focus on a person's current social situation. That social situation includes the other people in the environment, their attitudes and behaviors, and their relationship to the individual. To understand violent crime, social psychologists might consider what kinds of interpersonal situations create feelings of anger that may increase violent behavior. One social psychological explanation is that frustrating situations make people angry and increase their tendency to act aggressively. This explanation is called the **frustration-aggression hypothesis.** It predicts that when people are blocked from achieving a desired goal, they feel frustrated and angry and are more likely to lash out. This effect of frustration is one explanation for violent crime.

The frustration-aggression hypothesis can also explain how large-scale economic and societal factors create situations that lead to violence and crime. For instance, people who are poor and crowded into urban slums are frustrated: They cannot get good jobs, find affordable housing, provide a safe environment for their children, and so on. This frustration may produce anger, which can be the direct cause of violent crime. The frustration-aggression hypothesis focuses on the immediate social situation, the feel-

These demonstrators hold strong and opposite views about whether or not abortion should be legal. What individual, interpersonal, or societal factors might explain which viewpoint a person supports?

ings and thoughts such situations produce in people of many different backgrounds, and the effects of those subjective reactions on behavior.

Each of these three approaches (societal, individual, and interpersonal) is worthwhile and indeed essential if we are to understand complex social behavior fully. A single question—What causes violent crime?—can be answered in many different ways. This book introduces you to the social psychological perspective on human behavior.

Historical Roots of Social Psychology

In the early 1900s, three major theoretical perspectives were developed by pioneering psychologists, each of which has left a mark on contemporary social psychology.

Sigmund Freud, the founder of **psychoanalytic theory,** was fascinated by the rich mental life of the human animal. Freud proposed that behavior is motivated from within by powerful internal drives and impulses, such as sexuality and aggression. He also believed that adult behavior is shaped by unresolved psychological conflicts that can be traced to childhood experiences in the family. Psychoanalytic theorists seek to understand the inner forces, both conscious and unconscious, that energize and direct behavior.

A second major theory, **behaviorism,** offered a very different perspective on human experience. As developed by Ivan Pavlov, John B. Watson, B. F. Skinner, and others, behaviorism focused on the observable behavior of humans and other animals. Behaviorists were not interested in subjective thoughts and feelings; they preferred to study what they could observe and measure directly, that is, overt behavior. Behaviorists examined ways in which the environment shapes the behavior of animals, and they proposed that current behavior is the result of past learning. Behaviorists identified a series of principles to explain the specific processes through which this all-important learning occurs. Although much of their research was conducted with rats and pigeons, behaviorists believed that the same principles applied to humans.

The perspective of **Gestalt psychology** was developed by Wolfgang Kohler, Kurt Koffka, Kurt Lewin, and other European psychologists who immigrated to the United States in the 1930s. Their focus was on the way individuals perceive and understand objects, events, and people. In their view, people perceive situations or events not as made up of many discrete elements but rather as "dynamic wholes." Think about your best friend. When you last saw her, did you perceive her as a collection of arms, legs, fingers, and other features? Probably not. More likely, you perceived her as a total unit that integrates the relationships among her various body parts into the familiar "whole" or person you know and like. This emphasis on perceiving the environment as a whole that is more than the sum of its parts is known as "Gestalt psychology," from the German word for "shape" or "form."

Each of these three important theories arose from the work of a few charismatic individuals who inspired fierce loyalty to their ideas and, often, an equally fierce rejection of other viewpoints. These pioneers modeled their theories on those of the physical sciences. Their goal was to explain and predict all human behavior, and they wanted theories as detailed, universal, and complete as, for example, atomic theory in physics. Many of these theories were applied to the analysis of social behavior. The idea of developing general theories is important, but in the long run, the problems that are studied by social psychologists have proved to be too complex to be explained by any one general theory.

Even so, social psychological approaches to a wide variety of different problems have been guided by a few basic ideas that are easily traced back to the general theories of the past. In contemporary social psychology, the legacy of psychoanalytic theory can be seen most clearly in the analysis of motivation and emotion in social life. Social psychologists recognize that behavior is influenced by personal motives and by the emotional reactions individuals have to situations and other people. The legacy of behaviorism is our continuing concern with how learning shapes social behavior. Social psychologists are interested, for example, in how we learn to be helpful or to obey authority or to espouse conservative political views. Finally, the legacy of Gestalt psychology is found in the current emphasis on social cognition, the study of how we perceive and understand our social world. Basic Gestalt principles have been greatly expanded in recent years, as discussed in Chapter 2, Volume 1.

Theories in Social Psychology

In the following sections, we introduce some of the major contemporary theories in social psychology. These sections are not intended to be comprehensive or detailed. Rather, we want to convey the essence and particularly the contrasts among these theories, so that we can refer to them in later chapters. To permit a clear comparison of the theories, we will apply each approach to the specific problem of understanding violent crime.

Consider this situation: At 3 A.M. one morning, a police officer sees a high school dropout, Larry, coming out of the rear door of a liquor store with a bag full of money. The store, like everything else in the neighborhood, has long been closed for the night. The officer yells at Larry to stop and put his hands up. Larry turns, pulls a pistol from his pocket, and shoots the officer, wounding him in the leg. Larry is later apprehended and ultimately sent to jail. The statistics predict that Larry's stay in jail will not be productive or happy; it will be costly for society, and the chances of his committing further crimes are fairly high. We will refer to Larry as we describe major contemporary theories in social psychology.

Motivational Theories

One general approach focuses on the individual's own needs or motives. Both everyday experience and social psychological research provide many examples of the ways in which our needs influence our perceptions, attitudes, and behavior. For example, to enhance our self-esteem and satisfy a need to feel good about ourselves, we may blame others for our failures and take personal credit only for successes.

The Freudian, or psychoanalytic, view of human motivation emphasizes the importance of a few powerful inborn impulses or drives, especially those that are associated with sexuality and aggression. In contrast, social psychologists consider a much more diverse range of human needs and desires. Social psychologists also emphasize ways in which specific situations and social relationships can create and arouse needs and motives. For example, the experience of moving away from home to go to college often creates feelings of loneliness among young adults. Geographical moves disrupt established social networks and sources of companionship, and they arouse unmet needs for intimacy and a sense of "belonging." The desire to create a group of friends at college may lead new students to join clubs, go to social events, and talk to strangers in the cafeteria. Unmet needs for companionship can also lead some students to seek distractions from this discomfort by throwing themselves into their studies or by abusing alcohol or drugs. The core idea is that situations can create or arouse needs, which, in turn, lead people to engage in behaviors to reduce those needs.

To understand Larry's behavior in robbing the liquor store, a social psychologist who was using a motivational approach would try to uncover Larry's psychological needs. Was he motivated by a need for money, perhaps to buy food or to support a drug habit? Or was the robbery a way to gain status in Larry's peer group? Did Larry shoot the police officer out of fear or anger? A social psychological analysis might go further, to try to identify in detail ways in which Larry's social environment fostered the particular needs and motives that led to the robbery and shooting. Social psychologists would also want to study other young men who have committed armed robberies, in order to try to arrive at generalizations about the links between motivation and criminal behavior.

Learning Theories

The central idea in learning theory is that a person's current behavior is determined by prior experience. In any given situation, a person learns certain behaviors that, over time, may become habits. When presented with the same situation, the person tends to behave in the same habitual way. For example, when a traffic light turns red, we typically stop, because that is how we have learned to respond in the past. As applied to social behavior by Albert Bandura (1977) and others, this approach has been called **social learning theory.**

There are three general mechanisms by which learning occurs. One is **association,** or classical conditioning. Pavlov's dogs learned to salivate at the sound of a bell because they were presented with food every time the bell was rung. After a while, they would salivate to the sound of the bell even in the absence of the meat because they associated the bell with meat. Humans sometimes learn emotions by association. After a particularly painful visit to the dentist, the mere mention of the word "dentist" or the sound of any kind of drill may arouse anxiety.

A second learning mechanism is **reinforcement,** a principle studied by B. F. Skinner and others. People learn to perform a particular behavior because it is followed by something that is pleasurable or that satisfies a need (or they learn to avoid behavior that is followed by unpleasant consequences). A child may learn to help other people because her parents praise her for sharing her toys and smile approvingly when she offers to help with chores. Or a high school student may learn not to contradict his math teacher in class because each time he does, the teacher frowns, looks angry, and snaps at him.

A third learning mechanism is **observational learning.** People often learn social attitudes and behaviors simply by watching other people, known technically as "models." Children learn regional and ethnic speech patterns by listening to the speakers around them. Adolescents may acquire their political attitudes by listening to their parents' conversations during election campaigns. In observational learning, other people are an important source of information. Observational learning can occur without any

One of the most powerful mechanisms of learning is imitation. Like this boy, children often imitate a parent or other adults they admire and respect.

external reinforcement. However, whether or not people actually perform a behavior that is learned through observation is influenced by the consequences the action has for them. For example, a little boy may learn a lot about baby dolls from watching his sisters but may be discouraged from playing with them himself because his traditional parents say, "Dolls aren't for boys." **Imitation,** or **modeling,** occurs when a person not only observes but actually copies the behavior of a model.

The learning approach seeks the causes of behavior in the past learning history of the individual. To return to the example of Larry shooting the police officer, we might find that in his previous encounters with the police, they had been rough, rude, antagonistic, suspicious, and unsympathetic. Perhaps Larry had been reinforced in the past for responding violently to situations involving conflict with authority. Or perhaps his father often acted in violent ways so that Larry learned to imitate a violent model. The learning theorist is especially concerned with past experience and somewhat less with the details of the current situation.

Cognitive Theories

The cognitive approach emphasizes that a person's behavior depends on the way he or she perceives the social situation. Kurt Lewin applied Gestalt ideas to social psychology, emphasizing the importance of the social environment as perceived by the individual—what Lewin called the person's "psychological field." In Lewin's view, behavior is affected both by the individual's characteristics (such as ability, personality, and genetic dispositions) and by the social environment as he or she perceives it.

A core idea in the cognitive perspective is that people tend spontaneously to *group* and *categorize* objects. In a library, you see a row of books on a shelf as a unit, not as so many individual books. You probably perceive other people in the library in groups, perhaps as students and librarians, or as the line of people at the checkout desk, or as a couple in love. At home, you experience the pile of dirty dishes in the kitchen sink as an oppressive heap, not as individual dishes. We tend to group objects according to simple principles, such as similarity (dishes look more like each other than like the stove and refrigerator, so we group the dishes together), proximity (books stacked in a pile go together; the isolated books strewn all over the library table do not), or past experience (Santa Claus and Christmas trees go together, and so do doctors and stethoscopes, but Santa Claus and stethoscopes do not).

Second, people readily perceive some things as standing out ("figure") and some things as simply being in the background ("ground"). Typically colorful, moving, noisy, unique, nearby stimuli stand out as figure, whereas bland, drab, stationary, quiet, common, faraway stimuli constitute the background. For example, our attention is drawn to cheerleaders at a football game not because they are so numerous—there may be only a dozen in a crowd of nearly 100,000 people—but because cheerleaders move a lot, yell, wave their arms, and wear colorful uniforms.

These two principles—that we spontaneously group or categorize the things we perceive and that we focus attention on the most prominent (figural) stimuli—are central to our perception of physical objects and of the social world. As social thinkers, we try to arrive at meaningful interpretations of how people feel, what they want, what kinds of people they are, and so forth. In recent years, the cognitive perspective in social psychology has been stimulated by new developments in cognitive psychology, that is, the study of how people process information. As applied to social psychology, research on social cognition focuses on how we put together information about people, social situations, and groups to make inferences about them (Fiske & Taylor, 1991). Social cognition researchers examine the flow of information from the environment to the person.

Cognitive approaches differ from learning approaches in two major ways. First, cognitive approaches focus on current perceptions rather than on past learning. Second, they emphasize the importance of the individual's perception or interpretation of a situation, not the objective "reality" of the situation as it might be viewed by a neutral observer. To return to Larry's run-in with the law, cognitive approaches would emphasize the importance of the way Larry interpreted his situation. How did Larry perceive his actions in taking the money? When the police officer shouted at Larry to stop, how did Larry interpret the event? He probably perceived the officer as someone whose job it is to arrest people and who is likely to be prejudiced against people like him. He may have seen the officer as threatening, biased, or perhaps even cruel. Ultimately, it was Larry's interpretation of the situation that led him to shoot the police officer.

Decision-Making Theories

Decision-making theories assume that individuals evaluate the costs and benefits of various actions and pick the best alternatives in a fairly logical, reasoned way. They choose the alternative that gives them the greatest rewards at the least cost. Decision making involves weighing the pros (benefits) and cons (costs) of possible alternatives and then adopting the best one. The relative strengths of the pros and cons determine the final decision. To return to Larry's situation, let's suppose that he has the choices of fleeing, surrendering, or shooting. He thinks that if he flees, he may be shot, which adds up to a considerable cost. If he surrenders, he will go to jail, another major cost. However, he may think that by shooting the police officer, he can get away—and with the money, too.

Expectancy-value theory extends the notion of costs and benefits by adding an assessment of the likelihood that each alternative will happen (Edwards, 1954). This theory holds that decisions are based on the combination of two factors: (1) the value of each possible outcome or alternative and (2) the probability, or "expectancy," that each outcome will actually result from the decision. Larry may try to flee even though he might get shot and killed, a major cost indeed. But he may estimate that the officer is not very likely to hit him with a bullet in the dark and in a backyard with many obstacles. So the probability of being shot is low. Going to jail is not as bad as being shot, but surrendering means he is almost certain to go to jail. The probability that surrender will lead to prison is very high.

Sometimes the decisions we make actually do follow fairly well the rational procedures suggested by decision-making theories. For example, in deciding which of two colleges to attend, a student might list the pros and cons associated with each, assess the importance of each factor listed, and come up with some kind of score that indicates which college is better. However, social psychologists also recognize that in real life, judgments and decisions do not always follow strict rationality. As discussed in Chapter 2, Volume 1, people often use shortcuts that enable them to make decisions, form judgments, or solve problems quickly and efficiently, but not always thoroughly and according to strictly rational standards. In addition, many judgments and decisions are swayed by motivational factors, such as emotional reactions or personal goals. The high school senior trying to decide between two colleges may come up with a formal "decision" based on the pros and cons of each school, but if the answer doesn't "feel right," that is, doesn't fit with his or her emotional leanings, the senior may ignore the score sheet in favor of emotional preferences. In short, rational decision-making models do not always apply to everyday decision making and problem solving. There are important limits on the degree to which people actually use rational principles in their daily lives.

Interdependence Theories

Interdependence theories shift the focus of analysis from the behavior of one individual to the behavior of two or more individuals who interact with each other. When people interact, they influence each other. For example, as a father helps his young son get dressed, he might show him how to button his shirt and be rewarded for his efforts by an appreciative hug. When two people have mutual influence on each other's thoughts, feelings, or behaviors, they are interdependent. In technical terms, **interdependence** means that the outcomes one person receives depend at least in part on the behavior of the other and vice versa. As any parent knows, children do not always appreciate attempts to help them get dressed. So, instead of hugging his father, the young boy in our example might have protested angrily that he could do it himself and run out of the room. The outcome of this parent-child interaction—whether or not father and son are in a pleasant mood and how quickly the boy gets dressed—depends on the actions of both partners.

A prominent example of an interdependence approach is **social exchange theory.** The principles of social exchange build on the work of both learning theorists and decision-making theorists. Social exchange theory analyzes the interaction between people in terms of the benefits and costs the individuals exchange with each other. Sometimes people make explicit exchanges. For example, you may agree to help your roommate learn Spanish in return for help with your advanced calculus course. Or in the heat of an argument, you and a friend may trade insults. But even when we are not aware of it, the process of interaction creates benefits (information, smiles of approval, money, feelings of being loved, etc.) and costs (boredom, disapproval, feelings of being misunderstood, etc.) for the people involved.

Social exchange theory analyzes interpersonal interaction on the basis of the costs and benefits to each person of the possible ways he or she can interact. For example, the interactions between Larry and the police officer might turn hostile because of their conflicting interests. Larry would benefit from escaping, while the police officer would benefit from arresting him. In contrast, an exchange theory analysis of the interaction between a nurse and a patient might focus on the benefits to the patient from cooperating with the nurse (the patient gets the right care and is helped toward recovery) and the benefits to the nurse of being friendly (the patient cooperates and the nurse gets a reputation for doing a good job). In this case, the interests of both parties converge on sharing a cooperative and friendly interaction. Social exchange theory is particularly useful for analyzing bargaining situations in which two parties must come to an agreement despite their separate interests. It has also been elaborated by Harold Kelley and others to apply to personal relationships among friends and family. Social exchange theory is discussed in detail in Chapter 4, Volume 2.

Sociocultural Theories

In recent years, social psychologists have paid increasing attention to how people's diverse social backgrounds influence their thoughts, feelings, and behavior (Fiske, Kitayama, Markus, & Nisbett, 1998). Consider the pace of life. In some cultures, punctuality is important and the general speed of life is relatively fast. In other cultures, people have more casual attitudes about time and a slower pace of daily life. Robert Levine has studied these cultural differences in the pace of life. In one study, Levine (1988) asked college students in the United States and Brazil when they would consider a friend late for a lunch appointment. Americans said a friend would be late after 19 minutes, but Brazilians gave the friend nearly twice as long, not considering a friend late until 34 minutes after the time of the appointment.

Edward Hall (1959) described unspoken cultural rules about the use of time as a "silent language" that we learn through experience in a culture. Lack of familiarity with cultural differences in time can create problems when people travel to other countries. For example, American Peace Corps volunteers reported having more trouble getting used to the relatively slow pace of life and lack of punctuality in other countries than they did in adjusting to unfamiliar foods or different standards of living (Spradley & Phillips, 1972).

In seeking to understand differences such as these, psychologists have come to recognize the importance of **culture**—the shared beliefs, values, traditions, and behavior patterns of particular groups. These groups can be nations, ethnic groups, religious communities, or even teenage gangs and college fraternities. Culture is taught by one generation to the next through a process known as **socialization.** Children, for instance, may learn about their culture not only from parents and friends, but also from storybooks and television programs. New fraternity and sorority members are expected to learn the traditions, songs, and secrets of their group from its senior members.

Social norms—rules and expectations about how group members should behave—are a building block of culture. Social rules govern a surprisingly broad range of behaviors, from how close we stand when talking with a friend to what we wear (or don't wear) at the beach. Some norms apply to everyone in a social group, regardless of his or her position or status. On a school campus, everyone is expected to obey traffic signs and to put litter in wastebaskets. But frequently the norms that apply depend on the individual's position, for instance, whether the person is a professor or a student. Professors are supposed to come to class on time, prepare lectures and lead class discussions, write and grade tests, serve on college committees, and so on. Different norms apply to students, who are expected to take notes in class, study for tests, write term papers, pay tuition, and so on.

The term **social role** refers to the set of norms that apply to people in a particular position, such as teachers or students. One perspective on social roles uses imagery borrowed from the theater. The individual acting in society is like an actor in a play. In the theater, the script sets the stage, defines the role that each actor will play, and dictates what actors say and do. Similarly, cultures present us with many preestablished social rules of behavior. For example, when children enter school, they learn many rules of classroom behavior, such as sitting quietly in their seats or raising a hand to speak. In marriage, traditional roles prescribe that the husband should be the breadwinner and the wife should be in charge of childcare and housekeeping.

The sociocultural perspective is useful in understanding behavior within a particular social or cultural context. To return to the example of Larry robbing a liquor store and shooting a police officer, we might find that Larry belongs to a teenage gang. Perhaps this group condones stealing money and accords higher status to gang members who carry a gun. His gang may have a shared history of violent encounters with the police, which led Larry to be suspicious and quick to fire his weapon. An analysis of the beliefs, traditions, norms, and other aspects of "gang culture" might help explain Larry's actions.

The sociocultural perspective also emphasizes comparisons of different cultures or social groups. Unless we attend specifically to cultural influences, we are likely to overlook their importance. We tend to assume that the behaviors of our own culture are "standard" or typical. One benefit of foreign travel is that it causes us to take a fresh look at aspects of our own behavior that we take for granted, such as our beliefs about punctuality and the use of time. Similarly, social psychologists are conducting cross-cultural studies as a way to learn how social behavior is affected by differences in cultural values, norms, and roles.

Larry's behavior reflects in part the larger U.S. culture in which he lives. As described in Chapter 2, Volume 3, the United States is one of the most violent societies on earth. American children watch countless acts of murder and mayhem on television and often engage in fierce competition at school and in sports. Further, life in many urban areas provides easy access to handguns and other weapons that can turn the expression of anger into a deadly act of violence. Larry's attitudes were shaped in part by exposure to cultural messages about violence, and his act of shooting the police officer was made possible by situational opportunities to obtain a gun and ammunition.

One goal of cross-cultural research on social behavior is to identify important ways in which cultures differ from each other. A particularly useful distinction contrasts cultures that emphasize **individualism** and those that emphasize **collectivism** (Triandis, 1995). The cultural values of U.S. and European societies emphasize the importance of personal independence and individualism. Western literature, from the *Iliad* to *The Adventures of Huckleberry Finn,* tells of self-reliant heroes who leave home to seek self-fulfillment (Triandis, 1990). In an individualist culture, a person's behavior is guided

Culture affects all facets of life from our favorite foods to our beliefs about masculinity and femininity. These traditional Moroccan women wear very conservative clothes in public to protect their bodies from view.

largely by individual goals rather than by the goals of collectives such as the family, the work group, or the tribe. If a conflict arises between an individual's personal goals and group goals, it is acceptable to put self-interests first. Further, a person's sense of self is based largely on individual attributes and accomplishments rather than on membership in social groups.

In contrast, collectivist cultures emphasize loyalty to the family, adherence to group norms, and the preservation of harmony in social relations with members of one's own group. The cultural values of many African, Asian, and Latin American societies emphasize collectivism. This can be seen in Asian literature, which often celebrates a hero who performs his duty to his family or to the emperor, sometimes in the face of strong temptations to pursue more pleasurable pastimes. In a collectivist culture, group goals are expected to take priority over individual preferences, and the self is defined largely in terms of group membership. Collectivist cultures value a person who can fit in comfortably with the group. Thus, a Japanese folk saying warns, "The nail that stands out gets pounded down" (cited by Markus & Kitayama, 1991, p. 224). Individualist cultures applaud individuals who stand out from others; Americans note that "the squeaky wheel gets the grease."

Sometimes what appears to be the same concept has different meanings in individualist and collectivist cultures (Triandis, Bontempo, Villareal, Asai, & Lucca, 1988). In the United States, "self-reliance" typically implies freedom to do what one wants, freedom from the constraints of the group. In a collectivist culture, "self-reliance" is more likely to mean not being a burden on others, not making excessive demands on one's family or friends.

In large and complex societies such as the United States or Canada, individuals are often exposed to more than one cultural group. In the United States, collectivist tendencies are strongest in the Deep South; individualist tendencies are strongest in the Mountain West and Great Plains (Vandello & Cohen, 1999). Further, Hispanic Americans tend to be more collectivist than non-Hispanics (Marin & Triandis, 1985). However, the longer that Hispanic Americans are exposed to Anglo-American culture, the more individualist they tend to become. Collectivism also tends to be strong among Asian Americans (Triandis, 1990). Sometimes individuals who live in two cultural worlds have concerns about which cultural patterns to follow. One tenth-grade

Chinese-born girl who immigrated to the United States at age 12 described her feelings as follows:

> I don't know who I am. Am I the good Chinese daughter? Am I an American teenager? I always feel I am letting my parents down when I am with my friends because I act so American, but I also feel that I will never really be an American. I never feel really comfortable with myself anymore. (Cited in Olsen, 1988, p. 30)

The topic of identification with ethnic groups is explored further in Chapter 4, Volume 1.

Sociocultural approaches provide a useful perspective on social behavior, both within our own culture and across cultures. Throughout this book, we present research that seeks to understand cultural and ethnic diversity. In addition to materials in the text, several chapters have a special feature called "Cultural Highlight" that illustrates an important aspect of human diversity.

Evolutionary Social Psychology

The emerging field of **evolutionary social psychology** applies the principles of evolution and natural selection to the understanding of human behavior and social life (Buss & Kenrick, 1998). Evolutionary social psychology draws on ideas that were initially advanced by Charles Darwin and later elaborated by biologists to explain social behavior in insects, birds, and other animals. Whereas cultural approaches emphasize the amazing diversity of human behavior around the globe, evolutionary approaches emphasize the shared human qualities that are part of our heritage as a species.

In the distant past, some behavioral tendencies, such as the avoidance of snakes or a liking for foods rich in protein and sugar, increased the chances of survival among our ancestors. Individuals who showed these tendencies had more children who survived to reproduce, and so these patterns gradually became part of our human genetic inheritance. According to evolutionary social psychologists, similar evolutionary principles explain the origins of many social behaviors as well, including the tendency for infants to form strong emotional bonds with their parents, our preferences for particular mates, and our willingness to help others in need. In other words, many of the behavioral tendencies that we see in humans today are the end products of the history of natural selection in our species.

Several ideas are central to evolutionary social psychology (Buss, 1996).

1. Many human tendencies and preferences are the result of natural selection. These are known as **evolved psychological mechanisms.** They can be seen as adaptive responses to specific problems that were encountered by our ancestors. Thus, a fear of snakes may have solved the problem of avoiding a dangerous hazard in the environment.

2. All human behavior reflects the joint influence of internal psychological dispositions (including evolved psychological mechanisms) and external situational demands. People are biological organisms that act in specific social contexts; both biological and social influences on behavior are important.

3. Some of the most important problems faced by our ancestors were social in nature. Humans are born and spend their lives in social groups. Consequently, many evolved psychological mechanisms have to do with relating to other people. These include a fear of ostracism by the group, an ability to cooperate with others, and a willingness to invest resources in one's children.

What might an evolutionary perspective say about the case of Larry, who shot a police officer during the robbery of a liquor store? Evolutionary social psychologists would emphasize that aggression is a common human response to threat and presumably is a pattern that was adaptive thousands of years ago. They might further note that around the globe, violence is more common among men than among women, so it is not surprising that our young criminal is male. Evolutionary theorists might add that although there is a universal tendency to respond to a threat with aggression, the threshold or degree of threat required to trigger this response appears to vary depending on personal experience and cultural values.

The evolutionary theory of natural selection is very general in scope, comparable in some ways to the all-encompassing theories of psychoanalysis, behaviorism, and Gestalt theory. Within social psychology, researchers typically study more focused theories that are derived from this general evolutionary perspective. For instance, the theory of reciprocal altruism makes predictions about our greater willingness to help relatives than strangers in need. The theory of sexual selection predicts that men and women will prefer different qualities in prospective mates. We will discuss these and other ideas from evolutionary social psychology in later chapters of this book.

Social Psychological Theories Today

Modern social psychologists often find that they cannot fully understand the topics they study by using any single general theory, such as social learning theory. Rather, it proves useful to combine and integrate ideas from different theoretical traditions. Instead of focusing primarily on overt behavior, thinking, or emotions, newer theorists seek to understand the interrelationships among behavior, thoughts, and feelings. For example, social learning theorists have come to appreciate the importance of subjective expectations in an understanding of human behavior. As you read about research on specific topics in social psychology, such as aggression or conformity, consider how current social psychological analyses try to encompass all facets of human experience, including behavior, cognition, and motivation.

Another trend is for social psychologists to develop theories that can account for a certain limited range of phenomena, such as helping a stranger in distress, forming a positive impression of another person, or conforming to peer pressure. These are called **middle-range theories** because they focus on a specific aspect of social behavior and do not try to encompass all of social life. The frustration-aggression hypothesis is one illustration of a middle-range theory. In this book, you will be introduced to many of these more focused theories. As you will see, these specific theories and models continue to reflect the influence of basic theoretical traditions.

Research Methods in Social Psychology

An exciting feature of social psychology is that it explores topics relevant to our everyday experiences. Social psychologists study love and altruism as well as conflict and prejudice. Personal experience often leads psychologists to study particular topics and to generate initial hypotheses about social life. For example, social psychological research on prejudice was sparked by intense concerns about discrimination against African Americans, Jews, and other ethnic minorities in the United States. However, although social psychological research often begins with personal experiences and social concerns, it does not stop at armchair speculation. A hallmark of social psychology is its commitment to scientific methodology.

Social psychology is an empirical science. This means that social psychologists use systematic methods to gather information about social life and to test the usefulness of theories. Sometimes research confirms our commonsense views about social life, and sometimes it does not. Consider these statements and decide if each one is true or false.

- In choosing friends and lovers, a fundamental principle is that opposites attract.
- When people are anxious, they prefer to be with other people.

- TV ads that try to frighten people usually backfire and are less effective than ads that do not arouse fear.
- If you pay a man to give a speech that goes against his own beliefs, he will usually change his mind to agree with the speech. The more money you pay him, the greater will be the change in his personal attitudes.

When it comes to friends and lovers, research supports the old adage that "birds of a feather flock together." Similarity is a key ingredient in friendship and marriage.

You may not agree with all these statements, but it is fair to say that they all sound plausible. Yet research presented in later chapters in this book shows that all of these statements are oversimplifications and several are false.

Why do our informal observations of social life sometimes lead us to wrong conclusions? Often, our own experiences are simply not representative of those of most people or those that occur in most social situations. Sometimes we are biased and misinterpret what happens; we see things as we want them to be, not as they really are. Sometimes we see correctly but remember wrong. In contrast, scientific research collects data in ways that reduce bias. Psychologists strive to observe representative groups of people and to keep track of the "numbers"; they do not rely on memory or general impressions. Psychologists are not always entirely successful in avoiding limitations and bias in their work. For example, psychology has been criticized for relying too often on white middle-class college students as research subjects—a group that is hardly representative of society at large. What is unusual about scientific research, however, is the conscious effort to identify and overcome bias.

Social psychological research has four broad goals.

- ***Description.*** A major goal is to provide careful and systematic descriptions of social behavior that permit social psychologists to make reliable generalizations about how people act in various social settings. Are men more aggressive than women? Are there typical reactions when a love affair ends? In thinking up solutions to problems, do people work better alone or in a group? A thorough knowledge of how people behave is essential.
- ***Casual analysis.*** Much research in psychology seeks to establish relationships between cause and effect. Do expensive TV ad campaigns actually influence how people vote in elections? Does a college education cause students to become more liberal in their social attitudes? Fundamental to all scientific inquiry is the search to identify cause-and-effect relations.
- ***Theory building.*** A third goal is to develop theories about social behavior that help social psychologists to understand why people behave the way they do. As researchers learn more about general principles and the specifics of particular types of behavior, they gain a better understanding of social life. Theories help psychologists to organize what they know about social behavior as well as suggest new predictions that can be tested in further research.
- ***Application.*** Social psychological knowledge can help to solve everyday social problems. For example, the application of social psychology may help people learn to control their own aggressive impulses or develop more satisfying personal relationships. It may also assist policymakers to find ways to encourage people to recycle aluminum cans and conserve water. Today, researchers are using social psychological principles to find ways to understand prejudice against people with AIDS and to help sexually active people to engage in safer sex practices.

Specific examples of social psychological research are described throughout this book. These examples include both classic studies that have been influential in the history of social psychology and very recent studies on the forefront of contemporary research. You will also find a special feature called "Research Closeup" that profiles research on a particularly interesting or timely topic.

The American population is becoming more and more ethnically diverse. This U.S. shopping mall advertises in Spanish, English, Chinese, and Korean. Yet ethnic minority groups are often underrepresented in psychological studies.

Selecting Research Participants

How do researchers decide which people to study? One obvious starting point is to study the people about whom they later want to generalize. If they want to generalize about women who work full time, they should study employed women. But clearly they will never be able to study all working women. So instead they study some smaller number of women, chosen in such a way that they are representative of the larger group. This is known as a *representative sample*.

The best way to ensure this general representativeness is to study a random sample of the larger population. In formal terms, a **random sample** means that each person in the larger population has an equal chance of being included in the study. If researchers selected a sample of telephone numbers from the phone directory at random (using a table of random numbers, for example), they could be assured that theirs was a random sample of all listed phone numbers in the area covered by that telephone book. The laws of probability assure us that a large and truly random sample will almost always be representative of the population within a certain margin of error. It will include approximately the same proportion of women, ethnic minorities, married people, older adults, and so forth as the larger population. The "Cultural Highlight" in this chapter describes the current ethnic and social diversity of the U.S. population.

Most of the time, social psychologists want their research results to apply to people in general, not only to college students in Boston or to first-grade children in Toronto or to people who use Laundromats in Nashville. Yet it is expensive to study random samples of the general population, as you can readily imagine. So social psychologists try to make realistic compromises between practicality and the goal of collecting data that can be generalized beyond the few people studied.

A common compromise is to use college students as subjects. It has often been said that American social psychology is based on college sophomores, because they are a readily available population. About 75 percent of all published articles in social psychology use undergraduate subjects (Sherman, Buddie, Dragan, End, & Finney, 1999). How dissatisfied should we be with this reliance on college student samples?

The need for a representative sample depends on the question asked. In some basic theory-testing research, the representativeness of the sample may not be crucial. For example, the frustration-aggression hypothesis should apply equally to schoolchildren, commuters driving to work, shoppers at a suburban mall, or college students. On the other hand, college students are not appropriate for all research. Suppose researchers are hired to study how best to introduce computers into business offices where the employees have worked together for years, are almost all older women, and have no more than a high school education. It would be entirely unreasonable to study this question with a sample of unacquainted college students who had no experience with office work and used computers regularly. For a research question of this sort, studies of college students would be misleading.

In general, college students are much younger, higher in social class, and better at test taking than the general population (Sears, 1986). Their attitudes may be less well developed and more open to change. As a result, using college students in studies in which any of these factors make a difference could be unwise. For example, studies of personality should take into account the facts that most college sophomores are still rather young and that their personalities have not developed as fully as have those of older adults. The same is likely to be true of their political and social attitudes. Although college students are convenient subjects, they are not always the most appropriate participants for social psychological research.

Psychological research has also been criticized for an overrepresentation of white males among research participants. Beginning in the 1970s, feminist psychologists documented a common tendency to use male subjects rather than females or samples that

Cultural Highlight: America's Diverse Population

For the most part, social psychological research has used white college student samples for its studies. Such samples are too narrow. The gap between the experiences of white educated young adults and the experiences of the rest of the population is substantial and is likely to widen in coming years.

According to the U.S. Census Bureau (2001), slightly over 70 percent of Americans are non-Hispanic whites, 13 percent are African or Caribbean Americans, 12 percent are Hispanics (of any race), 4 percent are Asian Americans and Pacific Islanders, and about 1 percent are American Indians or Alaskan Natives. However, demographers predict that the ethnic mix of the United States will change dramatically in the twenty-first century. Immigration is a major factor. Of millions of immigrants who came to the United States toward the end of the twentieth century, fewer than 20 percent came from Europe. Instead, four out of five came from Asia, Latin America, and the Caribbean (Immigration & Naturalization Service, 1989).

By the year 2025, it is estimated that non-Hispanic whites will make up only 62 percent of the U.S. population, Hispanics/Latinos will constitute about 18 percent, African Americans about 13 percent, and Asian Americans about 6 percent. The Native American population is expected to remain less than 1 percent.

The face of American society is changing in other ways as well. The public visibility of lesbians and gay men has increased dramatically. Although no one knows for sure the sexual orientation distribution of the American public, conservative estimates are that at least 7 to 10 million people are gay and lesbian and an unknown number of others are bisexual. In addition, the number of older adults is increasing steadily. In 1960, fewer than 10 percent of Americans were age 65 or older. Today that figure has increased to 13 percent. It is estimated that by 2025, nearly 20 percent of the population will be 65 or older. There is also growing awareness of the many people with physical disabilities. It is estimated that about 12 percent of Americans have a severe disabling condition that limits their daily activities, preventing them from going to school, keeping house, or having a job. These disabilities include not only being blind, deaf, or paralyzed but also other, relatively hidden conditions, such as arthritis, diabetes, and severe back problems that interfere with daily life.

These examples highlight the enormous social and cultural diversity of the American population. At the beginning of the twenty-first century, a challenge for social psychologists is to broaden their research so that social psychology becomes more truly a psychology of all the people.

included both sexes. Further, research on particular topics such as aggression and achievement motivation was almost entirely based on male subjects. Critics questioned whether theories based on male subjects would be applicable to females. In recent years, heightened awareness of gender bias and increased numbers of women students and researchers have improved the gender balance of research samples (Gannon, Luchetta, Rhodes, Pardie, & Segrist, 1992).

Ethnic minority groups have also been seriously underrepresented in psychological studies, a pattern that continues to this day. For example, Sandra Graham (1992) analyzed trends in published research on African Americans in six major psychology journals from 1970 to 1989. She counted the proportion of journal articles in which African Americans were the focus of the study, or in which data from two or more racial groups were compared. Overall, only 3.6 percent of the articles she reviewed met one of these criteria, and the proportion of articles on African Americans actually declined from 5.2 percent in the early 1970s to 2.0 percent in the late 1980s. Noting that the U.S. population is becoming more ethnically diverse, Graham (1992) cautions that "academic psychology cannot maintain its integrity by continuing to allow ethnic minorities to remain so marginalized in mainstream research" (p. 638). A psychology of college sophomores is unlikely to offer an accurate psychology of humankind, and it may not provide an adequate basis for applying psychological principles to social problems.

Correlational versus Experimental Designs

After an investigator has decided what research question to ask, another difficult decision remains: How will the study be conducted? There are two basic research designs:

correlational and experimental. In correlational studies, the researcher carefully observes and records the relationship between two or more factors. For example, a researcher might ask whether physical attractiveness is related to a student's popularity with other students. In a correlational design, the researcher does not influence the students' behavior in any way but merely records information about the attractiveness of each student and how much he or she is liked by other students.

In contrast, the hallmark of an experimental design is intervention: The researcher puts people in a controlled situation and assesses how they react (Aronson, Wilson, & Brewer, 1998). To study the link between physical attractiveness and popularity, a researcher using an experimental design might enlist the assistance of a paid confederate who is sometimes dressed to look very attractive and sometimes dressed to look very unappealing. The researcher might then bring student volunteers into the laboratory for a brief interaction with another student (really the paid confederate). After a short meeting, the degree to which the student likes the confederate is measured. In this experimental design, the researcher controls the student's exposure to an attractive versus an unattractive peer, the setting in which they interact, and the way in which liking for the peer is measured. The following sections take a close look at both correlational and experimental research designs and highlight the advantages and disadvantages of each.

Correlational research consists of observing the relationship between two or more factors, known technically as *variables*. Correlational research asks if there is an association between the variables. More specifically, when variable A is high, is variable B also high (a positive correlation) or low (a negative correlation), or is B's value unrelated (no correlation)? Height and weight are positively correlated because tall people tend to weigh more than short people. In contrast, the amount of clothing worn and the temperature on a given day tend to be negatively correlated: People usually wear less clothing on hot days. However, height and amount of clothing are probably uncorrelated; in general, tall people and short people probably wear about the same number of pieces of clothing.

A good example of correlational research comes from studies of whether or not watching violence on television is related to aggressive behavior. Correlational studies have examined the association between how much time a child spends watching violent programs on television and the amount of aggressive behavior in which the child engages. Are the children who watch the most violence on television also the most aggressive in their daily behavior? Huesmann (1982) found that elementary school children who watched violent programs the most were also described by their peers as the most aggressive. In this study, viewing violent programs on television was positively correlated with children's aggressive behavior.

There are several advantages to correlational designs. First, they enable researchers to study problems in which intervention is impossible. For example, scientists cannot randomly assign people to experience passionate love, earthquakes, or cancer, nor can we randomly assign people to live in big cities or to grow up in small families. Such factors are clearly beyond the control of even the most ingenious and dedicated researchers. Both ethical and practical considerations limit the opportunities that researchers have to intervene in the lives of others. In such situations, correlational designs offer the best possible method for understanding the connections among various facets of people's lives.

A second advantage of correlational research is efficiency. Correlational studies allow researchers to collect more information and test more relationships than they can in most experiments. When they use a correlational approach to study what causes some children to be more aggressive than others, researchers can collect information on a great many factors, including television viewing, family history, intelligence, personality, relationships with other children, and so on. Moreover, researchers can measure aggressive behavior in a number of different ways: in terms of teachers' impressions, their own observations of children in school, a child's reputation for aggressiveness among other children, parents' reports, and so on. They can then use statistical procedures to uncover associations among these many variables. The experimental method is relatively inefficient for collecting large amounts of data on many variables.

Although correlational research is helpful in describing the interrelationships among variables, it does not provide clear-cut evidence of cause-and-effect relationships. In correlational studies, the cause-and-effect relationship can be ambiguous in two ways. The **reverse-causality problem** occurs whenever two variables are correlated with each other, yet each one can just as plausibly be the cause as the effect. In this case, we know that variables A and B are related, but we cannot tell whether A causes B or whether B causes A. Studies that show a correlation between watching television and levels of aggressive behavior illustrate this problem. Such results could indicate that TV violence causes aggression in children. But the opposite might also be true: Perhaps children who are very aggressive in their daily lives are especially interested in watching people fight and so spend more time watching violent TV programs. In other words, perhaps children's aggressive behavior is the cause of their TV viewing patterns. A correlation between two variables does not, by itself, indicate which variable is the cause and which is the effect.

The other serious ambiguity in correlational research is the possibility that neither variable A nor variable B directly affects the other. Rather, some other unspecified factor may influence both of them. This is called the **third-variable problem.** For example, the correlation between TV violence and aggressive behavior may be created by a third factor. Perhaps disadvantaged families who live in cramped households and experience a good deal of frustration in their lives tend both to watch more TV and to be more aggressive. Among such families, TV viewing and aggressive behavior would be correlated, but the correlation might be due to a third variable—poverty and frustration—that caused both. The correlation between watching televised violence and aggressive behavior would be called spurious because it was artificially created by a third variable that was not considered. Television would have no causal role itself in producing aggressive behavior.

These two ambiguities are often, but not always, a problem in correlational studies. Sometimes psychologists can rule out the reverse-causality problem. For example, many studies have found a correlation between gender and aggressive behavior; such studies have found boys to be more aggressive than girls. In this case, we can be confident that aggressive behavior is not the cause of the child's sex. Here the direction of causality is clear: Something about being a boy versus being a girl affects a child's aggressiveness.

The third-variable problem is not always a fatal difficulty, because researchers can sometimes check to see whether the most plausible third variable is really responsible for the correlation they have observed. For example, they could add measures of frustration and anger in the child's family to Huesmann's (1982) correlational study of elementary school children. Then they could check to see whether the correlation of TV viewing with aggressive behavior was in fact due to home life. Does it hold both in angry, frustrated families and in happy, peaceful families? If so, researchers can conclude that the third variable (home life) was not responsible for the original correlation.

Of course, this procedure does not completely eliminate the third-variable problem. Some other third variable (now actually a fourth) could exist that researchers had not measured, such as verbal skills. Perhaps children with poor verbal skills prefer watching TV shows with a great deal of physical activity rather than slower-paced shows with more talking. Again, to test this possibility, the solution would be to measure this new third variable—verbal skill—and then see if the original correlation held up for both highly verbal children and those below average in verbal skills.

This process sounds as if it could go on and on. But at some point it ends because researchers can no longer think of any more plausible third variables—not because no more variables exist but because, for the moment, researchers accept the correlation as reflecting a cause-and-effect relationship. Eventually someone will think of another possible variable to be examined.

In an **experiment,** the researcher creates two (or more) conditions that differ from each other in clearly specified ways. Individuals are randomly assigned to one of these different conditions and then their reactions are measured. For example, in experiments on media violence, one group of children might be shown a violent film and another group shown a nonviolent film. All the children might then be placed in a test situation in which their aggressive behavior can be measured. If those who were shown the violent film behave more aggressively, we can say that filmed violence is a cause of aggressive behavior in this setting.

A study of media violence by Hartmann (1969) illustrates this experimental approach. Teenage boys were randomly assigned to one of two conditions. Half the boys watched a 2-minute film that showed two boys shooting baskets and then getting into an argument and finally a fistfight. A second group of boys watched another 2-minute film that depicted an active but cooperative basketball game. After seeing the film, each boy was asked to help out in what was described as a study of the effects of performance feedback on learning. The subject was supposed to be a "teacher" who would administer a shock to a "learner" every time that "learner" made a mistake in the learning task. The "teacher" could deliver as strong a shock as he wanted, within certain limits. (In reality, the shocks were fake, and the "learner" was a confederate of the experimenter.) The boys who had seen the violent film delivered stronger shocks than those who had seen the nonviolent one. In this situation, at least, observing filmed violence caused an increase in aggressive behavior.

The great strength of the experimental method is that it avoids the ambiguities about causality that plague most correlational studies. Experimenters randomly assign people to different conditions to see if there is any difference in their responses. If the experiment has been done properly, any difference in responses between the two conditions must be due to the difference in the conditions. In more formal terms, the factor controlled by the researcher (the "cause") is called the **independent variable,** because it is determined by the researcher. In the Hartmann study, the independent variable was the type of film the boys watched. The outcome, or "effect," that is being studied is called the **dependent variable,** because its value is dependent on the independent variable. In the Hartmann study, the dependent variable was the amount of electric shock the subject administered to another person. Experiments provide clear evidence that differences in the dependent variable are caused by differences in the independent variable.

In experimental research, much attention is given to the creation of the independent and dependent variables. The psychologist usually starts with an abstract or conceptual definition of the variable in question. For example, the variable "observing violence" might be defined as watching acts that hurt or are intended to hurt another person. The researcher must then go from this fairly general conceptual definition to an operational definition. An **operational definition** is the specific procedure or operation that is used to manipulate or measure the variable in the experiment. For example, the experimenter might create two versions of a film, one violent and another nonviolent. If the experimenter is attempting to manipulate only the amount of violence in a film, then the two films should not differ in other ways; for example, they should run the same length of time, they should both be either color or black-and-white, and so on. Control over the independent variable is crucial because it allows the experimenter to pinpoint the cause of any differences that emerge between the two groups of people.

The second essential feature of an experiment is that subjects must be randomly assigned to conditions—by the flip of a coin, by the cutting of a deck of cards, or, more commonly, by the use of a table of random numbers. **Random assignment** of subjects to conditions is crucial because it means that differences between subjects in all conditions are due solely to chance. If subjects in each group differ in some systematic way beforehand, researchers cannot interpret any later differences in behavior as being due

Table 1.1

Comparing Correlational and Experimental Research

	Correlational	Experimental
Independent variable	Varies naturally	Controlled by researcher
Random assignment	No	Yes
Unambiguous causality	Usually not	Yes
Exploratory	Often	Usually not
Theory testing	Often	Usually
Tests many relationships	Usually	Usually not

solely to the experimental conditions. The differences in behavior could be due to those preexisting factors and not to the independent variable. Table 1.1 compares correlational and experimental research designs.

Field versus Laboratory Settings

Another decision in designing research concerns where the study should be conducted: in a field setting or in a laboratory. Research done in the field examines behavior in its "natural habitat." Researchers might study factory workers' productivity right in the factory, or commuters' responses to an emergency on the subway train they normally ride to work, or college students' relationships with their roommates in a dormitory.

Laboratory research, in contrast, is done in an artificial situation, one that the research participant does not normally inhabit. Some laboratory research is conducted in a specially outfitted room in a psychology building at a college or research institute. The lab may have all kinds of special equipment, such as video monitors to show films to subjects, audio equipment to record conversations between subjects, one-way mirrors to permit observation of group interactions, physiological recording equipment, or computers. Or the laboratory may simply be a room or lecture hall where people can fill out questionnaires. The point is that the subject comes to a setting that is selected and controlled by the researcher. Both experimental and correlational research can be done in either the laboratory or the field, and each setting has advantages and disadvantages.

The major advantage of laboratory research is the control it permits over the situation. Researchers can be quite certain about what is happening to each subject. If they are doing experimental work, they can randomly assign the participants to conditions, expose them to specific experiences, minimize the effects of extraneous factors, and go a long way toward eliminating unwanted variations in the procedures. Laboratory researchers also have great control over the dependent variable and can measure results more precisely than is often possible in the field. Therefore, the laboratory is the ideal place to study the exact effects of one variable on another. All these advantages fall under the heading of **internal validity.** Internal validity is high when researchers can be confident that the effects they observe in the dependent variable are actually caused by the independent variables they manipulated in the experiment (and are not caused by other uncontrolled factors).

In field settings, it is generally difficult to assign subjects to conditions randomly, to be certain that they are all experiencing the same thing, and to get precise measures of the dependent variable. In particular, it is difficult to design pure manipulations of the independent variable and to obtain pure measures of the dependent variable. The researcher must find or arrange circumstances that produce specific differences between the conditions.

Social psychological research is not confined to the laboratory. As you will see in reading this book, studies have also been conducted at summer camps, in airport waiting rooms, on urban subways, and even at the beach.

In an ambitious field study of the effects of TV violence, Feshbach and Singer (1971) studied adolescent boys who lived in seven different boarding schools in California and New York. With the help of the school staff, the researchers were able to assign boys randomly to two different "TV diets." All boys watched selected prime-time TV shows for at least 6 hours a week for 6 weeks. In the violent TV condition, the boys watched shows with aggressive content, including westerns and crime stories. In the nonviolent condition, boys watched situation comedies and other nonaggressive programs. Staff ratings of the boys' behavior constituted the measure of aggression. Contrary to what you might expect, the researchers found that the boys who were shown the violent programs were actually somewhat lower in aggressiveness than boys shown the nonviolent programs. Watching TV violence seemed to reduce aggressive behavior. Why might this unexpected result have occurred?

The researchers discovered that most of the boys preferred the more violent programs. Therefore, those boys who were assigned to the nonviolent television condition may have been more frustrated than the other group because they were prevented from watching their favorite programs. Consequently, it is not clear whether the results are due to the content of the shows the boys watched or to differences in the level of frustration between boys in the violent versus nonviolent TV conditions. This problem would not arise in a laboratory study, because the researchers would not have had to interfere with the boys' normal television-viewing practices and therefore would not have induced frustration in one group and not in the other.

Another advantage of the laboratory is convenience and cost. It is usually much easier and cheaper for researchers to set up a study in a room down the hall from their office than to go to the places where people live or work.

The most obvious advantage of field settings is that they are more realistic and therefore allow results to be generalized more readily to real-life situations. This is called **external validity** to reflect the fact that the results are more likely to be valid in situations outside (external to) the specific research situation itself (Campbell & Stanley, 1963). External validity is high when the results of a study can be generalized to other settings and populations. Consider the differences between two studies described in this chapter: the Hartmann (1969) laboratory experiment on TV violence and the Feshbach and Singer (1971) field experiment on the same topic.

In Hartmann's laboratory study, the independent variable—filmed violence—was artificial. The researcher created a brief film that was especially prepared for the study. In Feshbach and Singer's field study, the independent variable was the violence actually shown on prime-time television all over the country. In Hartmann's laboratory study, the dependent variable—aggressive behavior—was artificial: the amount of shock delivered in the teacher-learner situation that was constructed especially for the study. In the Feshbach and Singer field study, the dependent variable was naturalistic and consisted of observers' ratings of how much physical and verbal aggression the boys engaged in during their normal interactions with peers and teachers. Suppose we want to generalize from these two studies to the effects of prime-time television on teenage boys' aggression in their everyday lives. The field study deals with exactly the kinds of TV violence, everyday aggressive behavior, and real-life situations of interest. So it would be more appropriate to generalize from the field study. The field study, therefore, has greater external validity.

Another advantage of work in the field is that researchers are sometimes able to deal with extremely powerful variables and situations that could not be studied in the laboratory. Researchers can observe people in extreme situations, for example, when they are waiting for open-heart surgery in a hospital or huddled together under artillery bombardment. Sometimes ingenious researchers are able to take advantage of "natural experiments"—cases in which the independent variable is manipulated by nature rather than by the experimenter. For example, experimenters could not randomly assign homeowners to a destructive natural disaster in order to see if this experience changed their perceptions of personal control over their lives. But Parker, Brewer, and Spencer (1980) were able to approximate this design by studying a community that had suffered a devastating brushfire. Chance factors such as rapid changes in the wind direction determined which homes were destroyed and which were saved and so provided a rough equivalent of random assignment to conditions of disaster and nondisaster.

Because research in the field deals with everyday life, it tends to minimize suspicion by the subjects. Their responses are more spontaneous and less susceptible to the kinds of bias that suspicion can produce in the laboratory. Whenever people know they are participants in an experiment, there is always the possibility that they are not behaving naturally. For instance, they may try to please the experimenter or present themselves in a socially desirable manner, or they may distrust the experimenter and not believe the experimental manipulation. Any of these effects could produce bias in the results or obscure any actual cause-and-effect relationships. Table 1.2 compares characteristics of field and laboratory research.

Methods of Data Collection

The next step is to decide on a technique of data collection. Basically, researchers have three options: (1) They can ask research participants to report on their own behaviors, thoughts, or feelings; (2) they can observe participants directly; or (3) they can go to an archive and use data originally collected for other purposes.

Self-Report. Perhaps the most common technique of data collection in social psychology uses self-reports. People can be asked their preference between two presidential candidates, as in national polls done before each election. Children can be asked to report on their perception of their classmates' aggressiveness, or on their own television-viewing behavior. The big advantage of self-report questionnaires or interviews is that they allow the investigator to measure subjective states such as perceptions, attitudes, or emotions. These can be inferred only indirectly from observational studies. For example, it would be difficult for observers to tell how lonely another person feels without getting that person's self-report. The principal disadvantage of self-report is that we must rely on people to give honest descriptions of their own internal feelings. People are often willing to give honest and full answers, especially when their privacy is carefully protected. But researchers also know that people sometimes disguise socially unacceptable feelings (such as racial prejudices) and that people are sometimes not fully aware of their own feelings.

Table 1.2

Comparing Laboratory and Field Research

	Laboratory	Field
Control over variables	High	Low
Random assignment	Almost always	Seldom
Convenience	Usually high	Usually low
Realism	Low	High
Impact of independent variables	Tends to be lower	Tends to be higher
Suspicion and bias	Tends to be higher	Tends to be lower
External validity	Low	High

Observational Research. Direct observation is a widely used research technique. For example, to study helping behavior, researchers have staged fake emergencies in public places to see how many people are willing to come to the aid of a stranger in distress. Marriage researchers have obtained permission to place microphones in homes and to record family interactions so that they can learn about the frequency of conflict, fighting, praising, and other types of interaction.

Archival Research. In **archival research,** the investigator uses data that were previously collected for another purpose. For example, in the 1940s, researchers wanted to examine whether whites' violence against blacks was associated with frustration based on economic difficulties. They used historical records to correlate cotton prices and lynching of blacks in the southern United States (Hovland & Sears, 1940). They found that the greatest number of lynchings occurred during the years with the lowest cotton prices. Perhaps the best-known archival data come from the U.S. Census, which has been conducted every 10 years for two centuries. But many specialized databanks also exist with the records of polls, surveys, and large-scale studies.

There are many advantages to using archival data. The most obvious is that this technique is inexpensive. The U.S. Census costs millions of dollars to collect, but the data can be used for next to nothing. Archival data also allow researchers to test hypotheses about changes in attitudes or behavior over time rather than be limited to one historical moment. We might want to know how many people say they would vote for a woman for president; the availability of archival data on that question over many years can provide a rich historical context for the findings. On the other hand, in almost all cases, archival data were originally collected with some research topic in mind other than the one researchers now wish to investigate. As a result, the questions are usually not exactly the ones the present researchers would ask, or they may be worded the wrong way for their purposes, or the participants in the study might not be exactly the group researchers would prefer. Nevertheless, data archives can often provide a useful source of data for social psychological research.

Bias in Research

All scientists are concerned about possible bias in their research, and social psychologists are no exception. Two kinds of bias are particularly troublesome in social psy-

Social psychologists are concerned about possible bias in their research. Here, a white woman interviews a Korean American teenager. How might the gender and ethnic background of these individuals affect their interactions and the information the participant is willing to reveal?

chology: the effects of the experimenter's behavior and bias associated with a subject's feelings about taking part in a study.

Experimenter Bias. Research participants are extremely susceptible to influence by the researcher. If the experimenter implies, consciously or otherwise, that he or she would like subjects to respond in a certain way, there is a tendency for participants to respond in that way. Subtle cues tend to be picked up by subjects and to influence their behavior. This problem is known as **experimenter bias.** For example, consider the studies of media violence in which subjects give electric shocks to another person after watching either a violent or a nonviolent movie. A well-intentioned but perhaps overly eager experimenter, expecting that subjects in the violent-movie condition might be the most aggressive, could subtly encourage these subjects to give more shocks by smiling, nodding, or making eye contact when they pushed the shock button. Similarly, the experimenter might frown or communicate disappointment to nonviolent-movie subjects who gave the shock because they violated the hypothesis.

There are two solutions to the problem of experimenter bias. One is to keep the people who actually conduct the research (often research assistants) uninformed about the hypotheses or about the experimental condition to which a particular subject was assigned. For example, in research on TV violence, the experimenter could have one researcher show the movies and a second researcher administer the shock task, arranging it so that the second experimenter did not know which movie each subject had seen. The second experimenter is said to be "blind" to the condition the subject is in.

A second solution is to standardize the situation in every way possible. If everything is standardized and there are no differences between conditions other than those that are deliberate, there should be no bias. In the extreme case, subjects might arrive for an experiment and find a written instruction on the door telling them to enter and sit down at a computer. All instructions might be given by the computer, and the subjects might respond by typing in their answers to questions presented on the screen. Subjects might actually complete the experiment before they met the experimenter. In this way, every factor in the situation would be absolutely standardized, and experimenter bias would be eliminated.

In actual practice, the solution to the problem of bias is usually a combination of the two procedures we have described. As much as possible, the researcher is kept "blind" to the subjects' experimental conditions. Also as much as possible, instructions are standardized by the use of written materials, audio- and videotapes, and computers.

Subject Bias. Another source of bias stems from the subject's motives and goals when serving in the role of a research participant. **Demand characteristics** are "features introduced into a research setting by virtue of the fact that it is a research study and that the subjects know that they are part of it" (Aronson, Brewer, & Carlsmith, 1985, p. 454). The basic idea is that the mere fact of knowing that one is being studied may alter one's behavior. Subjects may try to "figure out" the true purpose of the experiment and alter their responses on the basis of their guesses about the study. They may try to give the "correct" or socially desirable response—to portray themselves as smart or politically liberal or religious or sexually responsible, depending on their interpretation of the situation. If subjects' responses are biased in these ways, researchers cannot draw accurate conclusions.

Weber and Cook (1972) carefully analyzed the roles subjects adopt in laboratory experiments. They distinguished several different roles: "good subjects," who try to help the researchers by confirming the hypothesis; "negativistic subjects," who try to sabotage the experiment; "faithful subjects," who scrupulously follow the instructions and try to avoid acting on the basis of any suspicions about the nature of the study (either to help or to hurt the research); and "apprehensive subjects," who are anxious about their own performance. These biases are almost impossible to eliminate entirely, but they can be minimized in a variety of ways. The goal is to produce a situation in which subjects respond spontaneously without worrying about the correctness of their response or trying to figure out what the situation "demands." When possible, researchers may use unobtrusive measures, by which the subjects do not know that they are being studied. For instance, pedestrians who encounter a person who has fallen on a city street may never know that the person is actually a researcher conducting a study of helping behavior. Another approach is to guarantee participants that their responses will be anonymous; no one, including the researcher, will know how any individual responded.

Perhaps the most common approach is to try to keep subjects unaware of the goals and hypotheses of the study. For instance, a researcher interested in sex differences in initiating conversations with strangers might ask subjects to volunteer for a study of taste preferences. While the subjects are waiting for the alleged study to begin, their behavior in the waiting room might be observed, perhaps with the help of a confederate who behaves in a standardized way in the waiting room. In this situation, subjects would expect to participate in one type of study and might not suspect that the time they spend in the waiting room is of any interest to the researcher. All these techniques reduce the possibility that participants' reactions will be distorted or changed by their concerns about social desirability.

Replication. No single study, however beautifully crafted, is ever perfect. Each procedure has its own limitations. And researchers can virtually never test the entire population of interest to them, so there is always some margin of error in their ability to generalize their results. Because any single study is flawed, a hallmark of good research is **replication.** In its simplest form, replication means that researchers are able to reproduce the findings of others if they re-create their methods. This is a fundamental requirement for all science, that different researchers working in different settings can all produce the same effects. Of course, in social research, it is seldom possible to re-create precisely every aspect of a study because the subject population may be somewhat different, the social and political climate may have changed over time, and so on. Consequently, when social scientists are able to replicate results, they have much greater confidence in their accuracy.

In addition to conducting exact replications, it is important to conduct conceptual replications. In a conceptual replication, different research procedures are used to explore the same conceptual relationship (Aronson, Brewer, & Carlsmith, 1985). For example, we have seen that research concerning the effects of TV violence on aggressive behavior has been conducted in both lab and field settings, has used both correlational and experimental designs, and has used diverse measures of aggressive behavior and a wide variety of violent films. To the extent that all these different techniques yield similar results, researchers become increasingly confident that they understand the phenomenon in question. The "Research Closeup" for this chapter discusses meta-analysis, a popular method for interpreting the results of many studies on the same topic.

The basic point is that researchers should be cautious about taking too seriously the results of a single study on a topic. Rather, they should ask whether any particular finding has been confirmed in other studies. And they should also ask how large and important the finding is in practical terms. For example, of all the possible variation in human aggression, how much can be attributed to TV violence? Are the sex differences we hear about so often really big enough to make a difference in everyday life? As you read magazines and newspapers or watch the news on TV, you will often hear about research on such diverse topics as the health dangers of cholesterol, the latest word on teen sex, the virtue of seatbelts, and the causes of child abuse. Use your knowledge of research methods and the importance of replication to be a sensible and cautious consumer of research reports.

Research Closeup: Meta-Analyais in Social Psychology

As the number of studies on a particular topic increases, researchers are confronted with a new problem: how to synthesize research findings to arrive at general conclusions. Consider work on sex differences in helping behavior. Eagly and Crowley (1986) identified no fewer than 172 separate studies that investigated male-female differences in helping behavior! How are researchers to handle this ever-increasing quantity of empirical research?

In recent years, statistical techniques called **meta-analysis** have been developed to help researchers review and synthesize empirical findings systematically (Miller & Cooper, 1991; Rosenthal, 1991). The first step is for the researcher to find as many studies as possible on the same topic. Then, meta-analysis uses statistical methods to pool information from all available studies. The goal is to arrive at an overall estimate of the size of the finding, for instance, the size of a particular sex difference. Researchers might find, for instance, that the average sex difference on a problem-solving test is less than a tenth of a standard deviation—quite a small effect that may not be of much practical importance.

In meta-analysis, statistics are also used to test for the consistency (homogeneity) of findings across studies. When results from different studies are found to be highly consistent, researchers can have much confidence in the finding. When results of studies differ, meta-analysis techniques direct researchers to look for other factors that may be important. For example, if 40 studies show that men are better at this type of problem solving and 40 studies show that women are better at this skill, scientists might suspect that some factor other than gender makes a difference. Perhaps men are better only when tested by a male experimenter, or only in group testing situations, or only if they come from middle-class backgrounds. Instead of merely commenting that the findings are inconsistent, the goal is to try to identify the reasons for the inconsistency. So additional analyses would be conducted that take these new factors into account.

As you read this textbook, you will find references to meta-analyses of numerous facets of social behavior.

Research Ethics

Until the mid-twentieth century, few people worried about the ethics of research with human participants. After World War II, however, the discovery of Nazi atrocities, such as the dangerous and often fatal medical experiments carried out by doctors in concentration camps on unwilling prisoners, came to light. Concerns were also raised by the discovery of unethical medical experimentation in the United States, such as the notorious Tuskegee case: In 1932, the U.S. Public Health Service began a 40-year study in Tuskegee, Alabama, on 399 poor and semiliterate African American men who had syphilis, a progressive disease that can lead to brain damage and death. The goal was to trace the effects of syphilis on untreated males over many years. The men were told they were being treated, but in fact they were never given medication, even though penicillin became available in the 1940s and was highly effective against the disease. Even as late as 1972, treatment was still being withheld from the survivors while the study continued.

In the field of social psychology, ethical concerns have often focused on the use of deception by researchers. Consider some of the lab studies of the effects of TV violence on aggression. Is it ethical for a researcher to tell a subject to administer what he or she believes are painful electric shocks to another person when, in fact, the shock machine is fake and the other person is a confederate? Might the experiment cause the subject to feel guilty for hurting another person? If at the end of the study the researcher explains that the shock machine was fake, will the subjects feel foolish that they were duped by the experimenter?

Studies that use deception have raised a number of ethical issues. When are researchers justified in deceiving subjects about the research they are participating in? When (if ever) is it legitimate to do harmful things to subjects? Is it justifiable to expose subjects to risks if the potential scientific value of a study is great? These questions have led to efforts within many professional associations to define ethical behavior. The

American Psychological Association (APA) first developed guidelines for the ethical conduct of psychological research in 1972 and revises these guidelines as new issues arise (APA, 1992). In addition, the U.S. government has also established procedures for the review of all research it funds. The government requires each university and research institution that receives federal funds to establish a committee of researchers to review all proposed research that uses human subjects. This institutional review board is responsible for ensuring that all research is conducted according to a set of general principles laid down by the federal government. Three important ethical issues in psychological research are informed consent, debriefing, and minimal risk.

Informed Consent. A subject must voluntarily agree to participate in research, without any coercion, and must understand what the participation involves. This is known as **informed consent.** The researcher has an obligation to tell potential subjects as much as possible about the study before asking them to participate. Subjects should be informed about the research procedures, any risks and/or benefits of the research, their right to refuse to participate, and their right to withdraw at any time during the research without penalty. Any exception to this general guideline must be approved by the institutional review board after careful examination of the planned research.

The requirement of informed consent sounds quite reasonable but sometimes creates problems for social psychologists. As we have just seen, it may be important not to tell subjects the true purpose of the study to avoid introducing bias into their responses. Even in the simplest research, subjects are rarely told the specific hypotheses that are being tested. Several of the studies we discussed in this chapter did not provide fully informed consent, and it is hard to see how they could have. Imagine what would happen if researchers first told subjects that the study concerned willingness to help strangers in distress and then tested to see if the subjects would help in an emergency. It is difficult to believe that this research would be valid.

Some people believe that deception of any kind in psychological research is unethical. They think it demeans the subjects and should never be used. A more moderate position that is endorsed by most research psychologists is that deception should not be used if at all possible or should be used only after a consideration of whether the benefits of the study outweigh any possible harmful effects. Subjects, however, should be volunteers. Perhaps they need not be told everything that will happen, but they should know that they are in a study and should freely give their permission. In other words, only someone who has given informed consent or consent based on trust should be exposed to potentially distressing conditions.

Debriefing. At the end of their participation in a study, subjects should always be debriefed. **Debriefing** means explaining in some detail the purposes and procedures of the research. Participants should be given an opportunity to ask questions and express their feelings. A friendly discussion between the researcher and the participants can help subjects to recover from any upset the research may have caused and to learn from their research experience. When research deals with very sensitive topics, it may be important for the researcher to suggest ways in which participants can learn more about the topic by reading or consulting with experts. Sometimes researchers offer to send participants written information about the results of the study once the research findings have been analyzed.

Minimal Risk. A third ethical guideline for research is to minimize potential risks to the subjects. **Minimal risk** means that the possible risks of participating in the research are no greater than those ordinarily encountered in daily life. What kinds of risks can social psychological research pose?

One of the most important risks is the invasion of privacy. An individual's right to privacy must be respected and valued. Researchers who study especially sensitive topics, such as sex, drug or alcohol use, illegal behavior, or religious beliefs, must protect the subjects' right to withhold such information and/or to have their responses kept in strict confidence. On the other hand, public behavior and events on the public record do not have to be protected as carefully. Anyone can go to the local courthouse and look up information on births, marriages, and deaths. Threats to privacy, like all risks involved in social psychological research, can change over time as the society itself changes. For example, people are much more willing to discuss details of their sexual relationships now than they were a generation ago. Today there is widespread concern about keeping the results of AIDS testing confidential, because disclosure that a person has been infected can jeopardize his or her health insurance, employment, and standing in the community. Responsible researchers protect the privacy of subjects by guaranteeing confidentiality and often by having the person participate in the study anonymously.

The other main category of risk in social psychology research comes from stresses of various kinds. Subjects in some studies may become bored, anxious, or fearful. Some studies may threaten the individual's self-respect. As we will see in Chapter 3, Volume 1, many studies in recent years have investigated the causal explanations that people have for their own successes and failures. Such studies frequently require that subjects be exposed to success or failure at an experimental task. A gratuitous failure experience in a psychology experiment is no fun. Being deceived is itself an unpleasant experience for some people. Smith and Richardson (1983) surveyed students who participated in psychology experiments at the University of Georgia. Twenty percent of students reported experiencing some harmful consequence, such as being deceived, feeling humiliated, experiencing physical discomfort, or being angered. Such reports were almost twice as common among students who had participated in deception experiments as among those who had not. Most students did not report harm, of course, but a substantial minority did.

How much risk should a subject be exposed to? The first and most important principle is once again informed consent. If at all possible, subjects must be allowed to make that decision for themselves, based on adequate information. This decision is similar to the decision people face when electing to undergo surgery: Ultimately, the decision must be in the hands of the patient, and it must be as informed a decision as possible.

It is not always possible to inform a subject fully about the exact nature of a study. In such cases, the researcher and the institutional review board must decide how much risk to allow. As stated above, the risks faced in the research should be no more severe than those likely to be encountered in normal life. Being threatened with an injection may be frightening, but it is a usual occurrence. Being threatened with isolation for 10 hours is also frightening, but it is not a common occurrence; most people never face this threat. So researchers would be more hesitant to deceive a person about isolation than about a harmless injection.

Finally, another criterion many researchers and review boards use in evaluating risk is that the subjects should leave the study in essentially the same state of mind and body in which they entered. That is, participation in the research should have no substantial effects that carry over once the subject has finished the study. Whether a study is pleasant, interesting, and enjoyable or mildly unpleasant, boring, or tedious, the subjects' state of mind, knowledge of themselves, and general attitudes should not be altered by the experiences. This guideline, if followed closely, ensures that participants will not be exposed to excessive risk.

At its best, social psychological research offers the joy of new discoveries about human experience. The thoughtful use of scientific methods can do much to advance our understanding of social life and social problems. But psychological research also carries with it the responsibility to treat research participants with sensitivity and high ethical standards and to repay their valuable assistance by sharing the research results with the public. The chapters that follow offer a guided tour of the major findings and theories in social psychology.

Summary

1. Social psychology is the scientific study of how people think about, influence, and relate to others. Social psychologists often emphasize factors in the immediate social situation that affect behavior.
2. Major theoretical approaches in social psychology include motivational theories, learning theories, cognitive theories, decision-making theories, and interdependence theories. These are not necessarily contradictory. Rather, each emphasizes one aspect of the causes of behavior without necessarily claiming that the others are unimportant or irrelevant.
3. A sociocultural perspective emphasizes how behavior is affected by cultural values, social norms, and social roles. Cultures differ in the relative emphasis they give to individualism and collectivism.
4. The emerging field of evolutionary social psychology applies the principles of evolution and natural selection to the understanding of human behavior and social life. Evolutionary approaches emphasize the shared human qualities and evolved psychological mechanisms that are part of our heritage as a species.
5. Today most social psychologists are working to develop middle-range theories or models to explain specific aspects of human behavior, such as the frustration-aggression hypothesis.
6. We all know a great deal about social behavior from our daily observations and experience. Systematic research is necessary to test which of our intuitions are right and which are wrong. Social psychological research has four goals: description, causal analysis, theory building, and application.
7. Research participants should represent the people about whom researchers seek to generalize. A random sample is ideal but costly; therefore, many researchers use convenience samples such as college students. Critics warn that an overreliance on white middle-class college students may bias research results and limit their generalizability.
8. Correlational research asks whether two or more variables are related without trying to manipulate either variable. Correlational research can deal with many variables at once and can investigate phenomena that cannot usually be manipulated in the laboratory, such as crime, divorce, or rape. But correlational research usually does not allow strong causal conclusions to be drawn.
9. In an experiment, subjects are randomly assigned to conditions that differ only in specific, deliberately varied ways (independent variable). If there is any difference in the resulting behavior (dependent variable), it is due to the independent variable controlled by the researcher. Experiments permit unambiguous causal statements.
10. Laboratory research provides more control and greater internal validity, but research in field settings is closer to the real world and often has greater external validity. The most common sources of data in social psychology are self-reports, systematic observations of behavior, and data archives.
11. Great care must be taken to avoid bias in research, including experimenter bias and demand characteristics of the research situation. Because any one study is inevitably limited, replication is an essential feature of good research.
12. Social psychologists face many ethical issues in doing research. They must protect the welfare of subjects and respect their privacy. Current guidelines emphasize obtaining informed consent and exposing subjects to no more than minimal risk.

Critical Thinking

1. The topics studied by social psychologists—love, prejudice, conformity, altruism, and so on—are of interest to many scholars and to the general public. What features distinguish a social psychological approach from other research disciplines such as sociology or clinical psychology? What distinguishes the work of social psychologists from the writings of poets, novelists, philosophers, or newspaper columnists?
2. The "Cultural Highlight" for this chapter discusses changing trends in the population of the United States. Summarize these trends. Then suggest three ways in which these changes may have encouraged social psychologists to consider sociocultural theories.
3. Explain the reverse-causality problem in correlational research. Describe two hypothetical examples of correlational findings in which the direction of causality would be uncertain. Describe two examples of correlations in which a single direction of causality is highly likely.
4. A researcher hypothesizes that lonely college students (as measured by a paper-and-pencil loneliness ques-

tionnaire) are less likely than students who are not lonely to initiate a conversation with an unfamiliar peer. Briefly describe an experimental design for testing this hypothesis. Then briefly describe a correlational study to test the same hypothesis. Evaluate the pros and cons of these two designs.

5. Many researchers believe that deception is sometimes necessary in psychological research and can be ethical if appropriate safeguards are followed. Others argue that deception can never be justified and should not be used. Take one side of this debate; present and defend your position.

Key Terms

archival research 24
association 7
behaviorism 5
collectivism 11
correlational research 18
culture 10
debriefing 28
decision-making theories 9
demand characteristics 25
dependent variable 20
evolutionary social psychology 13
evolved psychological mechanism 13
expectancy-value theory 9
experiment 20
experimenter bias 25
external validity 22
frustration-aggression hypothesis 4
Gestalt psychology 5
imitation 8
independent variable 20
individualism 11
informed consent 28
interdependence 9
internal validity 21
meta-analysis 27
middle-range theories 14
minimal risk 28
modeling 8
observational learning 7
operational definition 20
psychoanalytic theory 5
random assignment 20
random sample 16
reinforcement 7
replication 26
reverse-causality problem 19
social exchange theory 10
socialization 10
social learning theory 7
social norms 11
social psychology 3
social role 11
third-variable problem 19

IN THE NEWS

President Performs Ceremonial Duties

In May, 2001, President G. W. Bush met with Tibet's exiled spiritual leader, the Dalai Lama.

U.S. Naval Academy graduate leaps with joy after receiving his diploma from President G. W. Bush in May, 2001.

A picture is said to be worth a thousand words, and photojournalists rely on this truth to convey much about our social and political world. From the many pictures they take, they cull the ones that convey something important about a person: an inadvertent reaction to a newsworthy event, an emotion, a humorous interaction, or an ominous posture. Photojournalists know that we form impressions of others from their nonverbal behavior, and that others, in turn, read our posture, facial expressions, and other cues to infer our responses to them.

The pictures shown above are well-publicized photos of President George W. Bush's historic meeting with the Dalai Lama on the left and his participation in the Naval Academy's commencement ceremony on the right. What impression of the Dalai Lama does the president seem to hold? What information is the Dalai Lama conveying? In the right-hand photo, what emotions are being conveyed by the graduating midshipman (who was reported to have planted a kiss on the president's cheek shortly after this photograph was taken)? What is the president conveying in his posture and gaze? Come back to these questions after you've read the chapter.

CHAPTER 2

PERSON PERCEPTION: FORMING IMPRESSIONS OF OTHERS

Focus of This Chapter

Most of the time we have more than a snapshot about others. People use whatever information is available to form their impressions of others—to make judgments about their personalities or from hypotheses about the kinds of persons they are. In this chapter we deal with this process, which is called person perception: how we form impressions of people, what kinds of information we use in arriving at those impressions, how accurate our impressions are, and what biases affect our impressions.

In thinking about how people form impressions of others, it is useful to keep in mind six quite simple and general principles:

1. People form impressions of others quickly on the basis of minimal information and go on to impute general traits to them.
2. Perceivers pay special attention to the most salient features of a person, rather than paying attention to everything. We notice the qualities that make a person distinctive or unusual.
3. Processing information about people involves perceiving some coherent meaning in their behavior. To a degree, we use the context of a person's behavior to infer its meaning, rather than interpreting the behavior in isolation.
4. We organize the perceptual field by categorizing or grouping stimuli. Rather than seeing each person as a separate individual, we tend to see people as members of groups—a person wearing a white lab coat is a doctor, even though she may have features that make her quite different from other doctors.
5. We use our enduring cognitive structures to make sense of people's behavior. On identifying a woman as a doctor, we use our information about doctors more generally to infer the meaning of her behavior.
6. A perceiver's own needs and personal goals influence how he or she perceives others. For example, the impression you form of someone you will meet only once is different from the impression you form about your new roommate.

What Information Do We Use?

Our knowledge and expectations about others are determined by the impressions we form of them. A glance at someone's picture or at an individual passing on the street gives us ideas about the kind of person he or she is. Even hearing a name tends to conjure up images of what its owner is like. When two people meet, if only for an instant, they form impressions of each other. With more contact, they form fuller and richer impressions that determine how they behave toward each other, how much they like each other, whether they will associate often, and so on.

Roles

When one seeks ways to organize information about people, role schemas probably take precedence over other kinds of information such as traits. There are many ways to be extroverted (e.g., such as being a comedian, a political leader, or a bully), but there are relatively fewer ways to fulfill a concrete role (such as being a politician). Consequently, role schemas are informative, rich, and well articulated, providing greater information across a wide range of dimensions. Roles are also more distinctive than traits, leading to more distinctive associations. Knowing that someone is a cheerleader, for example, says a lot about exactly how he is outgoing and in what situations he is outgoing, whereas merely being told that he is an extrovert does not convey nearly as much information.

Moreover, role schemas are more useful than traits for recall (Bond & Sedikides, 1988). To see the advantage of role in memory, think of all the people in a particular seminar that you are taking. How easy was that? Now think of all the self-centered people you know. How easy is that? Chances are that social groupings lead to the generation of more names more quickly than do traits. People tend to think of others within a role context first, and only then according to personality traits.

Physical Cues

Our first impressions draw on other people's appearance and behavior to infer qualities about them. Such factors can lead us to form remarkably detailed impressions. The observation that a person is wearing conservative clothes, for example, may lead to the imputation of a variety of other characteristics, such as being conservative politically. We also use behavior to draw inferences about people. We observe a classmate helping an elderly person across the street and infer that he is kind. We even infer personality traits from a person's face (Hassin & Trope, 2000), expecting baby-faced individuals to behave in a warm, affectionate, honest, and even weak way (Zebrowitz, Andriolotti, Collins, Lee, & Blumenthal, 1998).

Salience

People direct their attention to those aspects of the perceptual field that stand out (the figure) rather than to the background or setting (the ground; Nelson & Klutas, 2000). This is termed the **figure-ground principle.** In the case of impression formation, the main implication is that the most salient cues will be used most heavily. If a student appears in a wheelchair the first day of class, everyone else in the room is likely to form an impression that is most heavily influenced by the fact of the person's physical disability. Clothing, hair style, and perhaps even age, race, and sex will all be secondary.

What determines the **salience** of one cue as opposed to another? A number of clearly specifiable objective conditions make cues stand out. Brightness, noisiness, motion, novelty are the most powerful conditions, according to Gestalt principles of object perception (McArthur & Post, 1977). A man in a bright red sweater stands out in a crowded classroom, and the sweater is his most salient feature. The student who stands up shouting in the middle of a lecture and leaves the room draws our attention because she is noisy and moving when almost everything else in the classroom is quiet and stationary. Anything that makes a cue objectively unusual in its context makes it subjectively more salient and more likely to be noticed.

Salience has a number of consequences for person perception. First, salient behaviors draw more attention than do subtler, less obvious ones (Taylor & Fiske, 1978). Second, salience influences perceptions of causality in that more salient people are seen as having more influence over their social context (Taylor & Fiske, 1975). The student who sits in the front row of the classroom and asks an occasional question is more likely to be perceived as dominating the discussion than the student who sits in the back and contributes just as much.

Because salient stimuli draw the most attention, they also produce extreme evaluative judgments, and they produce more consistency of judgment. These effects of salience have been described as "top of the head" by Taylor and Fiske (1978) because they seem to occur at the relatively superficial level of simply directing our attention. As might be expected, therefore, they seem to be strongest when the stimuli are sufficiently interesting and exciting to attract the perceiver's attention. The effects of salience appear to be rather general, occurring in important situations as well as unimportant ones (Borgida & Howard-Pitney, 1983; Taylor, Crocker, Fiske, Sprinzen, & Winkler, 1979).

From Behaviors to Traits

We move very quickly from observable information, such as appearance, behavior, and even gestures, to personality trait inferences about what the person is like (Mae, Carlston, & Skowronski, 1999; VanOverwalle, Drenth, & Marsman, 1999). Referring to traits is a more economical and general way of describing a person than is referring to behaviors. If someone asked you what your roommate is like and you had to recount each behavior you could remember, it would take you a long time, and the person to whom you were describing your roommate might not become much better informed by the process. Instead, you would use traits to summarize aspects of your roommate ("He is a good-natured, sloppy night person with a penchant for loud rock music"). This process appears to occur spontaneously, even automatically, as behavior is perceived (Uleman, Hon, Roman, & Moskowitz, 1996). These traits, in turn, can act as bases for predicting future behavior (Newman, 1996).

The fact that we move from behaviors to traits so quickly is compounded by the fact that traits imply each other. On observing a person patting a dog in a friendly manner, we may infer that she is kind, and from our inference of kindness, we may infer that she

Which person in this group is most salient? Does the white girl stand out? Salient people attract attention, we remember more about them, and we often interpret their behavior in stereotyped terms.

is friendly, warm, and helpful (Sedikides & Anderson, 1994). From a very simple incident of behavior, then, we can infer almost a whole personality. The implications that traits have for other traits is called **implicit personality theory.** People use traits to describe others from the moment they first observe them, although the more they know someone, the more likely they are to use traits to describe the person (Park, 1986). Nonetheless, there are individual differences in the degree to which people make trait inferences. People who demonstrate a high need for structure—that is, a need to have organized, coherent, and distinct patterns of information—are more likely to make spontaneous trait inferences than individuals who do not demonstrate this quality (Moscowitz, 1993).

Which Traits?

The trait inferences that we make about other people fall out along two important dimensions. We tend to evaluate others in terms of their task-related qualities or intellectual competence and in terms of their interpersonal or social qualities (Kim & Rosenberg, 1980). Trait inferences are made quickly, virtually spontaneously, on the basis of minimal information about a person and then often persist long after the information on which they were originally based has been forgotten.

Central Traits. Debate has raged over whether some traits are more central than others. For example, the pair of traits "warm-cold" appears to be associated with a great number of other characteristics, whereas the pair "polite-blunt" is associated with fewer. Traits that are highly associated with many other characteristics have been called **central traits** (Asch, 1946).

In a classic demonstration of the importance of traits, Kelley (1950) gave students in psychology courses personality trait descriptions of a guest lecturer before he spoke. Half the students received a description containing the word "warm," and the other half were told the speaker was "cold"; in all other respects, the lists were identical. The lecturer then came into the class and led a discussion for about 20 minutes, after which the students were asked to give their impressions of him. The results are shown in Table 2.1. There were great differences between the impressions formed by stu-

Table 2.1

Effect of "Warm" and "Cold" Descriptions on Ratings of Other Qualities

	Instructions[a]	
Quality	**Warm**	**Cold**
Self-centered	6.3	9.6
Unsociable	5.6	10.4
Unpopular	4.0	7.4
Formal	6.3	9.6
Irritable	9.4	12.0
Humorless	8.3	11.7
Ruthless	8.6	11.0

[a]The higher the rating, the more the person was perceived as having the quality.

Source: Adapted from H. H. Kelley (1950). *Journal of Personality, 18,* p. 434. Used with permission of Duke University Press.

People form impressions of each other quickly. They use minimal information, such as sex, appearance, or a brief interaction to draw inferences about each other. What information do you think these students are using to form impressions of each other?

dents who were told the lecturer was warm and those who were told he was cold. In addition, those students who expected the speaker to be warm tended to interact with him more freely and to initiate more conversations with him. The different descriptions affected not only the students' impressions of the lecturer, but also their behavior toward him.

Categorization

Social categories, such as gender, race, and social class, influence our perceptions as well. Perceivers do not respond to salient stimuli in isolation; they immediately and spontaneously perceive stimuli as part of some group or category. For example, we do not see that unshaven, dirty, disheveled man in the park with worn-out shoes and a couple of old shopping bags as just another human being; we immediately categorize him as a derelict. The **categorization** or grouping process is immediate and spontaneous and does not take any time or thought. At the crudest level, we categorize on the basis of natural similarities in appearance. We tend to assign people to the category of "men" or "women" on the basis of their physical characteristics, usually culturally defined differences in appearance (hair length, makeup, type of clothing). The same is true of assigning people to other social groupings such as racial categories.

What are the consequences of categorization? Determining that an individual is a member of a particular category may lead to social judgments about that person that are consistent with the category-based stereotype (Baron, Albright, & Malloy, 1995; Corneille & Judd, 1999; Jones, 1990). The observation that someone is an African American may call up a stereotype about African Americans in general (Devine, 1989). Categorizing a person also speeds information-processing time. For example, Brewer, Dull, and Lui (1981) presented participants with photos of people in three different categories—"grandmother," "young woman," and "senior citizen"—along with verbal labels clearly identifying their category. Then they presented the participants with additional information about each target person and measured how long the participants took to incorporate the information into their impressions. Information consistent with the prototype of the category ("kindly" for "grandmother") was processed faster than information inconsistent with it (such as "aggressive" for "grandmother").

Once we regard a person as a member of a social category, the way in which we process information about that person may change (McConnell et al., 1994). When we form impressions about individuals in isolation, we tend to use a piecemeal approach, in which we examine the individuating information about the person and form it into

Are these people acting in isolation or are they working together? We organize our perceptions by categorizing and grouping people, and in so doing we see them as part of a structured whole.

an overall impression. However, if we place a person in a category, often our impression of the person is based on that category, and the person's individual characteristics are assimilated into the overall impressions we have of that category (Brewer, 1988; Fiske & Neuberg, 1990). On the whole, perceivers seem to have a preference for category-based judgments over individuated judgments (Pendry & Macrae, 1994). This preference seems to exist because category-based evaluations are simpler and more efficient: They draw on our already-existing impressions about social groups. Categorization can also lead to predictable sources of error.

The Continuum Model of Impression Formation

As the previous discussion implies, our impressions of other people can range from stereotypical, category-based impressions to much more individuated impressions based on information about particular behaviors. This distinction has been called **dual processing.** Under conditions when people are motivated to make impressions quickly or when people need to form their impressions rapidly, they will often use their schematic, stereotypic and category-based modes of inference to form their impressions of others. Under such conditions, a bus driver may be little more than a bus driver to us. Usually people attempt to make category-based inferences before they process individual information because it is easy to do and because the cues that suggest categories (such as sex or race) are often highly salient.

Under conditions that motivate us to learn about an individual, our impressions are constructed piecemeal from the available data. Motivated to be accurate, we attempt to understand another's goals. When efforts to use categories to understand another person fail, we also turn to individuated processing. When the bus driver is quoting Shakespeare and singing Puccini, we are motivated to learn a little more about him (Fiske & Neuberg, 1990).

The continuum model of impression formation integrates what we know about how people form their impressions of others, and it acknowledges the fact that under some circumstances, we use rapid, heuristic-based processing, furnished by the categories of which a person is a member or a rapid determination of that person's traits (Ruscher, Hammer, & Hammer, 1996). When we need to be accurate, the person does not fit our categories, or we have other reasons for wanting to know a person more thoroughly, we construct our impressions more carefully, in a systematic, piecemeal fashion (Verplanken, Jetten, & van Knippenberg, 1996).

Context Effects

Social judgment is also strongly dependent on the context in which it is made (Bless & Wänke, 2000). There are two major types of contextual effects on social judgments: contrast and assimilation. **Contrast** refers to a biasing effect on judgments away from the environmental context. Thus, for example, photographs of faces are rated as much less attractive when they are preceded by exposure to a very attractive face (Wänke, Bless, & Igou, 2001). **Assimilation** refers to the biasing of a judgment in the same direction as a contextual standard. For example, simultaneously presenting a highly attractive person and a less attractive one tends to produce more favorable ratings for the less attractive face than if the other attractive face is not present for comparison (Geiselman, Haight, & Kimata, 1984).

What determines whether contrast or assimilation effects occur? Assimilation of impressions to the context is more likely to occur when people are processing information about another person at a relatively superficial or stereotypic level; it may be less likely to occur when the behavioral information about a target person is processed more thoroughly and systematically (Thompson, Roman, Moskowitz, Chaiken, & Bargh, 1994), as when people are motivated to be accurate (Stapel, Koomen, & Zeelenberg, 1998).

Social context is itself informative with respect to impresssions. Specifically, when people receive information about another person's traits and behaviors, they often focus on the pragmatic implications of the information; that is, they focus on why the information was conveyed (Wyer, Budesheim, Lambert, & Swan, 1994). For example, if your roommate tells you something negative about a mutual friend, it may somewhat modify your impression of that friend, but it will also cause you to question why your roommate made the remark. Thus, information about another does not always have the same impact. It depends on the context in which it is delivered and the purpose that is discerned for its delivery (Wyer et al., 1994).

For many behaviors, context information may not be appreciated. Context may be subtle, and so when the perceiver attempts to infer the characteristics of a target individual, he or she may not observe the role that the context or situation plays in the elicitation and maintenance of the particular behavior. Inferring the role of context in producing behavior appears to be a secondary process that occurs after people have inferred the dispositions of another person (e.g., Trope & Liberman, 1993).

Integrating Impressions

We move quite quickly from observations of people's appearance and behavior to inferences about their personality. How do we combine these separate inferences into an overall impression? What are the most important aspects of impressions, and how do we put together information that may seemingly be inconsistent, such as the observation that our roommate is pleasant but self-centered?

Evaluation

The most important and powerful aspect of first impressions is **evaluation.** Do we like or dislike a person? Put more formally, the evaluative dimension is the most important of a small number of basic dimensions that organize our unified impressions of other people (Osgood, Suci, & Tannenbaum, 1957).

Negativity Effect. During impression formation, we tend to pay special attention to negative information (Ito, Larsen, Smith, & Cacioppo, 1998; Pratto & John, 1991). And when we come to form an overall impression of the person, that negative information is weighed more heavily (Coovert & Reeder, 1990; Taylor, 1991; Yzerbyt & Leyens, 1991). That is, a negative trait affects an impression more than a positive trait, everything else being equal (Vonk, 1993). This has been called the **negativity effect.** The main explanation for this fact is that negative traits are more unusual and therefore more distinctive. People may simply pay more attention to those negative qualities and give them more weight.

The impact of negative information depends in part on what kind of judgment is being made about a person (Reeder & Brewer, 1979). The negativity bias is very strong for moral traits. Thus, if a person engages in dishonest behavior, that is assumed to be very informative about the person's underlying morality. Positive behaviors, in contrast, are perceived to be performed by both moral and immoral persons. A positivity bias exists for competence judgments, because competent performances are performed only by highly competent people; negative information has less impact because even highly competent people may fail sometimes because of fatigue, lack of motivation, or a temporary obstacle (Skowronski & Carlston, 1987; Wojciske, Brycz, & Borkenau, 1993).

Positivity Bias. A general evaluative bias in person perception is to evaluate people positively, a phenomenon termed the **positivity bias** (Sears, 1983a). For example, in one study, students rated 97 percent of their professors in college favorably (i.e., above "average" on a rating scale), despite all the mixed experiences students have in their college classes (Sears, 1983a). How do we reconcile the positivity bias with the negativity bias? In fact, they work together. The reason we feel positively about most people is that most behavior is positive. People act in a generally good way toward each other, and situational norms dictate that people will behave appropriately in social situations. Moreover, when we have positive expectations about others, we tend to test those expectations and remember positive information better. Negative information, which initially attracts attention, also leads us to ignore or reject another person. And consequently we may limit both our contact with them and whatever additional information we might otherwise learn about them (Ybarra, Schaberg, & Keiper, 1999).

Emotional Information. Perceivers also notice emotionally charged information and make great use of it in their judgments about others. That is, we infer what people are like from the emotions they express. In fact, emotional information is one of the most difficult sources of information to ignore when perceiving others (Edwards & Bryan, 1997).

Which particular emotion is being communicated by a target also influences processing. In one study, participants saw a videotape of a person who was in a neutral, happy, or angry mood. The happy mood elicited rapid, heuristic, stereotypic processing of the person's characteristics, whereas a neutral mood elicited more systematic processing of the information that was conveyed by the target. Angry displays led to a processing style between these extremes (Ottati, Terkildsen, & Hubbard, 1997). However, when perceivers are highly accountable for their inferences, the judgment process is more systematic, regardless of the emotional cues in the situation (Lerner, Goldberg, & Tetlock, 1998; Ottati et al., 1997).

The Averaging Principle

Most of our impressions are not purely positive or purely negative but a mixture of impressions that vary in valence and content. How do we combine separate pieces of information about a person to form a simple overall impression? Our impressions of others seem to follow an **averaging principle** (Anderson, 1965). For example, suppose Susan has just met her blind date, John. She quickly perceives that he is witty, intelligent, and courteous—but very short and poorly dressed. She processes this information in terms of how positive or negative she thinks those traits are. Suppose she were asked to evaluate those traits on a scale from +10 (very positive) to –10 (very negative). She might feel that wit and intelligence are extremely favorable qualities and assign them the maximum value each (+10), that being courteous is quite favorable (+4),

Table 2.2

Susan Evaluates Her Blind Date, John

Individual Traits	Susan's Evaluation
Witty	+10
Intelligent	+10
Courteous	+4
Very short	–5
Poorly dressed	–9
Overall impression	+10/5 = +2.00

that being very short is somewhat unfavorable (–5), and that being poorly dressed is very unfavorable (–9). As the averaging model in Table 2.2 suggests, John would receive an overall evaluation that was approximately an average of the five traits; that is, he would be considered moderately positive (+2).

As a result of further research, Anderson (1968b) proposed a refinement that predicts impression formation even more accurately; the weighted averaging model. According to this model, people form an overall impression by averaging all traits but give more weight to those they believe are most important. For example, an administrator interviewing scientists as candidates for a laboratory job would probably weight "intelligence" more heavily than "attractiveness," but someone hiring an actor for a television commercial might reverse that priority. In summary, the best way to account for integrating our impressions of others is the weighted averaging principle.

Imputing Meaning

Perceivers try to arrive at a meaningful impression of whole persons, rather than to absorb each new piece of information separately. Their understanding of any new piece of information depends in part on the other information they have about the person. The meaning of "intelligent" in the context of knowing that a person is a "warm, caring therapist" will probably be quite positive. But the meaning of "intelligent" when the person is otherwise a "cold, ruthless foreign spy" will probably be more negative; it makes the person seem even more dangerous. Our perceptions of others' personal qualities undergo a **shift of meaning** when they are placed in a new context (Asch, 1946; Zanna & Hamilton, 1977).

Imputing Consistency

People tend to form evaluatively consistent characterizations of others, even when they have only a few pieces of information. Because evaluation is the most important dimension in person perception, it is not surprising that we tend to categorize people as good or bad, not as both. We may then go on to perceive other traits as consistent with this basic evaluation. This tendency toward evaluative consistency is called the **halo effect.** If a person is likable, we assume that she is also attractive, intelligent, generous, and so on. If she is bad, she is assumed to be sneaky, ugly, and inept.

Resolving Inconsistencies. Sometimes the information we have about other people is internally inconsistent. For example, you may have an impression of your roommate as a kind and generous person—and then you may be told by a mutual acquaintance that your roommate is conceited and a snob. How is incongruent information incorporated into overall impressions?

Information that is incongruent with our impressions often gets remembered. You are not likely to soon forget your acquaintance's negative impression of your roommate. Why is this the case? Because in order to integrate this information into your overall impression, you had to do a lot of work. You had to think about why the incongruent information occurred, whether the acquaintance's report is trustworthy, why your roommate might have behaved in this way on this particular occasion, and the like. As a result of the complicated process people go through to understand inconsistent information, it comes to play a more important role in their overall impression than does information consistent with the impression they hold (Hastie & Kumar, 1979; Trafimow & Finlay, 2001). Indeed, when we are kept from being able to do the cognitive work required to make inconsistent information more comprehensible, as by being kept too cognitively busy with other tasks, the bias for remembering inconsistent information is eliminated (Macrae, Bodenhausen, Schloerscheidt, & Milne, 1999).

Of course, it isn't always possible to make an impression of a person entirely evaluatively consistent. A man may be very nice to his friends but treat his dog quite badly. A woman may be very outgoing with her friends but become quiet when she is with strangers. When incongruent information is confined to a particular situation, the situational specificity helps people recall them (Trafimow, 1998). In addition, when traits are at least mildly congruent or evaluatively consistent with each other, they are easy to integrate (Hampson, 1998). When they are incongruent and difficult to reconcile with each other, people sometimes leave them unintegrated and recognize the incongruency (Casselden & Hampson, 1990).

Schemas

As already noted, much of the time we process information about others using the stereotypes or preconceptions we hold about the categories that define people (such as gender and occupation). Another word for these preconceptions or stereotypes is "schemas." A schema is an organized, structured set of cognitions, including some knowledge about the object, some relationships among the various cognitions about it, and some specific examples (Taylor & Crocker, 1981). Schemas help us to process complex bodies of information by simplifying and organizing them. They can help us to remember and organize details, speed up processing time, fill in gaps in our knowledge, and interpret and evaluate new information. Several types of schemas figure importantly in person perception in forming impressions of others.

Person schemas are structures about people. They can focus on one particular person, for example, Abraham Lincoln. The schema might include such elements as his being deliberate, honest, serious about his duties, and concerned for oppressed people. Person schemas can also focus on particular types of people. For example, our schema of an "extrovert" might include such elements as "spirited," "outgoing," "enthusiastic," and "self-assured." The reasons we develop schemas for individuals is to help us gather information about those individuals and to guide our subsequent social interactions with them (Mayer, Rapp, & Williams, 1993). Figure 2–1 presents a diagrammable representation of a schema for a "cultured person."

People also have role schemas. These represent the organized, abstract concepts we have of people in a particular role, such as cowboy, professor, receptionist, or devoted lover. Sometimes these schemas are unrealistic. If our schema for "devoted lover" includes elements such as always understanding, always supportive, never angry, never childish, and always concerned first with the other person's happiness, we could be in trouble. Not many people will live up to that schema.

Other schemas focus on groups. The most familiar is the group **stereotype,** which attributes specific traits to a particular group of people. (Stereotypes are discussed in some detail in Chapter 1, Volume 2.) Other group schemas include schemas for group leader and group follower. Perceivers form inferences about others based on the particular group

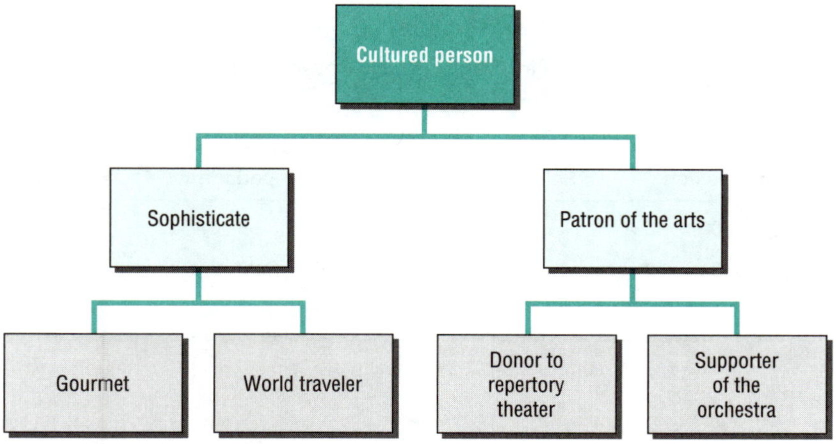

Figure 2–1 A Schema for a "Cultured Person."

Source: Adapted from Cantor and Mischel, 1979..

role they hold. For example, occupying the leadership role, even without having any attendant legitimacy, power, authority, or responsibility, may trigger a role schema that leads to the assumption of greater responsibility for group performance (Kerr & Stanfel, 1993).

Prototypes. In drawing inferences about another person, we often draw on the **prototype** of the schema. The prototype is an abstract ideal of the schema. In our category for football player, for example, we probably have an abstract idea of what the person's body type is, what he does in his free time, and perhaps even what fraternity he belongs to. When you categorize a new person as a football player, you may compare his attributes with those of the prototype for the schema.

Exemplars. When we learn the abstract attributes of categories, we also learn particular instances or examples of the category that we have actually encountered. In many cases, then, we categorize objects and people by seeing if they resemble the exemplars that we store in that category. For example, if you are evaluating a new partner as a possible long-term boyfriend or girlfriend, usually you compare the person not only with your prototype for the ideal boyfriend or girlfriend, but also with "old flames," particular past boyfriends or girlfriends who made your heart beat faster for a time (Fiske et al., 1987).

As can be seen, we rely on a complex mix of ways for recognizing and classifying people and their behavior. When we have very little information, we are most likely to fall back on prototypes for particular categories (e.g., what the typical police officer is like). When we have a little more information, we are likely to use both exemplars and prototypes to help us understand a person (e.g., what roommates are like in general and what your roommate last year was like) (Judd & Park, 1988; Linville, Fisher, & Salovey, 1989). For categories about which we have a great deal of information, we are likely to use our more well-developed and formal schemas (Sherman & Klein, 1994), although examples of specific behaviors may be drawn on as well (Budesheim & Bonnelle, 1998).

Motivated Person Perception

So far, we have discussed person perception as if it were a relatively rational process of taking in information about others and organizing it according to particular principles. Our goals and feelings about other people also influence the information that we gather about them.

Table 2.3

The Impact of Goals on Recalling a Person's Attributes: Expecting to Interact Led to Greater Recall Than in Any Other Goal Condition

Recall	Anticipated interaction	Impression	Self-comparison	Friend comparison	Memory
Target	4.38	4.00	3.31	3.38	3.00
Average of four other people	1.80	2.33	2.53	2.22	2.23

Source: Devine, Sedikides, and Fuhrman (1989), p. 686.

Goals

One factor that influences how we gather information about others is the goals we have for interacting with them. Psychologists have studied goals and their impact on person perception by manipulating them experimentally, such as by telling participants either to form a coherent impression of a person (impression formation goal) or to try to remember the separate bits of information they might be exposed to (remembering goal). Generally speaking, under impression goal conditions people form more organized impressions of others than when their goal is simply to remember the information (Matheson, Holmes, & Kristiansen, 1991).

Anticipating future interactions with somebody creates very different social goals from simply trying to learn about that person, and research shows that people remember more and organize the information differently when they expect to interact with someone in the future. For example, Devine, Sedikides, and Fuhrman (1989) asked participants to learn information about five people under various goal conditions. Either they anticipated interacting with the target, were told to form an impression of the target, were told to compare themselves with the target, were asked to compare the target with a friend, or were simply asked to recall the target's attributes. As Table 2.3 shows, anticipating interactions with the target in the future produced the greatest recall of the target's behavior. Paradoxically, compared to all the other goal conditions, simply being instructed to remember the target's attributes produced the lowest recall.

The dual processing distinction between rapid, heuristically based information processing and more systematic, piecemeal use of information is also relevant to motivated person perception. We noted that social perceivers often use rapid, heuristically based processing when their inferences are not particularly important to them, but they are able to switch to the more systematic style of processing when inferences are important. For example, we may be trying to decide if a certain student should be our lab partner, if we should hire a friend to tutor us in chemistry, or if we should go out with the persistent person in math class. Circumstances like these tend to foster efforts to form accurate impressions.

The need to be accurate usually produces more extensive and less biased information gathering about a person (Boudreau, Baron, & Oliver, 1992). In one study (Neuberg, 1989), students were asked to interview a job candidate. Half were led to expect that the candidate would be unpleasant, and the other half were given no expectation about the interviewee. Cross-cutting this expectation, half the students were encouraged to form accurate impressions about the target; the others were not. Students who did not have a goal of accuracy formed impressions of the person that were relatively negative and thus consistent with the expectation they had been given. However, participants who had been encouraged to be accurate formed more positive impressions, actively undermining the expectation they had been given through their more extensive and less biased efforts to gather information about the target. Thus, the goal to be accurate generally leads to more thorough and systematic processing of information about people than is true under conditions when accuracy is not a goal (Chen, Shechter, & Chaiken, 1996).

The type of impression one forms of another person also depends on the kind of interactions one anticipates having with that individual. Outcome dependency—that is, the situation in which achievement of an individual's own goals depends heavily on the behavior of another person—typically leads the individual to form a careful impression of the other (Vonk, 1999). Participants whose goals do not depend on the behavior of another person are more likely to form their impressions quickly and casually.

Another powerful goal is communication. The process of gathering information for another person greatly influences not only what information people communicate to that other person, but also the impressions they finally form themselves. Sedikides (1990) asked participants to form their own impressions of a target and then to communicate either positive, negative, or neutral information about the target to a third individual. Communication goals completely determined the information that was provided to the third individual, so that they overrode the participant's own impressions. In fact, participants actually reformulated their own impressions in the direction of the positive, negative, or neutral impression they had been instructed to convey (Skowronski, Carlston, May, & Crawford, 1998).

When people communicate information about a target individual to a listener, they not only modify their own perceptions about the target, but they also systematically affect the impressions formed by the listener (Malle, Knobe, O'Laughlin, Pearce, & Nelson, 2000). Specifically, when we transmit information about another person, we typically omit information about mitigating circumstances that may have influenced the behavior and instead present the behavior as if it represented characteristics of the target individual. The result is that listeners may make more extreme positive or negative judgments of target individuals than the tellers do themselves (Baron, David, Brunsman, & Inman, 1997).

The influence of social goals on the kinds of impressions that people form of others is substantial. Moreover, these effects appear to occur without intention or awareness (Chartrand & Bargh, 1996). People who have a particular social goal when they interact with another person appear to make inferences that are consistent with their goals about the other person, even when they do not intend to do so or are completely unaware that they are doing so (Uleman & Moskowitz, 1994).

The Perceiver's Cognitive and Emotional State

So far we've concentrated primarily on what information the perceiver extracts from a person but the perceiver also contributes to the person perception process in a variety of ways. Often when we form impressions of others, there is little else on our mind; and so we can focus our attention closely on the other person's behavior and infer what he or she is like. At many times, though, we are simultaneously pursuing other tasks—trying to present ourselves well, preparing for some future activity, thinking about something that happened the day before—and so our attention is not fully focused on the person about whom we are forming an impression.

When we are busy—namely, otherwise preoccupied—we are more likely to see other people's personal qualities as stable and enduring dispositions. As we listen to a professor give a boring lecture, we may assume that he is always dull and humorless, instead of realizing that his role may make him so, at least for the short term. This bias occurs because people fail to consider external influences on another's behavior (Osbourne & Gilbert, 1992; see also Weary, Reich, & Tobin, 2001).

We all have different things that we notice in other people. One person may be especially focused on whether someone is attractive, whereas another person may focus especially on whether that person is smart. Indeed one of the reasons that the same person can provoke so many different impressions in others is that those others are each interested in or engaged by particular qualities of the person.

One factor that influences how we react to others is whether we see ourselves as similar to them. For the most part, seeing another person as potentially similar is a source of attraction, but when the other person shares a characteristic that we fear in ourselves, we may instead psychologically distance ourselves from the person or avoid her or him altogether (Schimel, Pyszczynski, Greenberg, O'Mahen, & Arndt, 2000).

Sometimes the qualities we use to evaluate others are salient in our minds for reasons having nothing to do with the person being evaluated. For example, if Ellen has just left her boyfriend, Todd, because he is so controlling, she may evaluate all new dates in terms of how controlling they seem to be; this tendency to use an activated trait for evaluating others is remarkably resistant to correction (Staple, Koomen, & Zeelenberg, 1998). Compared to Todd, everyone else may come out looking less controlling (Moskowitz & Skurnik, 1999).

Our prior expectations about another person matter, too. When the social perceiver holds an expectation about the outcome of an interaction, he or she may use that expectation as a basis for evaluating a target (Weary, Tobin, & Reich, 2001).

How we think about traits also influences how we perceive others. Some of us are "entity theorists," who believe that traits are fixed and may grab at global trait judgments and see them as strong determinants of behavior. Others of us are "incremental theorists," who believe that traits are more malleable qualities. Entity theorists, not unexpectedly, make stronger inferences about the behavior of a target and seek more information about his or her character to support their strong theory about the person's behavior (Gervery, Chiu, Hong, & Dweck, 1999). Entity theorists are more inclined to see others in terms of their dispositions or traits, and they predict and notice negative behavior. In contrast, those with a more situational orientation are more likely to notice and remember positive behavior (Ybarra & Stephan, 1999). They form their impressions of others quite quickly, at the time they interact with them, whereas incremental theorists are more likely to form their theories based on their memories of those individuals (McConnell & Leibold, 2001).

Sometimes we use our own internal state as a basis for judging other people; the result may be systematic errors. When people are emotional, they are more likely to attend to emotional information and use that in their impressions (e.g., Halberstadt & Niedenthal, 1997). For example, when we are aroused, we tend to perceive other people in a more extreme manner than when we are not aroused (Stangor, 1990). If you have just finished playing a brisk tennis game and you meet someone who strikes you as sleazy, your impression of the person as sleazy is likely to be more extreme than if you have just come from reading a book.

The perceiver's impressions are also influenced by his or her own specific emotional state. Being in a bad mood might lead us to form a less positive impression of a person (e.g., Edwards, Weary, VonHippel, & Jacobson, 2000; Gasper & Clore, 2000; Strack & Neumann, 2000), and when we are in a good mood, we tend to see another person more positively. These biasing effects of mood are especially strong when the other person is behaving neutrally (Stangor, 1990; see also Isen, 1999, for a review).

Mood may influence not only the content of impressions we form of others but also the process we use in forming them. Specifically, a negative mood makes people more likely to use piecemeal processing in impression formation than to use categorical processing, whereas people in a more positive mood use category information (Edwards & Weary, 1993) and are susceptible to making strong trait inferences about the causes of others' behavior (Forgas, 1998).

To summarize, then, the process of putting together information about people often depends on motivational factors, including our particular goals, the affective state that we are in, or a motivation to hold a particular belief about another person.

Attributing the Causes of Behavior

One of the most important inferences we make about other people is why they behave as they do. What causes one individual to be shy at a party and another to be outgoing? What prompts the romantic breakup of two people who seemed so close? **Attribution theory** is the area of psychology concerned with when and how people ask "why" questions. Theorizing about causal attributions—that is, how and why people infer what causes what—began with Fritz Heider (1958). He argued that all human beings have two strong motives: the need to form a coherent understanding of the world and the need to control the environment. In order to achieve understanding and control, we need to be able to predict how people are going to behave. Otherwise, the world is random, surprising, and incoherent.

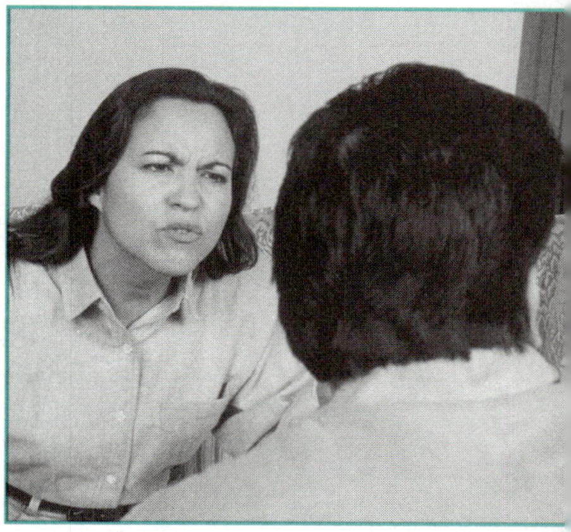

Causal attributions help us predict and control the environment. They determine our feelings and reactions to others, and they help influence our future behavior. If you encountered these two people, you would want to know what was wrong.

To keep our world predictable and controllable, we do not need to ask "why" questions all the time. Many of our causal attributions are virtually automatic, implicit in the impressions we form of other people and situations, as we have seen (Krull & Dill, 1998). However, sometimes a particular person or a set of circumstances catches us up and makes us pay special attention to what is going on, in order to try to understand why events are unfolding as they are or why they occurred as they did. In particular, we are especially likely to make causal attributions when something unexpected or unpleasant happens, because unexpected or negative events create a need for greater predictability (Kanazawa, 1992; Wong & Weiner, 1981). Unexpected and negative events especially, then, elicit a search for causal attributions, because by making them, we restore a sense of predictability and control over the environment.

Jones and Davis's Correspondent Inference Theory

One of the most important tasks of causal attribution is to understand why people do what they do. People engage in a variety of actions, but only some of those reveal their personal qualities (Hilton, Smith, & Kim, 1995). For example, if your new roommate smiles and greets your mother graciously, this behavior is unlikely to be very revealing about her. Most college students know that this is the courteous way to greet someone else's parents. What information about your roommate will tell you what she is really like? That is, under what circumstances do we infer that another's actions reflect real dispositions, such as traits, attitudes, and other internal states, and when do we assume that others are simply responding to the external situation? The terms we will use to describe these very different kinds of attributions are **dispositional or internal attributions** and **situational or external attributions**.

Jones and Davis (1965) developed **correspondent inference theory,** which details how we infer whether a behavior of a person is due to that person's personal characteristics or to momentary situational influences. Essentially, we use the context in which a person's behavior occurs to infer whether that behavior is a result of some temporary influence of the situation or of an underlying disposition, such as a trait. Actions perceived to be reflective of underlying dispositions lead to correspondent inferences; that is, they are judged to be meaningful and useful for illuminating a person's character.

A first important factor a social perceiver uses to infer the causes of another person's behavior is the social desirability of that behavior. Socially undesirable behavior leads people to infer an underlying disposition, whereas socially desirable behavior is not clearly revealing of personal characteristics. For example, if Kate is applying for a job at a summer camp and knows that having people skills is an important requirement, and if she behaves in an extroverted manner during the interview, it is difficult to know whether she is really socially skilled or simply appearing so to create a positive impression during the job interview. However, if Kate behaves in an introverted, rather shy and retiring manner, the interviewer could infer with some confidence that Kate is introverted. Otherwise, why would she behave in that way when the situation calls for different behavior?

Another important basis for inferring dispositions is knowing whether an individual's behavior is freely chosen or situationally constrained. Behavior that is freely chosen is more informative about a person's underlying characteristics than is behavior that is not chosen. For example, if you are a reporter for the student newspaper and are asked to write a story favoring the right to bear arms, readers would be unwise to infer that you hold a positive attitude toward the use of guns. However, if you were told you could write on either side of the issue and chose to write in favor of guns in the home, your readers could more confidently infer that your article reflected your true attitude (see Jones & Harris, 1967).

People consider the intended effects or consequences of another's behavior when inferring the causes of behavior. When a person's actions produce many desirable outcomes, it is hard to know the person's actual motives, but when the behavior produces a distinctive consequence, a motive may more confidently be inferred. For example, if you give up a desirable high-paying summer job in Boston in favor of a lower-paying, less attractive job in Oregon, your interest in being in Oregon over the summer would be evident to anyone observing your behavior. The distinctive features of people's choices are often used as a basis for inferring their underlying qualities through what is termed the "analysis of noncommon effects."

For example, if you are choosing between two graduate school programs that are equally reputable, both at good universities that have offered you the same stipend, and you choose the program that has an internship, one might infer that the training received during an internship is important to you.

Another condition that can help a social perceiver determine whether an action is produced by a person's dispositional qualities is knowing whether the behavior is part of a social role. Behavior that is constrained by a role is not necessarily informative about a person's underlying beliefs or behaviors. If a firefighter helps to put out a fire, we do not infer that he is helpful; he is simply doing his job. But if a stranger from the street helps put out a fire, we more confidently infer his helpfulness.

Finally, we interpret others' behavior on the basis of our preexisting expectations about their true dispositions (Jones & McGillis, 1976). For example, if you know that your roommate is politically liberal but you observe her nodding agreeably at her parents' conservative statements over dinner, you may nonetheless continue to believe

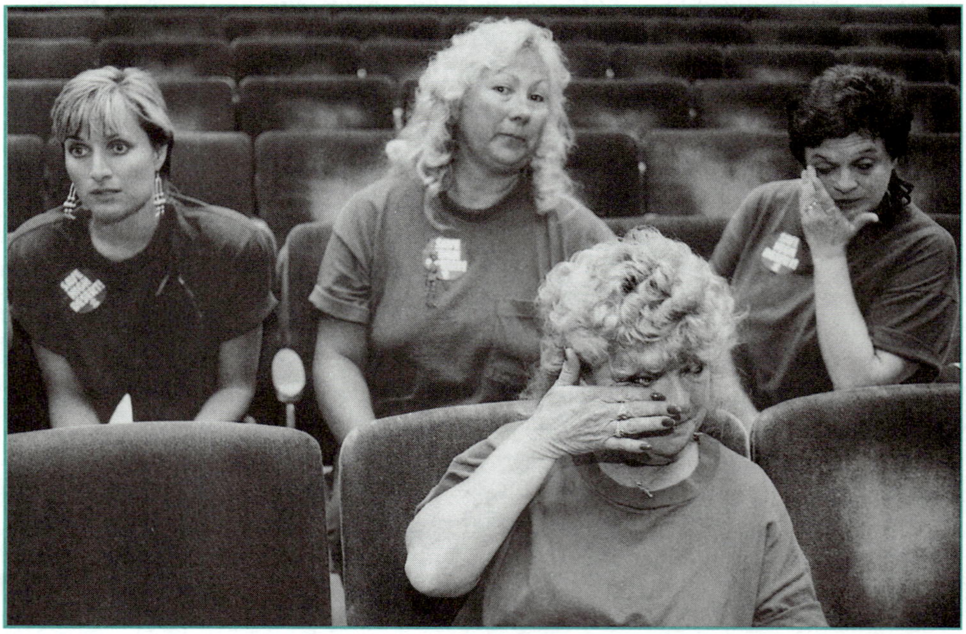

Unexpected or negative events that leave people uncertain are most likely to lead them to ask why the event occurred. Workers who are laid off may be in great need of an adequate causal explanation.

When a firefighter puts out a fire, we do not infer that he or she is being helpful. But when private citizens help to put out a fire, we infer helpfulness, because such behavior is not part of their social role.

that she is a strong supporter of liberal politics and make an external attribution for her nodding, namely, that she is trying to avoid an argument with her parents.

In summary, then, often we are in the position of wanting to know why a person committed a particular action. The goal of our attributional search is a dispositional attribution, that is, trying to find a stable internal quality of the person that explains the action. To arrive at a dispositional attribution, we use cues about the person in the situation as well as our past knowledge about the person and, taken together, this knowledge helps us infer others' dispositional qualities through the observation of their behavior.

Kelley's Covariation Theory

Sometimes, during the search for causal attributions, we have the opportunity to gather additional evidence. Is the professor really as stern and humorless as she seems? If so, it will be a long semester. Harold Kelley's (1967) **covariation** model refers to the fact that people try to see if a particular effect and a particular cause go together across different situations. In order for something to be the cause of the behavior, it must be present when the behavior occurs and absent when it does not. Kelley suggests that we use three types of information to validate our tentative causal attributions: consistency, distinctiveness, and consensus.

Suppose your friend Mary tells you about a comedian she saw the night before. She says that he was the funniest comic she'd heard in years and that you should definitely go to see him. Before doing so, you may want to know if the comedian really is funny or if there is something unusual about Mary or about the situation that night, such as the mood she was in, the people she was with, or the drinks.

Kelley suggests that we ask at least three questions:

1. Is the behavior distinctive? That is, does Mary laugh at any comedian, or does she laugh really hard at this one?
2. Is there consensus? Do other people act the same way in the situation? Did other people like this comedian as well?
3. Is the behavior consistent? Did Mary react this way only on this particular evening, or does she find him funny in other situations as well?

Consensus is one of the sources of information people use to make causal attributions. If everyone laughs at a comedian, we infer that he is funny, but if only a few people laugh, we infer that he is not funny.

For us to infer confidently that the comedian caused Mary's enthusiastic recommendation, three tests have to be passed: high distinctiveness, high consensus, and high consistency. Her reaction has to be distinctive to this comedian and not to others, other people have to like him, too, and she has to react similarly to him in other situations. To make an internal attribution—that is, for her laughter to be attributed to her, rather than to the comedian—we should see low distinctiveness, low consensus, and high consistency: Mary laughs at all comedians, no one else laughs at this comedian, and she laughs in a lot of situations. These predictions are illustrated in Table 2.4. The basic predictions of Kelley's theory and the use of consistency, consensus, and distinctiveness to draw causal attributions have been widely confirmed by research. However, it appears that we are at our best when we are assessing covariation along just one factor rather than several at a time (Fiedler, Walther, & Nickel, 1999). What this finding suggests is that we tend to simplify the attribution process.

Sometimes there are several possible causal explanations for behavior, and we need guidelines to determine which attribution is correct. Kelley (1972) discussed a second major principle used for making causal attributions, termed the **discounting principle.** We are less likely to attribute an effect to any particular cause if more than one potential cause is likely. If an insurance salesperson is nice to us and offers us coffee, we may not want to conclude that he or she is intrinsically friendly. We may, instead, suspect that the salesperson wants our business. If a stranger brings us a glass of water and a cookie after an automobile accident while we are waiting for the police to come, we are likely to infer that she is being kind; she has no other reason for being nice to us. By and large, research findings do seem to follow the patterns described by the covariation and discounting principles (e.g., Cheng & Novick, 1990; Morris & Larreck, 1995).

Biases in the Attribution Process

So far, we have described the process of making causal attributions as a fairly rational and logical one. We look at a person's behavior and reasonably infer the causes from the systematic knowledge we have of that individual and the circumstances in which the behavior occurred. But is the attribution process always this reasonable? Considerable research suggests that there are several prominent biases in the ways we make causal attributions.

Fundamental Attribution Error. Generally speaking, we are more likely to attribute others' behaviors to their general dispositions—that is, to their personality traits or attitudes—than to the situation they are in. This tendency is called the **fundamental attribution error** (Ross, 1977). When we ask the clerk in the college administration

Table 2.4

Why Did Mary Laugh at the Comedian?

	Available Information			
Condition	**Distinctiveness**	**Consensus**	**Consistency**	**Most common attribution**
1	High—she didn't laugh at anyone else	High—everyone else laughed, too	High—she always laughs at him	Stimulus object: The comedian (61%)
2	Low—she always laughs at comedians	Low—hardly anyone else laughed	High—she always laughs at him	Person: Mary (86%)
3	High—she didn't laugh at anyone else	Low—hardly anyone else laughed	Low—she has almost never laughed at him	Context: (72%)

Source: Adapted from McArthur (1972).

Table 2.5

Attitude Attributed to Writer

Condition	Pro-Castro	Anti-Castro
Experiment 1		
Choice	59.6[a]	17.4
No choice	44.1	22.9
Experiment 2		
Choice	55.7	22.9
No choice	41.3	23.7

[a]A high score indicates a pro-Castro position attributed to the writer.

Source: Jones and Harris (1967), pp. 6, 10.

building for help and he seems impersonal and brusque, we assume that he is a cold, unfriendly person and ignore the fact that his whole day must be taken up with anonymous complaining students. It probably is his job, not his personality, that makes him act this way (Sabini, Siepmann, & Stein, 2001; Ross, 2001).

As an example of the fundamental attribution error, consider a study by Jones and Harris (1967) that looked at attributions about the attitudes of people who had written essays on a controversial topic, in this case, an essay about Cuba under the rule of Fidel Castro. Students were given copies of essays and were told that the essay writers had freely chosen to take either a pro-Castro position or an anti-Castro position; or they were told that the essay writers had been assigned the position and had no choice about which perspective to adopt in the essay. Even when the writers had been assigned the essay position, observers overestimated the role of internal dispositions (the writers' true position on Castro) and underestimated the strength of the external situation (i.e., the lack of choice about what position to take) to explain the position taken in the essay. Data from Jones and Harris's two very similar experiments are shown in Table 2.5.

Research suggests that attributions of dispositional qualities to others on the basis of their behavior may be made spontaneously and without awareness, perhaps even automatically, when we observe or hear about these others' behavior (Gilbert & Mallone, 1995). Using information about the situational context to qualify dispositional inferences seems to be part of a second, less spontaneous, and more thoughtful process that involves correcting the initial disposition or inference (Gilbert, McNulty, Giuliano, & Bentson, 1992; Wegener & Petty, 1995). Often, we do not get to this second stage of correction, unless the contextual information is very compelling or salient (Trope & Gaunt, 2000).

People also fail to reach the correction phase when they are cognitively "busy," that is, thinking about their future activities, trying to make a good impression, or engaging in other tasks that consume attention (e.g., Gilbert, Pelham, & Krull, 1988; see also Trope & Alfieri, 1997). When we are busy, we focus on the most salient or meaningful aspects of the situation and pay less attention to nonsalient contextual factors. As a result, we are especially likely to make dispositional attributions for others' behaviors. When we are not busy, however, we can take in at least some of the qualifying contextual information that may have produced another person's behavior and use it to correct our extreme dispositional inferences. Most of us are cognitively busy most of the time, however. If anything, then, research may underestimate the strength of the fundamental attribution error.

Attributions and attributional biases are also qualified by the culture in which attributions are made. Research suggests that people from different cultures may share the correspondence bias, at least to some degree; that is, when one is observing a person's behavior, there is a tendency to impute a dispositional quality to it (Krull, Loy, Lin, Wang, Chen & Zhao, 1999; Choi & Nisbett, 1998). However, when asked what the ultimate cause of a person's behavior is, individuals from Western cultures are more likely to credit dispositional factors as the ultimate cause—that is, the fundamental attribution error—whereas members of other cultures may take situational and contextual factors into greater account.

One important study that demonstrated this cross-cultural limitation was conducted by Joan Miller (1984). She asked people of different ages—people from the United States and Hindus from India—to explain some common events. She found that people in the United States were more likely to use internal, dispositional attributions, but that Hindus were more likely to invoke the external context. For example, a person from the United States who was asked to explain a neighbor's cheating on her taxes said, "That's just the type of person she is. She's very competitive." But a Hindu said, "The man is unemployed. He is not in a position to give that money." According to the Hindu respondents, the situation, rather than internal dispositions, explains behavior.

The well-documented tendency to explain behavior in terms of enduring dispositions, appears to be a more pronounced bias in the United States and much of Western Europe. In Eastern countries, such as India (Miller, 1984), China (Morris & Peng, 1994), and Japan (Markus & Kitayama, 1994), the role of context and situational factors as causes of behavior is far more likely to be acknowledged.

The Actor-Observer Effect

One of the more interesting aspects of the fundamental attribution error is that it applies when we explain the behaviors of other people, but not when we explain our own behavior. This phenomenon is called the **actor-observer bias.** It refers to the fact that when we observe other people's behavior, we tend to attribute their behavior to their dispositional qualities, but when we explain our own behavior, we explain it in terms of situational forces (Jones & Nisbett, 1972).

In one of the earliest demonstrations of this bias, Nisbett, Caputo, Legant, and Maracek (1973) asked male students to write a paragraph on what they liked most about the women they dated and why they had chosen their major. They were then asked to answer the same questions as if they were their own best friend. Responses were scored for the extent to which the behavior was attributed to the actor's disposition (such as "I need someone I can relax with") and the extent to which the behavior was attributed externally, to aspects of the girlfriend (such as "She's smart and fun") or to the major ("Chemistry is a high-paying field"). The participants gave more situational reasons for their own behavior and more dispositional reasons for a friend's behavior.

Why do actors and observers give different explanations for the same events? One reason is that actors and observers have access to different information and may come to different conclusions (see Johnson & Boyd, 1995). Actors know more historical information about their own behavior in different situations than do observers. They know their behavior has varied across situations and may therefore be more likely to attribute it to a particular situation. In other words, they see themselves as behaving differently in different situations, whereas an observer has only the one situation to go on.

Another explanation is that the difference may be due to different perspectives. The visual field of the observer is dominated by the actor, and the special salience of the actor may lead the observer to overattribute the actor's behavior to dispositions. The actor, however, is looking not at her own behavior, but at the situation—the place, the other people, their expectations, and so on. The actor's own behavior is not as salient as it is to an observer; instead, the situation is more salient and therefore more causally potent.

Under certain circumstances, the actor-observer effect is weakened. For example, when we feel empathy for person whose behavior we are observing, we tend to explain the behavior the way that the other person does, namely, in terms of situational factors (Regan & Totten, 1975). We are more likely to attribute positive outcomes to dispositional factors and negative outcomes to situational factors, regardless of whether they are committed by actors or observers (Taylor & Koivumaki, 1976). Empathy may be the exception, rather than the rule, however, as the next bias suggests.

False Consensus

People tend to imagine that everyone responds the way they do. We tend to see our own behavior as typical. This tendency to exaggerate how common our own behavior and opinions are is called the **false consensus effect.**

In an early demonstration of this effect, students were asked if they would walk around their college campus for 30 minutes wearing a large sandwich board with the message "Eat at Joe's." Some students agreed; others refused. Both groups estimated that about two thirds of the other students on the campus would make exactly the same choice that they did. Clearly, both groups could not be right (Ross, Greene, & House, 1977). This false consensus effect has been found in a broad array of situations (Kulig, 2000).

Why does the false consensus effect occur? One possibility is that people seek out the company of others who are similar to them and who behave as they do (Krueger & Zeiger, 1993). Consequently, estimates of the beliefs and behaviors of others may simply reflect the biased sample of people one has available for social inference. Another possibility is that our own opinions are especially salient, and so our beliefs about consensus are increased because our own position is the only one we are thinking of (Marks & Miller, 1987). A third possibility is that in trying to predict how we might behave or think in a certain situation, we resolve ambiguous details in our mind in a way that favors a preferred course of action. We fail to realize that our own choices are a function not simply of the objective situation, but of our construal of it as well (Gilovich, 1990). For example, the person who imagines that others will point and laugh if she appears in a sandwich board will probably refuse to wear one and assume that others, anticipating the same harassment, would do the same. A fourth possibility is that people need to see their own beliefs and behaviors as good, appropriate, and typical, and so they attribute them to others to maintain their own self-esteem. Research suggests that all these explanations may play some role in the false consensus effect (Fabrigar & Krosnick, 1995; Marks & Miller, 1987).

On certain personal attributes, people show a **false uniqueness effect** (Marks, 1984; Snyder & Fromkin, 1980). For example, when people are asked to list their best abilities and estimate how others stand on these abilities, they usually underestimate their peers' standing. We need to feel distinctive and to feel that we are uniquely good at some of our abilities. Highly valued skills and abilities, then, show this false uniqueness effect, whereas attitudes and opinions are more likely to show a false consensus effect.

The Self-Serving Attributional Bias

After your football team has soundly beaten an opponent, how often do you hear a gratifying, "Gee, you're better than we are, aren't you?" Usually you hear that it was bad luck, the field conditions were poor, and they'll beat you next year. On the other hand, when you have just been badly beaten, the smug look and condescending "bad luck" from the opponent are particularly grating, because you know that they do not believe it was bad luck at all; they think they are better. The tendency to take credit for success and deny responsibility for failure is known as the **self-serving attributional bias** (Miller & Ross, 1975). Evidence for the self-serving attributional bias is extensive, although there are a couple of qualifications.

People are more likely to credit themselves for success and blame others for failure in relationships that are casual, rather than close. In close relationships, they do not take more credit than their partner for success or blame the partner more for failure in joint tasks (Sedikides, Campbell, Reeder, & Elliot, 1998).

Overall, there is more evidence that people take credit for success than that they deny responsibility for failure. People are sometimes willing to accept responsibility for failure, especially if they can attribute it to a factor over which they have personal control, such as effort. By so doing, they can preserve the belief that they will not fail in the future. Even though the self-serving attributional bias plays fast and loose with the facts, it may actually be quite adaptive. Attributing success to one's own efforts, particularly one's enduring characteristics, may make people more likely to attempt related tasks in the future (see Taylor & Brown, 1988). For example, in one study, unemployed workers who attributed their firings to external factors made greater efforts to become reemployed and were actually more likely to find jobs than those who attributed their firings to their personal characteristics (Schaufeli, 1988).

Biases: Where Do They Come From?

Why are there such reliable biases in the attribution process? There are several reasons. Some biases represent cognitive shortcuts, ways of cutting through masses of information quickly to reach a good explanation. The tendency to attend to salient stimuli and to attribute behavior to internal dispositions may simply make the process of forming causal attributions more rapid and efficient. Other attributional biases come from people's efforts to satisfy their own needs and motives. In addition to needing a coherent understanding of the world, we need to feel good as well. The self-serving and false consensus biases enhance self-esteem and the perception that we can control our lives. In short, our attributional biases come from a combination of cognitive and motivational needs.

Accuracy of Judgments

How accurately do people perceive others? Our impressions of others—our friends and family, for example—are rich and detailed, leading us to be confident that we know what they are like (Gill, Swann, & Silvera, 1998). But do we really? As we will see, this is a thorny question. On the one hand, people must be reasonably accurate in their judgments of others for society to function as smoothly as it does. On the other hand, having considered various evaluative and cognitive biases to which person perception is subject, the research suggests that under many circumstances, person perception may be quite inaccurate. The answer is that we are both accurate and inaccurate.

People perceive external, visible attributes fairly accurately. A man in a blue uniform with a gun strapped to his side is a police officer, and we must treat him accordingly. Person perception becomes more difficult, however, when we try to infer internal states, such as traits, feelings, emotions, or personalities. Research on accuracy has, accordingly, focused on the judgments people make about internal states and on the cues used to make those judgments and how those cues are combined (Park, DeKay, & Kraus, 1994).

Judging Personality

Considerable research has examined how accurate people are in judging others' personality traits, such as dominance or sociability. The results of this work suggest that accuracy is compromised by several factors. First, people's perceptions of others are sometimes determined more by their idiosyncratic preferences for particular personality dimensions than by objective attributes of the person being evaluated. For some people, knowing how intelligent a person is is important, whereas for another person, being trustworthy or not might be more important. Second, it is difficult to measure personality traits, and so it is difficult to establish the proper criteria for accuracy. A third problem has to do with how consistent people's personality traits are, especially for predicting their behavior. Often, personality traits predict behavior in only a limited set of circumstances. If a man cheats at pool but is scrupulously honest in dealing with his coworkers and subordinates, is he an honest or dishonest person?

Because of the difficulty in establishing criteria for accuracy, research has focused on when people agree about traits of others (Funder, 1987). Some traits have behavioral manifestations that are especially observable, and observable traits show high levels of agreement. For example, people show a lot of agreement in their ratings of whether someone is extroverted or not (because extroversion is easy to observe), but less agreement on whether the person is honest or conscientious—traits that are more difficult to observe and confirm or disconfirm clearly (Park & Krauss, 1992).

Accuracy has also been measured by whether a rater's judgments of another person match that person's own self-perception. For example, if you were asked to rate your roommate Suzie's friendliness, your rating would be compared with Suzie's self-rating to show how much you agree. Generally speaking, agreement between peer ratings and target ratings depends on how well the two people are acquainted (Kenny & Acitelli, 2001; Malloy & Albright, 1990). When you know a person better, you are more likely to see the person the way that person sees himself or herself. When you know a person less well, agreement may be high on publicly visible qualities, but not on qualities less open to observation (Fuhrman & Funder, 1995; Funder, Kolar, & Blackman, 1995).

Accurate perception of another person's attributes can be improved when we have information about the situation in which the trait occurs. For example, if people learn that an individual has a particular goal in a situation, they are more likely to make a trait inference from observation of behavior. Thus, for example, if Linda wants to make the field hockey team and trips an opponent during practice, one may infer her ruthlessness with greater confidence than if she trips an opponent in the absence of a particular goal.

Perceivers agree more on the likability of specific target persons than they do on their traits or other attributes (Park, 1986). When one person talks about another's warmth and sense of humor and someone else talks about his kindness and good-naturedness, the only disagreement may be one of semantics. Perceptions of specific personality traits are another matter. People use more idiosyncratic trait definitions when they are making judgments about ambiguous traits than when they are making judgments about traits that have lots of observable referents. When people are forced to use the same trait definition for ambiguous traits, their agreement increases (Hayes & Dunning, 1997).

Somewhat surprisingly, even strangers are able to rate others in a manner consistent with those others' self-perceptions after relatively brief exposures to their behaviors. However, stranger-self agreements seem to occur primarily for behaviors that have many observable referents, such as extroversion, intelligence, and warmth (e.g., Borkenau & Liebler, 1993; Levesque & Kenny, 1993). Sharing a cultural background usually leads to more accurate inferences than if the perceiver and the perceived come from different cultures (Coleman, Beale, & Mills, 1993), Accuracy can be improved by inducing empathy because when we feel empathy for others, we seem to get inside their heads, see the world as they see it, and more accurately infer the content of their thoughts and feelings (Gesn & Ickes, 1999). The most consensus about a target's attributes is found when perceivers share information about targets who behave consistently across situations (Malloy, Agatstein, Yarlas, & Albright, 1997). The lowest consensus occurs when perceivers do not communicate with each other and have different kinds of information about targets who behave differently in different situations.

People are more likely to agree on another person's characteristics if that person's behavior is not overly variable (Biesanz, West, & Graziano, 1998). People are also more likely to reach consensus about another person's attributes if their outcomes are dependent on their inferences (Bernieri, Zuckerman, Koestner, & Rosenthal, 1994; Paulus & Bruce, 1992). Participants in one study (Flink & Park, 1991) were told that they would observe eight of their peers being interviewed and then choose one of the interviewees to teach them a game (outcome dependency). The judges then rated each of the targets on a number of attributes. Outcome dependency greatly increased the consensus among the judges and reduced idiosyncratic judgments based on factors irrelevant to the judgment, such as liking. Outcome dependency also seemed to make judges more sensitive to the variability in a person's behavior across situations. That is, they noticed when a person was inconsistent and when he or she was not. Consequently, impression accuracy improved. (Wright & Dawson, 1988).

Unfortunately, though, when we attempt to predict future behavior, we fare rather badly. That is, for the most part we are overconfident about predicting the behavior of both other people and ourselves (Dunning, Griffin, Milojkovic, & Ross, 1990; Vallone, Griffin, Lin, & Ross, 1990). This inaccuracy seems to be due to two factors. First, when people express high confidence that certain things will happen to themselves or others in the future, it is rarely warranted. As confidence increases, the gap between accuracy and confidence widens. For example, when California college students were asked to indicate how likely it was that their roommate would take his or her first job in California, many students expressed high confidence in this outcome; many of them were wrong, because finding and accepting a first job depend on many factors in addition to the geographic locale in which you might want to live. Second, predictions that are statistically unlikely are very rarely accurate. Thus, for example, when asked how likely it was that most of their close college friends would be from outside their dorm, those students who said "highly likely" were usually wrong; people usually form friendships on the basis of propinquity, namely, who lives close by (Vallone et al., 1990).

Recognition of Emotions

Much of the work on the accuracy of person perception has focused on the recognition of emotions—on whether a person is happy or afraid, horrified or disgusted. In a typical study, a person is presented with a set of photographs of people portraying different emotions and asked to judge what those emotions are. More recent research has made use of videotaped clips of emotional reactions. Research shows that there is virtual universal recognition of several facial expressions of emotion in both literate (Ekman, 1972; Izard, 1971) and preliterate (Ekman & Friesen, 1971; Ekman, Sorensen, & Friesen, 1969) cultures.

Why are we fairly accurate in our perception of emotional states? In 1871, Charles Darwin proposed, on the basis of his evolutionary theory, that facial expressions convey the same emotional states in all cultures. His argument was that universal expressions have evolved because they have great survival value: They allow animals to communicate

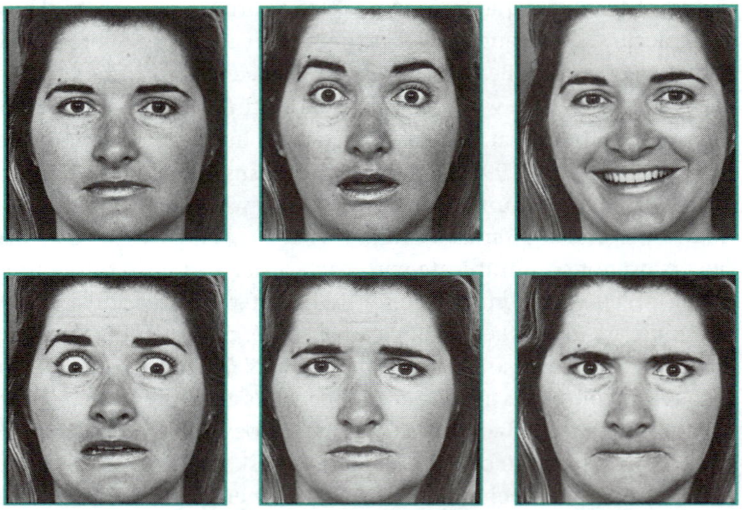

Figure 2–2 Examples of Stimuli Used in the Study of Perceptions of Emotion.

Each picture portrays a different emotion. Try to identify them before looking at the answers.

(Top, left to right: neutral, surprise, happiness. Bottom: fear, sadness, anger.)

emotions and thereby control the behavior of others. Ekman and Friesen (1975) maintained that this universality is manifested in facial affect programs, biologically hardwired sets of cues that allow one person to know the emotion of another (Wehrle, Kaiser, Schmidt, & Schere, 2000). In fact, virtually all species of Old World monkeys and apes have been found to use facial gestures to signal dominance or submissiveness. Differing eyebrow positions seem to be crucial: Typically the brows are lowered on dominant or threatening individuals and raised on submissive or receptive individuals (Keating et al., 1981). As another example, Craig and Patrick (1985) induced pain by immersing participants' hands and wrists in icy water just at freezing temperature. They found consistent responses across cultures, including raising the cheeks and tightening the eyelids, raising the upper eyelids, parting the lips, and closing the eyes or blinking. The evolutionary argument is that there may be a link between the facial expressions used by subhuman primates to communicate with and control other species members and those used by humans for the same purpose. If so, presumably the same link between emotion and facial expression would exist among humans across all (or most) cultures.

Of course, not all individual emotions can be discriminated well, but people can typically distinguish the major groups of emotions using facial cues. In an early study, Woodworth (1938) suggested that emotions can be arranged on a continuum; the relationship between any two emotions is distinguished by the distance between them on this continuum. The continuum of emotions is:

1. Happiness, joy
2. Surprise, amazement
3. Fear
4. Sadness
5. Anger
6. Disgust, contempt
7. Interest, attentiveness

People seem to be quite good at distinguishing emotions in categories that are 3, 4, or 5 points apart—they rarely confuse happiness with disgust or surprise with contempt (e.g., Rozin, Lowery, & Ebert, 1994). But it is almost impossible to discriminate emotions in the same category or only one group away. Happiness and surprise are frequently confused, as are anger and disgust, for example.

Two basic dimensions of emotional expression are pleasantness and arousal (Russell & Bullock, 1985), and people are reasonable judges of emotional states within the categories that these dimensions form. For example, positive emotions such as excitement and happiness are easily distinguished from negative ones such as fear, anger, and disgust. Among the positive emotions, arousing ones such as excitement can be distinguished from nonarousing ones such as contentment. Similarly, negative arousing emotions such as fear and anger can be distinguished from nonarousing ones such as sadness. On the whole, though, the pleasantness dimension is more easily discriminated than the arousal dimension.

Nonverbal Communication

People make judgments about others on the basis of more than emotional expression. In fact, much communication occurs nonverbally, and the effects of nonverbal communication on impressions of others can be extremely potent. In a study by Amaby and Rosenthal (1993), students were presented with 30-second silent video clips of

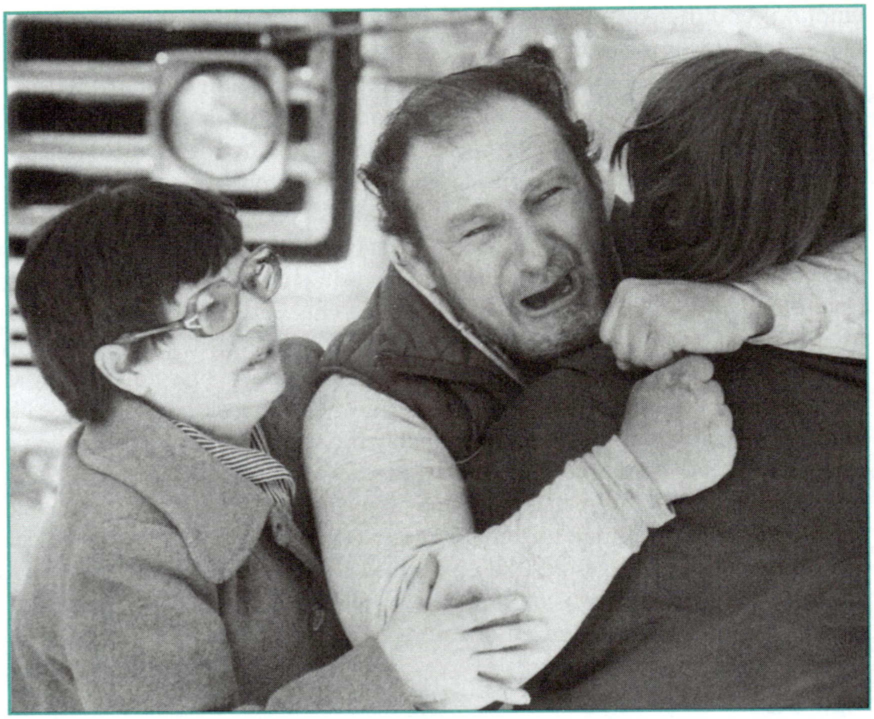

Because certain emotional expressions are universal, most people looking at this picture would assume that the man is deeply unhappy about something. In fact, he has just learned that his family was killed in a fire.

college professors' lectures and then had them rate the professors on a variety of personal qualities. Students were able to make reliable ratings of the professors' qualities, ratings that showed a fair degree of consensus and were significant predictors of end-of-semester student evaluations of those teachers. The impact of even small amounts of nonverbal behavior can be substantial indeed.

Generally speaking, people communicate information about themselves through three main channels. The most obvious is verbal communication, the content of what a person says. The other channels are nonverbal and provide a set of much subtler cues. Nonverbal communication comes to us through a visible channel, which includes such features as facial expression, gesture, posture, and appearance. It also comes to us through a paralinguistic channel, namely, the remainder of the speech signal when the content has been removed, such as the pitch, amplitude, rate, voice quality, and contour of speech.

The Visible Channel

Some of the main nonverbal cues of the visible channel are expressed through distance, gesture, and eye contact.

Distance. In general, the more friendly and intimate a person feels toward another, the closer he or she will stand. Friends stand closer than strangers (Aiello & Cooper, 1972), people who want to seem friendly choose smaller distances (Patterson & Sechrest, 1970), and people who are sexually attracted to each other stand close (Allgeier & Byrne, 1973). Although most people do not think much about personal space, we are all aware that standing close is usually a sign of friendship or interest. It may be one of the most important and easiest ways of telling someone you have just met that you like him or her. The other person is immediately aware of your interest, and if not interested, he or she will probably move farther away to make that clear.

Gestures. In recent years, many popular books have been published on **body language.** These books suggest that people can tell exactly what others are thinking by observing their bodily movements and posture. An open palm is an invitation, crossed legs are defensive, and so on. Clearly, bodily gestures and posture carry information. There are straightforward, direct gestures and very subtle ones. Many bodily movements are generally accepted and convey specific information or directions—the gestures for "stop" and "come" are examples, as are gestures for "sit down," "yes," "no," "go away," and "good-bye." Various obscene gestures have well-known meanings. In a sense, all these gestures are a sign language.

Gestures have meaning mainly when observers and participants understand the context, and especially when they understand the culture. An open palm is not always an invitation: Sometimes, putting a hand up with palm out means "stop," not "go"; the reverse gesture, with the palm in and the fingers moving toward the body, means "come" or "enter." The meaning of gestures depends on context, on the person doing the action, on the culture, and on the recipient of the communication (Bavelas, Chovil, Coates, & Roe, 1995).

The importance of nonverbal communications and gestures in particular has now made its way into the popular culture. Media experts who "handle" political candidates often work as much on those candidates' gestures and other nonverbal communication as on the content of their presentation. During the 1988 campaign season, Roger Ailes, George Bush's media consultant, was quoted in *Newsweek* (Warner & Fineman, 1988, p. 19) as telling Bush during a rehearsal for one of the debates, "There you go with that f-ing hand again. You look like a f-ing pansy!" (cited in DePaulo, 1990).

Eye Contact. Eye contact is an especially interesting form of nonverbal communication. As with other forms, the meaning of eye contact varies greatly and depends on the context. At the minimum, eye contact indicates interest or lack of it. In movies, couples stare into each other's eyes to portray love, affection, or great concern. An otherwise casual conversation can become an expression of romantic interest if one of the speakers maintains eye contact. In other cases, a stare may be a challenge or a threat, as when two athletic opponents try to stare each other down (Ellsworth & Carlsmith, 1973). It is perhaps not surprising that eye contact can have seemingly contradictory meanings, for example, friendship or threat. In both cases, eye contact indicates greater involvement and higher emotional content. Whether the emotion is positive or negative depends on the context; the nonverbal cues themselves have no fixed meaning.

Conversely, avoiding or breaking the contact is usually a sign that the person is not interested. Indeed, when someone does not make eye contact during a conversation, we tend to interpret this as an indication that he or she is not really involved in the interaction. However, there are obvious exceptions to this general principle. Someone who is conveying bad news or saying something painful may avoid eye contact. Lack of eye contact can sometimes mean the person is shy or frightened as well.

Facial Expressions. Facial expressions also can be intended to communicate to others. One interesting case of this is mimicry. It has often been observed that people (and chimpanzees) physically mimic the responses of others. Darwin noted that in particular, people mimic distress when others are feeling it. It is possible that this mimicry is an expression of sympathy for the victim; the mimic may want the other person to know that distress about the painful experience is shared.

To test this idea, Bavelas, Black, Lemery, and Mullett (1986) had undergraduate women individually view a person accidentally drop a heavy TV monitor on an already injured finger, one with a heavily taped splint on it. In some cases, the victim, a (badly bruised) confederate, then looked directly at the observer; in other cases, no eye contact was made. Most of the observers in turn displayed an expression of pain, but it quickly faded in the absence of eye contact. Moreover, the observers were considerably

People from different cultures have different customs regarding touching and other nonverbal communication during casual conversation. These North American women, for example, are comfortable not touching, whereas the two men on a street in Spain stand close together and touch repeatedly during their conversation.

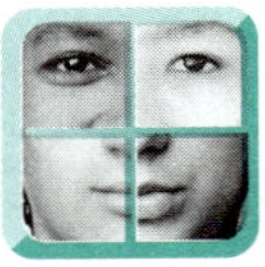

Cultural Highlight

A Smile Is a Smile Is a Smile? Cross-Cultural Differences in the Meaning of the Smile

Every day, visitors to the Department of Motor Vehicles line up to have their pictures taken for their identification cards and drivers' licenses. When asked to give a big smile, most people willingly do so. However, as a California Department of Motor Vehicles photographer reported, one day when he asked a Japanese man to smile, the man refused. What went wrong? The answer lies in the different information that is conveyed in a smile.

In the United States, a smile is usually regarded positively as an indication that the person wearing it is a kind and friendly individual who can be trusted. Historians have suggested that because the United States was once a frontier society in which there was little formal law enforcement, the ability to communicate to another person that one was friendly, intended no harm, and could be trusted was very important. This behavior seems to have persisted, inasmuch as people in the United States are generally regarded as among the friendliest people on earth.

In contrast, among Asians, the smile may convey very different information. The Japanese man who refused to smile for his driver's license picture believed that the smile would indicate that he did not take his driving responsibility seriously. The picture was for a government document, and to smile would convey a frivolous attitude toward an important activity (Dresser, 1994). A Korean proverb similarly conveys the sentiment: "The man who smiles a lot is not a real man." Among many Asian societies, including Japan, Korea, and India, people may smile when they are embarrassed, sad, happy, apologetic, angry, or confused. Therefore, the smile is not distinctively associated with friendship or happiness, as it is in the United States.

Different cultural interpretations of the smile can create problems (Dresser, 1994). Korean shopkeepers who interact with non-Korean customers are sometimes perceived as hostile because they do not smile. People from the United States are sometimes regarded as childlike and a bit silly because they do. When Japanese government officials are photographed with dignitaries from the United States, they sometimes smile, but largely because they have been coached that U.S. audiences value such behavior. Thus, a behavior as simple as a smile may have multiple meanings in different cultures and may be used as a basis for inferring a variety of personal or cultural characteristics.

more likely to smile when eye contact was made, probably in an effort to be reassuring. The facial expressions of the observers in the eye contact condition were in fact rated as more "knowing" and "caring" than were those of the observers in the no-eye-contact condition, a finding suggesting that the former were successfully communicating feelings of empathy and sympathy.

Paralanguage. Variations in speech other than the actual verbal contact, called **paralanguage,** carry a great deal of meaning, especially emotional meaning (Banse & Scherer, 1996). Voice pitch, loudness, rhythm, inflection, and hesitations convey information. Parents can often tell whether their baby is hungry, angry, or just mildly cranky by the sound of his or her cry. Dogs bark in different ways, and each type of bark means something different to someone familiar with the animal. And of course, the significance and meaning of adult speech depends in part on these paralinguistic factors.

A simple statement such as "You want to move to Japan" can mean entirely different things depending on emphasis and inflection. Say it aloud as a flat statement with no emphasis, and it sounds like a mere statement of fact. Say it with an inflection (rising voice) at the end, and it questions the wisdom of going to Japan; you are expressing doubt that it is a good place to move to. Say it with added emphasis on the first word, and it turns into a question as to whether or not the person addressed is qualified; you are raising doubts about whether or not the person is capable of getting along in such a foreign country. The short phrase "I like you" may indicate almost anything from mild feelings to intense passion, depending on its paralinguistic characteristics. Interpretation of paralinguistic cues depends on individual habits and characteristics as well as on ethnic customs, as the "Cultural Highlight" suggests.

Multiple Channels

Which of these three channels of communication—verbal, visible, or paralinguistic—provides the most information about a person's real emotions? Typically, and not surprisingly, people tend to form more accurate judgments about another person when they have access to all channels of communication (Chawla & Krauss, 1994). But generally, the verbal channel—that is, the information that people convey about themselves—seems to be much more influential for inferences about people, (e.g., Berry, Pennebaker, Mueller, & Hiller, 1997).

The question of which channels communicate most powerfully becomes important, however, when the observer is receiving conflicting cues from different channels. How do you interpret your girlfriend's feelings when she says she loves you but moves away from you and won't look at you? The verbal and visible channels of her communication seem to conflict. We turn next to this issue.

The Problem of Deception

A particularly important area of conflict between verbal and nonverbal cues is judging when people are lying or otherwise trying to deceive observers. Police, judges, and jurors are constantly trying to learn the truth from people who try to mislead them. Closer to home, college students report telling about two lies a day during the course of normal social interactions with others (DePaulo, Kashy, Kirkendol, Wyer, & Epstein, 1996). Are people successful or unsuccessful liars, especially to people whose feelings they were attempting to spare (DePaulo & Bell, 1996)?

Nonverbal Leakage

People sometimes betray the fact that they are lying through nonverbal cues even when they are successful in lying verbally. People attend more to what they are saying than to what they are doing with their bodies, reverting to **nonverbal leakage** (Ekman & Friesen, 1974). True emotions "leak out" even when a person tries to conceal them. For example, a student may say she is not nervous about taking a test but will bite her lower lip and blink more than usual, actions that often indicate nervousness.

Liars often betray themselves through paralinguistic expressions of anxiety, tension, and nervousness. It is sometimes possible to tell when someone is lying by noting the pitch of the voice. In general, the voice is higher when someone is lying than when he or she is telling the truth (Ekman, Friesen, & Scherer, 1976; Krauss, Geller, & Olson, 1976). The difference is often so small that an individual cannot tell simply by listening; however, electronic vocal analysis reveals lying with considerable accuracy. In addition, shorter answers, longer delays in responding, more speech errors, and more nervous, less serious answers are all characteristic of people who are perceived as liars or who are instructed to tell lies (Apple, Streeter, & Krauss, 1979; Kraut, 1978; Zuckerman, DePaulo, & Rosenthal, 1981). People also infer deception from "weird" nonverbal behavior. When an individual engages in odd nonverbal behavior, such as arm raising, head tilting, or staring that seems inappropriate to the perceiver, the perceiver is more likely to infer that the other's purpose is deceptive (Bond et al., 1992).

The concept of leakage implies that some nonverbal channels leak more than others because they are less controllable. The musculature of a smile, for example, is different when people are being truthful and when they are lying (Ekman, Friesen, & O'Sullivan, 1988). Several studies (e.g., Zuckerman et al., 1981) have found that the body is more likely than the face to reveal deception. Paralinguistic cues can also leak because, like the body, tone of voice is less controllable than facial expression. Liars, for example, may be better able to modify—that is, suppress and exaggerate—facial expressions than tone of voice (Zuckerman, Larrance, Spiegel, & Klorman, 1981). Typically, successful deceivers make eye contact with their listeners and inhibit smiling while they are delivering deceptive messages. The ability to deceive appears to relate to particular social skills connected to dominance (Keating & Heltman, 1994).

The leakage hypothesis proposes, then, that when people are trying to conceal something, they may be able to control their verbal content and facial expressions fairly well, but their deception may leak out in bodily gestures and paralinguistic cues. Nonverbal channels may leak more than verbal channels, because when conveying information verbally, a person both produces and hears exactly what he or she has said and consequently can make corrections. However, in the nonverbal channel, we usually do not see our nonverbal behaviors and consequently may be less able to regulate them (DePaulo, 1990). Thus, although we may try to regulate our nonverbal behavior, we may not always be successful, because we lack the kind of feedback that we get from our own verbal behavior.

Accuracy in Detecting Deception

Perceivers do quite consistently perceive deceptive messages as somewhat less truthful than truthful messages (see DePaulo, 1990, for a review), but rarely by an impressive margin (DePaulo, 1994; Frank & Ekman, 1997). Not surprisingly, people can detect the fact of lying better than we can figure out the nature of the liar's true feelings. Lies are easiest to detect when they are apparently motivated by ingratiation, that is, when the sender has a motivation to lie, such as communicating false agreement with an attractive partner of the opposite sex (DePaulo, Rosenthal, Green, & Rosenkrantz, 1982). Deception is harder to detect without any specific information about reasons to lie. It is especially difficult to discriminate lying from ambivalence, because some of the same nonverbal cues characterize both states.

Does it help to be warned explicitly that a target person may be lying? One would think so, because perceivers then would attend more closely to "leaky" channels, such as the face and tone of voice. However, it seems not to help very much. In a study by Toris and DePaulo (1984), involving simulated job interviews, the "applicants" were told to be honest in some cases and dishonest in others, while the "interviewers" were told to expect the applicant to try to convey a false impression in some cases or were given no warning. This warning of deceptiveness simply made the interviewers suspicious of 1everyone. Compared with interviewers who had not been warned to anticipate dishonest behavior, the warned interviewers perceived all applicants as more deceptive, and they were no more accurate than the unwarned interviewers in singling out the dishonest applicants from the honest ones. Moreover, they were less confident of their judgments than their unwarned counterparts.

Paradoxically, people may be somewhat better at discerning deception when they are less involved. Highly involved participants tend to process people's messages centrally, and they therefore attend more to the verbal message whereas less involved participants are more likely to pay attention to peripheral cues and attend more to nonverbal behavior (Forrest & Feldman, 2000). However, much of the time we may not be particularly motivated to notice whether a person is lying or not. In most social situations, deceptive self-presentations are likely to be taken at face value (DePaulo, 1990).

The Giveaways

When observers are able to discover deception, what cues do they use? Is the leakage hypothesis correct? Is the body less controllable than the face, and do people catch deception primarily through nonverbal bodily cues? Or is the voice—pitch, loudness, speed, and so forth—an even leakier channel than the body? Most of the research shows that all these cues help to expose a potentially deceptive communicator. However, they are really useful only when the observer also has access to the content of the person's speech.

Psychologists now know the specific behaviors that reliably distinguish lies from truth. Liars blink more, hesitate more, and make more errors when they are speaking, perhaps because it is arousing to lie. They tend to speak in higher-pitched voices, and their pupils are more likely to be dilated. Liars are more likely to feel guilty or anxious, and this may explain why liars fidget more, speak more hesitatingly and less fluidly, and make more negative and distancing statements than do those who tell the truth. The voice tone of liars also often sounds negative. Interchannel discrepancies are more likely to occur. For example, someone attempting to convey an impression of warmth may smile and make eye contact but lean away from the person with whom he is conversing, rather than leaning forward (DePaulo, Stone, & Lassiter, 1985a; for general reviews, see DePaulo, 1990; DePaulo, Stone, & Lassiter, 1985b; Zuckerman et al., 1981).

Paradoxically, one of the best sources of information regarding deception may be the sender's motivation to lie. Considerable research suggests that when people are motivated to get away with their lies, they actually become more obvious to observers (e.g., DePaulo, Kirkendol, Tang, & O'Brien, 1988; DePaulo, LeMay, & Epstein, 1991). Motivated liars seem to work harder to control their nonverbal behavior, sometimes attempting to suppress it altogether in a rigid effort not to give anything away. In other cases, they may deliberately try to control all their verbal and nonverbal behaviors. Both strategies fail because observers can perceive this rigid or controlled behavior through the nonverbal channels and more successfully discern the effort to lie (DePaulo, 1990).

Nonverbal Behavior and Self-Presentation

So far, our discussion has implied that nonverbal behavior is either spontaneous and unself-conscious or a potential source of leakage about deception. However, nonverbal behavior is also subject to a certain amount of self-regulation (DePaulo, 1992). Whenever people are motivated to convey a particular impression in a social setting, they often do so, in part, by managing their nonverbal behaviors.

Think about the last time a friend shared a problem with you. If you listened patiently and sympathetically, as most of us do, at least initially, you were probably aware of saying the right things, such as "That's too bad" or "That's a terrible way to treat anybody." You may also have been aware of the appropriate nonverbal behaviors, such as making eye contact with your friend while he talked and nodding sympathetically. You knew, for example, not to smile, but to look serious, and not to open your mail and skim it while he was explaining his problem. Although not intending to deceive your friend in any way, your nonverbal behaviors were clearly monitored, at least to a degree, so that you conveyed the appropriate sentiments and reactions to your friend's disclosures.

Over a lifetime, we learn a great deal about the self-presentation of nonverbal behavior—indeed, so much so that it becomes almost automatic in adulthood. For example, by the time we are in college, we may not have to think much about the fact that we should stop fidgeting, make extended eye contact, and look sympathetic when another person is telling us a problem. These behaviors may occur virtually spontaneously in response to a friend's distress. Cultural norms regarding how one conveys emotions to others are orderly and follow what psychologists call "display rules" (Ekman, 1992a, 1992b). Display rules govern not only which emotion should be conveyed in a particular situation, but also how the emotion should be conveyed.

Nonverbal behavior can also be used to further social goals. When he is talking with a woman he wishes to date, a man may smile a great deal, make extended eye contact, stand fairly close, and rest his hand against the wall behind his intended partner. Caught in a conversation with someone to whom he is not attracted, he stands farther away, glances from time to time around the room, maintains a more serious expression, and keeps his arms folded in front of him.

Gender

People vary in how effectively they use nonverbal communication. In particular, there are sex differences in the use of nonverbal behavior. Girls and women tend to be more expressive, more involved in their interpersonal interactions, and more open in the expression of emotion (DePaulo, 1992). They tend to use more nonverbal behavior in interacting with others, such as touching, eye contact, expressive body movements, smiling, and gazing. Women are also more accurate interpreters of nonverbal cues than are men (Hall, 1978). There are also gender differences in the communication of different emotions. Women are better able to communicate happiness, whereas men are better able to communicate anger (Coats & Feldman, 1996).

It is easy to interpret gender differences in sex-role terms. Generally, women have been regarded as the experts in the social and emotional areas of life, and nonverbal behavior can clearly help in this regard. However, some studies suggest that these sex differences develop very early in life, as early as 3 months of age (Malatesta & Haviland, 1982). Consequently, it is difficult to disentangle the roles of nature and nurture in attempting to understand these significant sex differences (DePaulo, 1992).

In conclusion, it appears that when people are motivated to convey a particular impression of themselves in a social interaction, they attempt to do so, in part, by controlling their nonverbal behaviors. Although sometimes people exhibit such behaviors to deceive others, more commonly people use them to convey an accurate impression of themselves and their feelings in a particular situation. Moreover, people seem to be fairly successful at exercising this nonverbal control, as long as they are not trying to convey a false impression.

Summary

1. People often decide very quickly what other people are like and base their decisions on minimal information, such as appearance or gender. They infer enduring qualities in others from brief exposure to behavior in limited situations.
2. The qualities we infer about another are influenced by physical features, salience, the social categories to which the individual belongs, and our own motives and goals for forming the impression.
3. The evaluative dimension is the most important organizing principle behind first impressions. People tend to decide first how much they like or dislike another person and then ascribe characteristics to that person that fit this pleasant or unpleasant portrait.
4. Various perceptual biases distort our judgments of others, such as the halo effect (we tend to think that a person we like is good in every dimension), the positivity bias (we tend to like most people, even some who are not so likable), and the negativity effect (more emphasis is placed on negative than on positive information).
5. People tend to form highly consistent impressions of others, even with very little information.
6. When combining information into an integrated impression, we tend to use a weighted averaging approach, in which all information is considered but certain information is given more importance. When we are able to identify a person as a member of a particular social group, we are able to use our schemas or stereotypes to draw inferences about them.
7. Attribution theory is concerned with how people infer the causes of social events. Although causal attributions can be made by most people for most events, people are most likely to ask "why" questions when something unexpected, unusual, or unpleasant happens. Causal attributions help people predict and control the environment.
8. To infer the causes of behavior, people use a covariation principle, meaning that they look for an association between a particular effect and a particular cause across a number of different conditions. A second important principle is that people discount the role of one cause in producing a given effect if other plausible causes are also present.
9. There are several systematic biases in the attribution process. The fundamental attribution error and the actor-observer bias both suggest that people ascribe a

greater causal role to more salient stimuli. People are also influenced by the need to provide causal explanations that protect their self-esteem. This need leads to the self-serving bias and the false consensus bias.

10. Our judgments of other people are not always accurate. In particular, we have a hard time judging people's emotions from their facial expressions. We can tell fairly easily if the emotion is a positive or a negative one, but we have difficulty telling which positive or negative emotion is being experienced. Nevertheless, there do seem to be some universal connections across cultures between certain emotions and certain facial expressions.

11. We use nonverbal cues, as well as verbal and visual ones, to infer the qualities of others. Nonverbal communication includes cues from both the visible channel (such as facial expressions, gestures, and posture) and the paralinguistic channel (cues in speech when the content has been removed, such as the pitch, rate, and delays of speech). Nonverbal cues not only help us form impressions but also enable us, under some circumstances, to detect deception.

12. Verbal communication is probably the single most important source of information about other people. However, visible and paralinguistic information makes an important additional contribution, particularly when the content helps us to interpret its meaning.

13. Deception leaks out in numerous nonverbal ways, such as nervous gestures or high-pitched and rapid speech. Observers can usually detect deception at levels slightly better than chance, but they need all three channels of communication to do so effectively.

Critical Thinking

1. When we first meet someone, what are some types of information that we are likely to pay particular attention to? After we know someone a little, what kinds of information are most likely to change our impression?

2. Sometimes we make attributions about the reasons for another person's behavior almost automatically from observing her or his behavior, whereas other times we are much more self-conscious and thoughtful in our causal processing, trying to think through why an event may have occurred as it did. Under which circumstances are we more thoughtful, and under which conditions are our attributions almost automatic?

3. Person perception is affected not only by the person we see, but also by our own needs and goals. What are some of these needs and goals, and why are they so important in the person perception process?

4. What are some of the factors that compromise our accuracy in person perception? Under what circumstances do we perceive others accurately?

5. Sometimes we know when someone is lying or attempting to deceive us. Think of a situation in which this has happened to you. How did you know the person probably wasn't telling the truth? Did you use nonverbal cues, and if so, which ones?

Key Terms

actor-observer bias 52
assimilation 39
attribution theory 47
averaging principle 40
body language 58
categorization 37
central traits 36
contrast 39
correspondent inference theory 47
covariation 49
discounting principle 50
dispositional attributions 47
dual processing 38
evaluation 39
false consensus effect 53
false uniqueness effect 53
figure-ground principle 34
fundamental attribution error 50
halo effect 41
implicit personality theory 36
negativity effect 40
nonverbal leakage 61
paralanguage 60
positivity bias 40
prototype 43
salience 34
self-serving attributional bias 53
shift of meaning 41
situational attributions 47
stereotype 42

In the News

The Nuns' Story

Recent research with nuns has helped scientists to identify some patterns of thinking associated with healthy cognitive functioning across the lifespan.

What have 678 nuns taught the world about social cognition? As a blitz of recent news stories attests, the answer is a great deal. University of Kentucky psychologist David Snowden has been studying this large group since 1986 to identify what aspects of early life are protective against the potential ravages of later life, including Alzheimer's disease and early death. Snowden began studying the nuns in 1986. He chose this group because sisters enter the convent at a young age and from then on have relatively similar lifestyles: They share living conditions, health care, and economic status, among other factors. For this reason, they provide a potential laboratory for understanding the factors that lead to premature senility and even death.

Early on in his investigations, Snowden stumbled on two metal file cabinets containing the personnel records of the women from the time they had first taken their vows. Each woman had completed information describing her background, parents and siblings, her reasons for joining the order, and the like, in short, a small autobiography filled with personal and social observation. Snowden discovered that these youthful autobiographies provided one of the important keys to the development of Alzheimer's disease.

The young women who had filled their essays with complex and dense ideas were far less likely to have deteriorated cognitively in later life than those women who wrote relatively simple factual statements about their background. Compare, for example, a statement of one of the lower-scoring nuns, "My father was born in the city of Ross in Ireland and is now a sheet metal worker in Oeau Claire," and the statement of one of the more complexly written autobiographies: "My father is an all-around man of trades but his principle occupation is carpentry, which trade he had already begun before his marriage with my mother" (*Time*, May 14, 2001, p. 59). The latter woman lived well into old age with no signs of senility while the brain of the first woman showed signs of deterioration when it was analyzed after her death.

CHAPTER 3

SOCIAL COGNITION: UNDERSTANDING THE SOCIAL WORLD

Focus of This Chapter

Snowden and his colleagues then turned their attention to emotions (Danner, Snowdon, & Friesen, 2001). They searched the early autobiographies for words suggesting positive emotions, such as happiness, love, hope, and contentment, and for words suggesting negative emotions, including sadness, fear, confusion, and shame. The sisters who expressed negative emotions early in life did not live as long as those who conveyed more positive ones.

Scientists don't know, of course, if expressing yourself in a complex fashion or thinking more positively about your life experience will prolong your life and mental functioning. At present, we know only that these aspects of life are associated with longevity and better mental functioning. As Snowden's work continues we will no doubt learn more about what keys social cognition holds to a longer and richer life.

In this chapter, we take up the complex topic of **social cognition**, the study of how people form inferences from the social information in the environment (Fiske & Taylor, 1991). Research on social cognition explores how people make social judgments about other individuals or social groups, about social roles, and about their own experiences in social settings. Making social judgments is more difficult than we might imagine. Often, the information available to us is incomplete, ambiguous, or downright contradictory. How do we use all this information to arrive at a coherent judgment? This is the core question in research on social cognition.

You might assume that social cognition involves seeing the world accurately and forming unbiased, clear assessments of the social life that swirls around us. In fact, however, one of the earliest discoveries that social psychologists made is that social cognition is often marked by apparent errors in biases. Certainly there are logical and correct ways to put information together to make wise and logical decisions, but people's social inferences often depart in quite predictable ways from logic and accuracy. As we'll see, though, these errors in biases are themselves informative about how we actually do form inferences about the social environment. First, let's look at a social situation to see how it is marked by these departures from logic and accuracy, and then we'll see how they've shaped our current view of how we form social judgments.

Imagine that you have completed college and are interviewing at a company for your first job. You have met the personnel director and some prospective coworkers. You also have toured the facilities, seen where your office would be, and learned a great deal about the work the company does and your prospective responsibilities to the company. How do you decide if this is indeed the kind of company you want to work for and if you would like the work itself and the people you would work with?

Social Inference

Any social inference is composed of several steps: gathering information, deciding what information to use, and integrating the information into a judgment. For example, as you are learning about your possible new employer, you are gathering information about the people, products, and general feel of the organization, and you are gathering information from people around you through the questions you ask and the types of facilities or people you request to see. When you return home and mull over your visit, you must then decide which of the multitude of information you received will be most relevant to your decision and then integrate that information into an overall impression or judgment concerning whether this company is the right one for you.

Gathering Information. When people gather information that is relevant to some inference they will ultimately form, they might plan to do so in an evenhanded and unbiased manner. However, research suggests that actual information gathering is often subject to several sources of bias.

Prior Expectations. Suppose you learn that a college acquaintance of yours, a tense, serious, humorless fellow, works for the company you are considering and finds it very much to his liking. If he likes the company so much, you might suspect that it is because he has found people there who are similar to him. Consequently, you might infer that everyone at the company must be stiff and uptight. Accordingly, as you learn about the company with this suspicion in mind, you might selectively gather information consistent with this prior expectation. You might note that prospective coworkers seem a little rigid or formal when you meet them and might conclude that indeed your classmate is typical of the people at this firm. But in doing so, you might fail to remember that most people are a little stiff or formal when they are meeting someone for the first time. Their formality might simply be due to the fact that you are a stranger to them, and they might actually turn out to be very friendly people. But with your prior expectations in mind, you might dismiss them as stiff and formal people without giving them a chance. This is how prior expectations can bias the process of gathering information.

Of course, prior expectations are very helpful in sifting through a lot of information that may otherwise be uninterpretable. They can provide structure and meaning for information that would otherwise be hard to interpret. However, sometimes prior expectations can cause us to draw inaccurate inferences. Four conditions are especially problematic (Nisbett & Ross, 1980). The first is faulty expectations. For example, your belief that the company is stiff and stodgy merely because it attracted one such individual to its ranks is likely to be incorrect. Therefore, letting this expectation guide your collection of information will probably lead you to incorrect answers. A second condition under which prior expectations can be problematic occurs when the social perceiver fails to recognize how prior expectations bias the collection of information. For example, you may be unaware that your impressions of your stodgy college classmate are actually guiding your judgments of your prospective coworkers.

What are these people doing? Helping an injured companion? Playing a game? Going through a survival exercise? Because much behavior is fundamentally ambiguous, social inference processes give social interaction structure and meaning.

This lack of awareness means that later on you will be unable to correct the biasing effect of your prior impression. Your judgments concerning your prospective coworkers will stray on the stodgy and serious side without your realizing that your own biases contributed to this inference. Third, prior expectations can create problems when they overrule consideration of information altogether. If you decide on the basis of your college classmate's attributes not to interview at the company, you have made this error. And finally, if information is inconsistent with what you want to believe, you are likely to scrutinize it far more carefully, potentially rejecting it in favor of information that supports what you want to believe (Ditto, Scepansky, Munro, Apanovitch, & Lockhart, 1998).

Biases in the Information. Once the social perceiver has decided what information is relevant to an inference, the information must actually be collected. The individual must determine which bits of information from the available wealth of data should be examined. For example, obviously you cannot meet everybody at the company during your job interview visit, and so the people you do meet will help give you an impression of the qualities of your prospective coworkers. But judgments made on the basis of limited information can be distorted when there are biases in the information. For example, if you are introduced to a particularly outgoing and friendly coworker, your impression of the attributes of the workers in the company may be falsely influenced toward the outgoing and friendly side.

Even when people are warned that information may be biased, they sometimes fail to understand the full implications of that bias. For example, in one study (Hamill, Wilson, & Nisbett, 1980), researchers told participants that they would be viewing a videotape of an interview with a prison guard. Some participants were told that this prison guard was typical of most prison guards, whereas others were told that he was very different from most prison guards. In the third condition, participants were not given information about how typical the guard was. Half the participants then saw a tape in which the prison guard appeared as a highly compassionate, concerned individual. The other half saw a tape that portrayed him as an inhumane, macho, cruel person. Participants were later asked a set of questions about the criminal justice system that included questions about what kinds of people become prison guards. The results showed that participants exposed to the interview of the humane guard were more favorable in their attitudes toward prison guards than were participants who saw the interview with the inhumane prison guard. More important, participants' inferences about prison guards were unaffected by whether or not they had been told that the interview with the prison guard was typical.

Small Sample. Inferences are also problematic when they are based on very little information. A small sample of information can actually produce a very biased picture (Schaller, 1992). For example, if you are introduced to only 2 of your prospective coworkers, who seem pleasant enough, but you will actually be working with 20 individuals, there is the possibility that these 2 are not typical of the larger group. The other 18 may not be quite as pleasant. Sometimes people forget that they are dealing with very little information, and they make confident inferences nonetheless (see Nisbett & Kunda, 1985).

Statistical versus Case History Information. Another distinction that is important in how people use information is between **statistical information** and **case history information.** Statistical information provides data about a large number of individuals, whereas case history information deals with only a few specific individuals. When people are exposed to both statistical information and a contradictory but colorful case history, the case history often has more influence on their judgment (Taylor & Thompson, 1982). This reaction occurs even when the statistical information is objectively more accurate. For example, one type of information you might want to gather during your job interview is about how quickly people advance in the company. Clearly, the most appropriate information to look at is the statistical information about promotion rates for all the employees and for those in your prospective division particularly. However, suppose you are told about Mark Comet, a particularly dynamic fellow who managed to go from clerk to associate vice president in 3 short years. It is very likely that the case history of Mark Comet's dramatic rise to fame and fortune within the company will bias your impression of how quickly people advance. It may lead you to ignore the more appropriate statistical information, which would suggest that people typically advance fairly slowly within the company.

Most of us seem to know that we really should use broadly based statistical information in making our judgments. People draw on statistics all the time when they are trying to make a persuasive argument, and a person who has statistical information available can often be quite persuasive. If a case history does not lead us to a strong conclusion, we are more likely to rely on the statistical evidence. However, generally speaking, when more engaging anecdotal case history evidence is present, people often ignore relevant statistical evidence and are instead persuaded by case histories (Bar-Hillel & Fischhoff, 1981; Beckett & Park, 1995).

Impact of Negative Information

Suppose that during the course of gathering information about your prospective company, you learned one or two negative pieces of information. For example, one disgruntled employee, about to be let go for poor performance, may question why you would ever want to work at this place. Chances are, you would attach some significance to this observation, perhaps more than it was worth. This is a common finding in research on judgments and decisions.

Negative information attracts more attention than positive information (Pratto & John, 1991). Consequently, negative information is weighted more heavily than positive aspects when judgments are made (Coovert & Reeder, 1990). In studies of all kinds, ranging from forming impressions about other people to evaluating positive and negative information in order to reach a decision or judgment, negative information figures more prominently (Taylor, 1991).

Integrating Information

The next task in the inference process involves bringing information together and combining it into a social judgment. When people's integrative capabilities are compared with rational models, it appears that the human judgment process is rather haphazard and does not closely follow the principles of a rational model.

Consider the example of college admissions. When there are many applicants and only a few openings, criteria must be developed for deciding which people to admit and which to reject. Most college admissions departments have a formula for admitting students that dictates how heavily to weight SAT scores, high school grades, letters of recommendation, the personal essay, and other sources of information. With such clear standards available, one would assume that the college admissions decision makers do a good job of using this formula to determine who will be admitted and who will not. However, studies show that when there are clear standards for combining information into a judgment, computers typically outperform human decision makers (Dawes, Faust, & Meehl, 1989).

Why is this true? Human decision makers have great faith in their abilities to make decisions. When asked what procedures they use to make decisions, they typically report that they are more consistent, use more pieces of information, and make more complex judgments than they actually do. The reason that computers typically outperform human judges is that the computer consistently uses criteria established by people, weights information in a standard way, combines the information according to the formula, and reaches a judgment. Human decision makers, in contrast, may be swayed by pet theories or stereotypes that influence the information they select. Extensive studies have pitted human judges against computers or other mechanical aids and have yielded the same conclusion. When people can specify the rules of inference they want to use to combine information into an overall decision or judgment, computers and other mechanical aids always do a better job of following these rules than human judges do (Meehl, 1954).

Imagine how this process might work after your job interview. A small group of individuals who met you during your visit is assigned the task of deciding whether to hire you. Each person has only a modest amount of information about you. One person

Decision making often involves collecting and integrating complex information. People typically think they are more consistent, use more information, and make more complex judgments than is actually the case.

points out that you seemed nervous under pressure, as evidenced by the fact that you dropped your roll on the floor during lunch. Another, however, argues that you could be a potential Mark Comet, given that you both have competitive tennis in your background. Another points out that your college transcript shows you have high grades in virtually every subject, suggesting great ability. The next person, however, complains that although you did well in everything, you have not shown any special talents. In short, then, each evaluator may have certain idiosyncratic ways of viewing the information derived from your brief visit that he or she considers relevant to the overall judgment of whether you should be hired. It is indeed unnerving to realize one's fate often depends upon this type of decision-making process.

Judgments of Covariation

In addition to putting information together to form coherent impressions of people and events, we are also concerned about figuring out what goes with what in social life. Many of our beliefs involve statements about the relationship between things. For example, the adage "All work and no play makes Jack a dull boy" implies that working too hard and being dull are related and that playing and not being dull go together. Similarly, the statement "Blonds have more fun" implies a relationship between being blond and having fun and between not being blond and having less fun. Technically, such ideas about the associations between things are called judgments of **covariation.**

In making judgments about covariation, people are prone to certain errors. Specifically, they tend to see things as going together when they think they ought to go together or when they share features that make them seem similar. Thus, when a relationship between two variables is expected, a person is likely to overestimate how closely related those two things are or impose a relationship when none exists. This process is called **illusory correlation.**

Illusory Correlation. Several factors can produce an illusory correlation (Klauer & Meiser, 2000). The first is associative meaning, in which two items are seen as belonging together because they "ought" to be, on the basis of prior expectations. Thus, members of minority groups are often seen as having attributes stereotypically associated with their group because of their membership, when, in fact, any given individual in the group may not exhibit the stereotypical behavior or may contradict it (Hamilton & Gifford, 1976). A second basis of illusory correlation is paired distinctiveness, in which two items are thought to go together because they share some unusual feature. For example, distinctive social groups, such as religious groups that dress differently, are especially likely to evoke distinctive, novel stereotypes (Mullen & Johnson, 1995), and social groups that do not appear to be any different from the people around them may be erroneously assumed to have less extreme attributes (Sanbonmatsu, Shavitt, & Gibson, 1994). Illusory correlations, then, can substitute for real correlations when people have expectations or theories about whether two factors go together.

Framing Effects

How decision alternatives are framed, that is, the terms in which they are cast, often strongly influence people's judgments. For example, if someone you admire tells you that a particular summer job will "be a great opportunity," you are likely to be disposed favorably toward the job even before you know what it is. In contrast, if someone tells you that "at least it's a job," you are likely to approach the position with some dread, feeling that at least it will pay the bills but it probably won't be very exciting.

Framing effects are well established in social cognition. One of the most common and influential ones is whether a decision is presented in terms of the gains it will create or the losses that might be incurred (Kahneman & Tversky, 1982). For example, research generally suggests that people become very cautious when alternatives are phrased in terms of their risks, but they are far more likely to take chances when the alternatives are framed in terms of gains (e.g., Roney, Higgins, & Shah, 1995). Consider the following example:

> Imagine the United States is preparing for the outbreak of an unusual Asian disease, which is expected to kill 600 people. Two alternative programs to combat the disease have been proposed. Assume that the exact scientific estimate of the consequences of the program is as follows: If Program A is adopted, 200 people will be saved. If Program B is adopted, there is a one-third probability that 600 people will be saved, and a two-thirds probability that no people would be saved. Which program would you favor?
>
> Now imagine the same situation with these two alternatives: If Program C is adopted, 400 people will die. If Program D is adopted, there is a one-third probability that no one will die, and a two-thirds probability that 600 people will die. (Based on Tversky & Kahneman, 1982).

Tversky and Kahneman presented these problems to college students. When the problem was framed in terms of lives saved, 72 percent of the participants chose Program A. However, when the program was phrased in terms of lives lost, 78 percent favored Program D, and only 22 percent favored Program C, which has the same outcome as Program A!

This result, that people are more risk-averse when decision alternatives are framed in terms of losses, has been found in many studies, and the implications are important. Such findings may affect how health warnings and information about other risks (e.g., the benefits of sunscreen use) should be presented and may illuminate systematic biases in the everyday decisions people make.

Emotion and Inference

Many of the errors and biases we have considered share an important feature. They represent evaluative beliefs. Often we form an emotional commitment to a particular theory or belief that overrides the information as we see it. We think we've done well on a job interview because we want the job so badly, for example. You might therefore assume that emotion is a process that derails cognition in the search for accuracy. In certain respects, you would be correct. However, emotion is also a vital part of decision making, and when people ignore their emotions or don't have access to their emotions, they may make decisions that work against their interest. We pick our partners, our jobs, even our college on the basis of the emotional cues we get from the decision-making context. This is not to say that our emotions are always on target. Like cognition, emotions can lead us astray, but the role that emotions play in all forms of social cognition is becoming ever more evident, as the next sections suggest.

Mood and Inference

Perhaps you have noticed that when you get a good grade on a test, you're nicer to your roommate, or that when you've had a nice time with your girlfriend or boyfriend, you're more likely to help someone who needs it. Or perhaps you've noticed that when you're feeling anxious, all of your activities seem more risky. These examples illustrate some of the effects that mood has on inference and behavior (Murphy & Zajonc, 1993).

How have psychologists uncovered the effects of mood on people's beliefs and behavior? Like Peter Pan teaching the Darling children how to fly, psychologists lead people to think happy thoughts by surprising them with an unexpected gift, inducing them to concentrate on happy experiences ("Think of Christmas, think of snow"), asking them to recall a time in the past when they were very happy, or having them read a series of statements that suggest a progressively happier state of mind. Before very long, people exposed to these techniques report that they feel more cheerful, even euphoric. Alternatively, psychologists can make people unhappy by getting them to think about times in the past when they were sad or having them read a series of statements that produce a progressively negative mood. But negative moods are harder to induce than positive moods, and once in them, people are more likely to try to escape negative moods.

What is the effect of mood on behavior? When we are in a good mood, we tend to be more sociable and more altruistic in our behavior. We spend more time with others and help others more, for example. What happens when we're in a bad mood? You might think that people in a bad mood would be more withdrawn and help other people less, and sometimes this is true. But often, people who are in a bad mood want to escape that bad mood, and so instead of acting in a way that is consistent with their bad mood, they try to work themselves out of it by being sociable, by helping others, or by engaging in other positive actions. A bad mood, or even just the stress of the day, can lead people to make decisions with short-term benefits but long-term adverse effects (Gray, 1999), and so the effects of mood on an immediate judgment have far from trivial effects. This means that the effects of positive mood on prosocial behavior are stronger than the effects of negative mood in producing antisocial behavior (Isen, 1999).

Mood also influences memory. Perhaps you have had the experience of receiving a piece of good news and then finding yourself remembering other past experiences of being happy, feeling good, or feeling competent. Under many circumstances, people remember material whose valence fits their current mood state (Fiedler, Nickel, Muehlfriedel, & Unkelbach, 2001). This effect is called **mood-congruent memory.** People tend to recall positive material when they're in a positive mood. Does mood-congruent memory work for negative moods as well? Sometimes people recall more negative material when they're in a negative mood. This seems to be especially true of people who are depressed (Lyubomirsky, Caldwell, & Nolen-Hoeksema, 1998). But remember that the effects of negative mood are more variable; sometimes people in a negative mood think of positive things, in part so they can work themselves out of the bad mood (Rusting & DeHart, 2000).

Mood also affects judgments. Cheerful people like just about everything better than people who are not in a good mood: themselves, their health, their cars, other people, the future, and even politics (see Fiske & Taylor, 1991, for a review). Do unhappy people dislike everything? Again, the evidence is mixed. Sometimes unhappy people make negative judgments about others, but other times they do not. Negative mood has a less reliable impact on judgments than does positive mood. Mood also influences the predictions people make about the future (DeSteno, Petty, Wegener, & Rucker, 2000). People who are depressed tend to be accurate in making pessimistic predictions but relatively off-base in predicting positive events. The opposite is true of people who are more optimistic (Shrauger, Mariano, & Walter, 1998).

Mood influences not only what we remember and how we evaluate our world but also how we make judgments. Happy people are expansive, inclusive, and impulsive in their decision making. They make decisions quickly, they work quickly at simple tasks, they make more unusual connections among the things they are thinking about, they have looser and less organized associations, they group more varied things together into the same category, and they think in a more stereotyped fashion (Isen, 1987; Park & Banaji, 2000). A negative mood seems to slow down the processing of information: People are more methodical and precise, they make decisions more slowly, they make more complex causal attributions, and they work more slowly, but they are not necessarily more accurate (Gannon, Skowronski, & Betz, 1994). These findings extend to people who are chronically in a good or a poor mood. For example, extroverted people are especially influenced by positive information, whereas people who are high in neuroticism are more responsive to negative information (Rusting & Larsen, 1998).

Happy people also do not like to receive negative feedback, and they are especially "loss-averse" (Esses, 1989). This means that risky choices that highlight the negative consequences of decision alternatives seem worse to people who are feeling happy (Isen, Nygren, & Ashby, 1988). People in a negative mood, on the other hand, do not seem to be as strongly affected by negative feedback, and potential losses may not loom as large for them either.

What, then, might be the effect of your mood on extracting and processing information from your job interview? If you were in a good mood at the time you visited the prospective workplace, you would probably pay disproportionate attention to all the positive features of the job and work environment. If you were in a bad mood, however, you might focus more on the apparent disadvantages of the position. Later, when you had to make a decision about the job, if you were in a good mood you might make the decision quite impulsively based on the positive features of the experience. On the other hand, if you were in a bad mood you might survey your impressions more methodically and even become quite bogged down in making the decision. In short, affective factors such as mood can influence judgment and decision making in important ways.

Automatic Evaluation

In recent years, social psychologists have provided compelling evidence that many social cognition processes occur virtually automatically and without awareness (Bargh, 1997; Batson, Engel, & Fridell, 1999). Essentially, the years of practice we have had responding to positive and negative cues in the environment have made our emotional, our cognitive, and even our behavioral responses to many cues automatic. We respond to these evaluative cues without needing to attend to them or think about them.

In a study that shows these automatic associations, John Bargh and his associates gave students word puzzles to solve very much like that shown in Figure 3–1. Students were told to circle any words that they saw in the puzzle. For some of the students, the words embedded in the figure related to aging and included such terms as "elderly," "slow," and "aged" (as is true in Figure 3–1). For others, the words were related to neutral topics ("corn," "classroom"). Bargh and his associates reasoned that for those students who received the word puzzle with the aging-related clues, the stereotype of the elderly would be automatically primed in such a way that it would effect future thoughts and behaviors. The results bore out this hypothesis. When leaving the experiment, those participants who had been primed with the stereotype of the elderly walked more slowly than the participants who had not been so primed (Bargh, Chen, & Burrows, 1996).

This automatic evaluation can occur very rapidly. In one study, Fazio, Sanbonmatsu, Powell, and Kardes (1986) presented participants with a series of word-pair sequences and asked them to judge whether the target adjectives were negative or positive. The first word, a prime, appeared for 200 milliseconds and the second, the

d	e	g	d	y	i	t	n	d	c	e	f
e	a	g	e	d	a	l	w	m	t	l	t
c	m	e	c	k	n	p	g	a	a	d	s
r	w	j	e	n	c	r	j	e	f	e	e
e	o	p	l	a	i	y	a	u	r	r	n
p	l	d	d	e	e	c	h	y	n	l	i
i	s	w	r	i	n	k	l	e	d	y	l
t	y	p	f	j	t	e	u	g	v	p	e

Figure 3–1 Word Puzzle (after Bargh, Chen, & Burroughs, 1996). See how many words you can find in this word puzzle. What do those words suggest? Puzzles like these have been used to prime concepts automatically, in this case a stereotype of the elderly.

How would you regard this scene if you were the girl's father? The boy's ex-girlfriend? The person who had arranged the first date between these two? The interpretations we make and the affect we experience are heavily determined by the motives we bring to social situations.

target, appeared 100 milliseconds after the prime had disappeared. Despite the very rapid speed at which this task had to be accomplished, participants' rating of the target word as positive or negative was much faster when the prime and target had the same evaluative content (both were negative or both were positive) than when they were incongruent.

Such evidence clearly shows that evaluation is one of the most rapid and fundamental judgments that we make that guides our processing of subsequent information. Automatic evaluation seems to come from the fact that evaluatively tinged stimuli are easily and quickly noticed and prompt the behavioral tendencies of approach or avoidance (Chen & Bargh, 1999; Wentura, Rothermund, & Bak, 2000). In essence, these early and rapid judgments set the stage for the actions we will take.

Chen and Bargh (1999) hypothesized that identifying something as good or bad arouses an action tendency to approach or avoid a situation or stimulus. In one study that showed this, they had participants respond to attitude statements either by pulling a lever toward them or by pushing it away from them. Consistent with the hypothesis, participants were faster to respond to negatively valenced words when they pushed the lever away from them (avoided it) than when they pushed it toward them (approached it) (Chen & Bargh, 1999).

Another example of this automatic evaluation-behavior link is the fact that people often nonconsciously mimic postures, mannerisms, and facial expressions of the people they interact with. If you doubt this, you can try an experiment. Smile at the person you are speaking to and see if your smile isn't reciprocated; then rest your hands on your hips and see if your partner doesn't mirror your behavior; then scratch you head and smooth your hair and see if your partner doesn't move his or her hand in that direction. This nonconscious mimicry is very common in social interaction, and it is a good example of the direct effect of the perception of other people's behaviors on our own behavior, usually without any awareness or intention on our part (Chartrand & Bargh, 1999).

In Chapter 2, Volume 1, we noted how goals can influence cognition, ranging from how we gather information to how we put it together. Goals can also influence behavior automatically. Habits may be thought of, in part, as an association between a goal and an action so that if a goal is primed, the action will occur automatically. Perhaps you've had the experience of thinking about something you need to do at school and discovering that you are now driving in that direction even though you were headed elsewhere. Or perhaps you made late dinner plans with friends and found yourself accidentally cooking dinner at your usual time. Habits do indeed seem to be a result of goal-dependent automatic behavior (Aarts & Dijksterhuis, 2000). The fact that many of our emotions, thoughts, and actions occur as automatic responses to cues that are rapidly and unconsciously processed is a very important insight from social cognition research. It helps to explain how human beings accomplish the vast amount of information processing that they seem to do so effortlessly. And it helps us understand why so often we are the creatures of our own habits.

Motivation and Inference

The particular content of one's motivation also influences inferences. How we process and put information together can be heavily influenced by the inferences we want to make. People often generate and evaluate information in a self-serving manner, constructing theories that are consistent with the belief that good things will happen to them and bad things will not (Dunning, Leuenberger, & Sherman, 1995; Kunda, 1987). For example, on learning that the divorce rate for first marriages is 50 percent, most people predict that they will not fall within that 50 percent group and will remain married to their spouse for life. They convince themselves that this is the case by highlighting their personal attributes that might be associated with a stable marriage and down-

Research Closeup

"I'll Get It Done by Friday": The Planning Fallacy in Action

How many times have you convinced yourself that you could complete a paper long before it was due, only to find yourself writing furiously the night before you have to turn it in? How many times have you promised yourself you would keep up with the course readings, only to find that you are going through chapters for the first time as you're studying for the course midterm? These experiences are familiar to most—perhaps all—college students, and they are examples of a well-established phenomenon called the **planning fallacy** (Buehler, Griffin, & MacDonald, 1997).

The planning fallacy refers to the fact that people consistently overestimate how quickly and easily they will achieve a goal and underestimate the amount of time, money, or effort that will be required to reach that goal. In a study that examined the planning fallacy (Buehler, Griffin, & Ross, 1994), college students were asked to list an academic project that had to be completed within the next week and to estimate when they intended to begin the project, when they expected to complete the project, and how many hours they expected to put into it. A week later, the students were asked if they had completed the project and when. Although all the students had estimated that they would complete the project comfortably in the time indicated, 1 week later more than half the projects remained uncompleted. Those that had been completed had typically taken, on average, nearly 5 days longer than had been estimated. So much for planning!

If our best-laid plans do not guide our behavior, what does? If you think back to when you typically complete a paper or project, you will realize that often the answer is "Right before it is due." Deadlines have a major impact on whether people complete projects and when they do so. Surprisingly, most of us are unaware of the effect of deadlines. When participants in the studies by Buehler and colleagues (1994) were asked about the factors that influenced when they completed their projects, most were oblivious of the role that deadlines had played. Yet well over two thirds of the participants finished their projects the day or night before they were due.

playing the significance of or actively refuting information that might suggest a vulnerability to divorce. Thus, for example, one might point to one's parents' enduring marriage, the close family life that existed in one's early childhood, and the fact that one's high school relationship lasted a full 4 years as evidence for a likely stable marriage. The fact that one's husband has already been divorced once, a factor that predicts a second divorce, might be interpreted not only as not leading to divorce in one's own case, but as a protective factor ("He does not want this marriage to fail like the last one, so he's working especially hard to keep our relationship strong").

When we are motivated to make a good decision or to reach a careful inference, do we do a better job or a worse job than if the inference matters less to us? Pelham and Neter (1995) undertook several studies to address this intriguing question. They manipulated motivation in several ways, including a financial incentive to be accurate, personal accountability for the decision made, and personal involvement in the decision. In the three separate studies, they found that higher levels of motivation increased the accuracy of judgments when those judgments were easy to make but decreased judgmental accuracy in the case of difficult judgments. Thus, a desire to be accurate does not necessarily translate into reality.

Another motivational factor that may influence the nature of social inference concerns one's assessment of one's knowledgeability or expertise in a particular area. If we consider ourselves to be experts on a topic, are we? And does that expertise actually translate into better judgments? For example, if you believe yourself to be very knowledgeable about cars, will that information translate into better or worse information gathering when you go to purchase one? Radecki and Jaccard (1995) found that people know less than they think and that their incorrect beliefs about their level of knowledge can actually hurt them. They found that people who perceived themselves to be knowledgeable gathered less information, with the result that they made poorer decisions. The "Research Closeup" represents another example of motivated inference.

Emotions guide the information we seek out and how we process it. What emotions do you think these women are experiencing as they are recalling the events pictured in the scrapbook

Suppressing Thoughts and Emotions

As the previous discussion has implied, we often try to regulate our emotions by engaging in a behavior that might restore a good mood or in some cases by simply trying to suppress emotion-laden thoughts. Perhaps you've tried to forget about an exam you took that you didn't think you did very well on, and despite your efforts, you kept thinking about the test. You are not alone. Suppressing one's thoughts is difficult, and many of these efforts not only fail but may actually produce a rebound effect (Wegner, 1994). Many people find themselves thinking about exactly what they're trying to forget.

Theoretical accounts of this process suggest that when you are trying to suppress a thought, you are simultaneously trying to find things to distract yourself and also automatically monitoring the environment for cues you might have to suppress. This is why, despite your best efforts, you may find yourself thinking about exactly what you're trying to forget. (For example, a stray remark about applying to graduate school by a friend might remind you about the test you just took); (e.g., Liberman & Forster, 2000.)

There are costs to this suppression (Richards & Gross, 2000). Trying to suppress an emotional response to an event involves a lot of effort, and as a result, not only do people find it hard to suppress these feelings, but their physiological processes are affected and they are more aroused (Gross & Levenson, 1997). Even the immune system may be influenced adversely (Petrie, Booth, & Pennebaker, 1998) when people are actively trying to avoid thinking about the difficult aspects of their lives.

Affective Forecasting

Imagine that the dean of your university has called you up, personally congratulated you on the grades you have achieved, and told you that you will have a scholarship for the remainder of your academic career. How would you feel, and how long would you feel that way? Most people are good at inferring how they would feel—elated and thrilled, for example—but they are typically rather poor at estimating how long they will feel that way. This bias gets in the way of a common phenomenon called "affective forecasting."

"Affective forecasting" refers to the ways in which we use our emotions to make decisions about the future. Generally speaking, people overpredict how long their emotional reactions to events will last. In most cases, we do not respond emotionally to an event as much as we thought we would (Gilbert & Wilson, 2000). We see our affective responses as more durable than they actually turn out to be. This seems to occur in large part because we overestimate the impact of one event on our future, thinking, or emotions ("I'll be so happy if the Lakers win this year") and fail to realize how much our thoughts and feelings about the future will be influenced by other intervening events that will also affect our emotional state (Wilson, Wheatley, Meyers, Gilbert, & Axsom, 2000; Gilbert, Pinel, Wilson, Blumberg, & Wheatley, 1998).

Inference: A Summing Up

Overall, how well does the social perceiver fare on tasks of social inference? The evidence we have considered suggests that when evaluated against appropriate standards, social inference suffers from some predictable errors and biases (Fiske & Taylor, 1991) as shown in Figure 3–2. This evaluation prompts at least two reactions. The first is concern over the disconcerting ways in which social perceivers let their prior expectations override and ignore relevant information. The second reaction is puzzlement. How do people manage in their social lives as well as they seem to if their social judgments are biased?

One answer to this question is that many of the rational models that psychologists expect people to use are very difficult to employ on a daily basis. Moreover, much of our social information is unreliable, biased, and incomplete, and it may not be presented to the average person in a way that is clear or usable. The conditions that maximize ac-

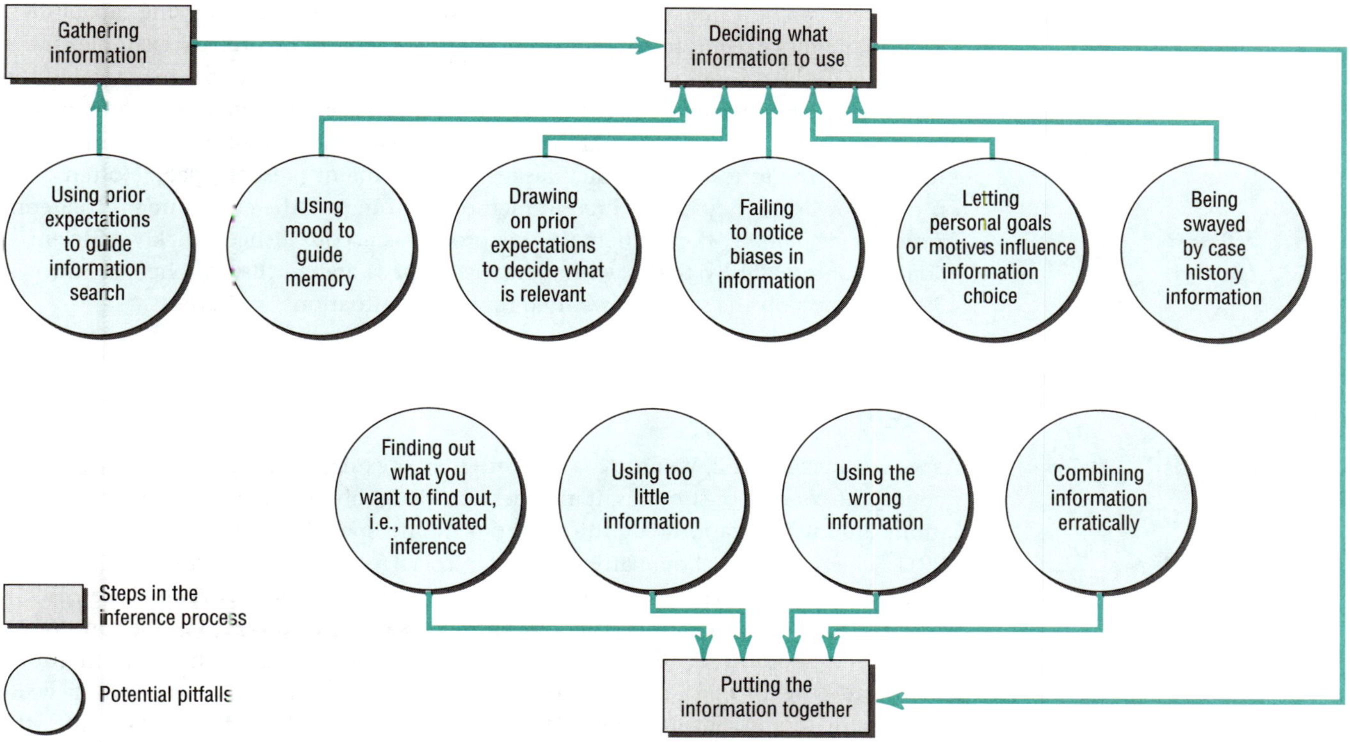

Figure 3–2 **Social Inference and Its Pitfalls.**

curacy seldom occur in real life, and accordingly, in many situations, social perceivers could not apply a rational model even if they were so inclined.

Perhaps most significant is the fact that it is often more important for people to be efficient—that is, to process information quickly—than to be 100 percent accurate. Consider the sheer volume of information that an individual encounters in a particular day. Even an act as simple as crossing the street requires watching the lights and signs, the flow of the traffic, and the pedestrians on one's own side and the other side of the street. If people truly had to make all their inferences using rational models of inference, they might still be plotting a course to follow across the street when the light changed back to "Don't walk." In other words, careful, complex, and rational decisions require time, and given the busy, stressful nature of the real world, time is a very expensive commodity.

Consequently, people draw on their preexisting conceptions of people and situations and use inferential shortcuts to make social judgments quickly and efficiently. This is not to say that the errors we have just documented in the social inference process are inconsequential. Indeed, they can often have problematic consequences. Moreover, people are not very good at discriminating their poor and biased evaluations from their good ones, nor do they respond with the vigilance one might expect when they are warned that their inferences may be biased (Stapel, Martin, & Schwarz, 1998). Training people in appropriate reasoning strategies can therefore be essential, leading people to make better inferences (Schaller, Asp, Rosell, & Heim, 1996). Improving the inference process, then, is an important priority for social cognition researchers. But it must be done in the context of understanding the processes people typically use (Nisbett, Fong, Lehman, & Chang, 1987).

To understand how the social perceiver actually forms inferences requires an important observation. The act of bringing information together and solving a problem, as we have noted, can be a time-consuming task involving substantial processing capabilities. However, memory seems to have an almost limitless capacity. Think, for example, of the number of popular songs to which you know all the lyrics. The number may total in the hundreds or even thousands. This important difference is fundamental to how people actually make inferences. Rather than engaging in elaborate and often time-consuming problem solving for each individual task the environment presents, people often draw on the knowledge they have stored in memory to interpret the environment that confronts them, namely, their schemas. This process is accomplished quickly, efficiently, and often automatically, that is, without intention or awareness (Bargh, Chen, & Burrows, 1996). It draws on the schemas we hold for people, situations, and events.

Schemas

As we saw in Chapter 2, Volume 1, a **schema** is an organized, structured set of cognitions about some concept or stimulus. It includes knowledge about the concept or stimulus, relations among the various cognitions about it, and specific examples (Fiske & Taylor, 1991). Schemas can be about particular people, social roles, or the self; attitudes about particular objects; stereotypes about groups; or perceptions of common events (Eckes, 1995).

Schemas about extremely common events are usually called **scripts** (Abelson, 1976). A script is a standard sequence of behavior over a period of time. One script might be called "ordering for a group in a Chinese restaurant." Everyone sits down, and the waiter brings the menus. Several people talk at once, giving their favorite dishes, while others say they never know what to have and would someone else just please decide. Then people go through the menu section by section, haggling over which soup to have, bargaining away their favorite beef dish (which no one else wants) for sweet and sour pork (which at least one ally does), and finally appointing the most self-confident and brash person to communicate the whole negotiated package to the waiter.

We could generate similar scripts for other ritualized series of events, such as having a baby, taking a shower, taking a final exam, or playing a basketball game. The essence of a script is in its boundedness in time, its causal flow (early events cause later ones), and its being a simple, coherent perceptual unit.

People have scripts for common, organized sequences of behavior, such as ordering food in a restaurant or paying for a purchase in a store. These scripts help us to anticipate what will happen next and to prepare our behavior accordingly.

Schemas and scripts are important because people draw on them to interpret the environment. That is, each time we are confronted with a new situation, instead of trying to understand it afresh, we draw on our knowledge of similar past situations. In this way schemas help us to process information. They help us to recognize what aspects of a situation or stimulus are important. They add structure and organization to information. Schemas enable us to remember information better, to organize details, and to process information relevant to the schema very quickly. Schemas can sometimes fill in gaps and knowledge as well as help us interpret and evaluate new information.

An exemplar is a model example of a category. Michael Jordan is an exemplar of the category, "basketball star."

Organization of Schemas

An important feature of schemas is that they often have some hierarchical organization. They have some abstract and general elements and some more concrete, specific ones that are linked to each other (Smith, 1996). Suppose we had a schema of a party. We know that parties are usually held in the late afternoon or evening, usually in someone's home. They have guests and usually a host and a hostess; they might have some food and some alcoholic drinks. Normally people interact by standing and talking to each other rather than by watching one common event (such as a singer). In short, we have in our minds a clear, well-developed, somewhat abstract picture of a party. It has a standard sequence—a number of elements with clear causal interrelationships.

At a more specific level, the schema might well have different categories of parties, all of which would be clearly distinct. For example, a wine-and-cheese party held at the opening of an art exhibition would be clearly different from the weekly Saturday night bashes at the country club, where all the local businesspeople and their spouses get together and drink too much, or from a formal diplomatic reception at a foreign embassy. At a still more specific level, our schema might include several specific parties we have attended, especially if those parties had some distinctive or memorable event (Trafimow & Wyer, 1993), such as the hostess being thrown into the pool by her guests. All told, we might have a hierarchical schema of a party that would include a general, abstract concept covering all kinds of parties we have gone to.

Many schemas contain **exemplars,** which are the most common or best examples of a schema. For example, your schema of "bird" probably includes being small, feathered, and mottled brown in color, with a long tail and little clawed feet. But the exemplar or best example of the category may be a robin or a blue jay (Smith & Medin, 1981). Exemplars need not correspond to all the schema's typical features and may, in fact, be rather different from those typical features, like the robin and the blue jay.

So far, our discussion of schemas makes them sound very orderly. However, the associations contained within a schema often more closely resemble a tangled web than a hierarchy (Cantor & Kihlstrom, 1987). For example, a politician, a con man, and a clown are all examples of extroverts. Being socially skilled is associated with each of them, yet being self-confident is associated with being a politician, or a con man, but not necessarily with being a clown. Thus, the more specific attributes embedded in a schema (socially skilled, self-confident) may overlap with many or few of the upper-level concepts (politician, clown, con man) (Andersen & Klatsky, 1987). Social categories, then, are very flexible and complex, and not always neat, tidy, and hierarchical.

Schematic Processing

Advantages

Schemas Aid Information Processing. Schemas are important because they help us process an enormous amount of information swiftly and economically. Indeed, schemas make processing more efficient in several different ways. They help us remember information and interpret new information, draw inferences from it, and evaluate whether we agree with it. They help us fill in gaps in our knowledge by suggesting what is likely to be true. They help us to perceive and label information that is either consistent or inconsistent with the schema (Sherman, Lee, Bessenoff, & Frost, 1998). And they help us prepare for the future by structuring our expectations about what is likely to happen. These advantages of schematic processing have been demonstrated in a wide variety of studies (see Fiske & Taylor, 1991).

Schemas Aid Recall. Memory often works best when we have a schematic representation of past events or people, because the schema will bring many details along with it (Hirt, 1990). For example, Cohen (1981) presented participants with a videotape of a woman and her husband sitting in their home. Half were told that the woman was a librarian and half that she was a waitress. Some of the features of the woman fit the schema of a librarian (as measured separately), such as wearing glasses, eating salad, drinking wine, and playing the piano. Others fit the schema of a waitress, such as having a bowling ball in the room, having no bookshelves in the room, and eating a chocolate birthday cake. Later the participants were asked to recall the details of the videotape. They remembered the schema-consistent details better, whether recall was assessed immediately or a week later (see also Madey & Gilovich, 1993).

But schema-inconsistent material is not always recalled poorly. Both schema-consistent material and schema-inconsistent material are remembered much better than items that are simply irrelevant to the schema (Brewer, Dull, & Lui, 1981; Hastie & Kumar, 1979), perhaps because it is difficult to learn material that is irrelevant to a schema.

Sometimes information that contradicts a schema is better recalled than information that is consistent with it, especially when a person has a very poorly developed or an extremely well-developed schema. People who are unfamiliar with a schema and attempt to learn it show an initial advantage in remembering schema-inconsistent information (Ruble & Stangor, 1986). Similarly, people who are highly familiar with a domain may more easily recognize inconsistencies. People with moderately well-formed schemas may be most attentive to consistent information (Higgins & Bargh, 1987). Consider, for example, the impressions that might be formed of Harry, a police officer who raises kittens and does needlepoint in his spare time. Those just meeting Harry and those who know him very well may be especially attentive to the schema-inconsistent behaviors, whereas those with a moderately well-developed conception of Harry may attend more to his schema-consistent behavior, such as his concern for abiding by the law or helping people in need (Borgida & DeBono, 1989).

Schemas Speed Up Processing. When people have a schema for a particular person or situation, it is easier for them to process information relevant to the schema. People who have watched a lot of soccer games, for example, simply see more and take in more information than people who know relatively little about soccer.

But schemas do not always speed up processing. In some cases, having a well-developed schema slows things down by introducing a more complex mass of information that must be processed (Fiske & Taylor, 1991). For example, an experienced soccer fan may spend a lot of time commenting on a dubious foul call because he or she knows that players often fake injuries, that apparent fouls may represent inadvertent stumbles, and that soccer action looks very different from different angles. To a novice, however, the referee's call of a foul might be sufficient to process what is happening in the game.

Schemas Aid Automatic Inference. Another important attribute of schematic processing is that some schema-related inferences appear to occur almost automatically, without any conscious effort. For example, when meeting an especially friendly person, you may automatically attribute to him other characteristics associated with friendliness, such as kindness and warmth, and may be completely unaware that you have done so. These automatic effects are most likely to occur if the information in the environment strongly suggests a particular schema, or if the schema involves a person or life domain about which you have strong emotional concerns (Bargh, 1994).

Schemas Add Information. A schema can help us fill in missing information when there are gaps in our knowledge. If we read about a police officer but have no information about his or her clothing, we imagine him or her to be wearing a blue uniform. We assume a nurse will be warm and caring, and that a queen will be rather aloof and haughty. Missing information is filled in by schema-consistent details, even when we must invent them.

Exemplars of schemas are often used to fill in missing information (Sia, Lord, Blessum, Thomas, & Lepper, 1999). For example, if "blue jay" is your exemplar, or best example, of the category "birds," then on briefly glimpsing some new bird, you may assume that the bird has a crest because the blue jay has a crest. If the exemplar of your category for birds is "robin," however, you might be less likely to assume that the new bird has a crest.

Schemas Aid Interpretation. Because schemas tell you how information in a particular domain relates to other information relevant to that domain, they help you interpret ambiguous situations. For example, a pediatrician diagnosing a child as having mumps can make a whole series of other inferences with confidence: how the child got the disease, what symptoms should be present, what the course of the disease will be, what treatment is best, and so on. For a person with no schema for mumps, none of this would be possible. Schemas allow confident inferences about matters that would otherwise not be clear (Read & Cesa, 1991). This effect seems to occur more for strong schemas than for weak ones, however. When people use weakly developed categories, such as "day people" versus "night people," the schema itself seems to be weakened by new and potentially irrelevant information (Fiske & Neuberg, 1990).

Schemas Provide Expectations. Schemas also contain expectations for what should happen. These expectations, in turn, can determine how pleasant or unpleasant we find a particular situation. When experience matches expectations, the result may be pleasant, whereas violations of expectations are often experienced as unpleasant. Suppose a black student who had worked to educate himself was nonetheless unable to find a job at his level of expertise. This experience might violate his expectations and would be likely to make him quite angry. A sense of deprivation relative to expectation has been cited as one of the causes of riots and other forms of social rebellion (Sears & McConahay, 1973).

Schemas Contain Affect. Affect consists of the feelings we have about the content of the schema. Consequently, use of a particular schema can produce an emotional response, called "schema-driven affect." For example, most of us have a fairly well-developed schema for "politician." It may include information about what the politician does in his or her job and what kinds of people are attracted to being a politician. The schema also includes any affective responses we have to the concept of politician. For example, some of us feel positively about politicians, thinking of them as helpful lawmakers; others may feel negatively about politicians, thinking of them as sly, self-serving, and power hungry. When information in the environment fits a particular schema, it triggers the affect attached to that schema (Fiske & Neuberg, 1990). The affect triggered by a schema is an efficient affective processing device: One can say, "I know that type and I know how I feel about him or her."

Under some circumstances, bringing a schema to bear on an object or an event can actually change the feelings one has toward that object or event. A series of studies by

Tesser (see Tesser & Conlee, 1975; Millar & Tesser, 1986) suggests that simply thinking about something with a schema in mind can intensify the affect one feels for that person or object. For example, if you feel that a professor belittled the comments you made in class, then the longer you think about it the more upset you are likely to become. Under other circumstances, however, schemas may make affect more complex, not more extreme (Linville & Jones, 1980; Linville, 1982). For example, if a good friend of yours snaps at you one day, this behavior may produce a fairly complex evaluation. You have so much information about your friend and about yourself that coming up with an explanation for this behavior may be difficult (Gilovich, 1987).

Liabilities of Schemas

All these advantages of schematic processing have their accompanying disadvantages, and many of them are precisely the errors and biases discussed at the beginning of this chapter. The tendencies to be overly accepting of information that fits a schema or theory, to fill in gaps in thinking by adding elements that do not belong but are schema-consistent, to apply schemas even when they do not fit very well, and to be unwilling to change schemas can all be liabilities. We can easily be misled by oversimplifications. Schematic processing has the advantage of speed and efficiency and of making events comprehensible and predictable; it has the disadvantage of leading to wrong interpretations, inaccurate expectations, and inflexible modes of response.

There are so many familiar examples of the dangers of this kind of stereotyping that it hardly seems necessary to belabor the point. Everyone knows that people frequently behave in ways contrary to the stereotype generally held about their groups. Yet schematic processing can lead the perceiver to ignore important information (von Hippel, Jonides, Hilton, & Narayan, 1993) or to reach some dangerously false inferences about individual members of the group. (We will discuss these issues in somewhat more detail in Chapter 1, Volume 2).

Mental Shortcuts: Using Cognitive Heuristics

As we've seen, efficiency pressures often lead people to fall back on their prior schemas or scripts for events to manage the rapid and complex flow of information in the social world. Still, we need a way to get from the information we see around us to the schemas. That is, we need to know which of these complex structures in long-term memory are appropriate for understanding any given social situation. This complex task is solved in part through the use of **heuristics** (Tversky & Kahneman, 1974).

The Representativeness Heuristic

Is John, the new guy in your math class, really the incurable romantic he seems to be, or is he a cad who moves on every woman he meets? The act of identifying people or events as examples of particular schemas is fundamental to all social inference and behavior. The question "What is it?" must be answered before any other cognitive task can be performed. A mental shortcut called the "representativeness heuristic" provides a rapid method for accomplishing this task.

Basically, the representativeness heuristic matches information in the environment against schemas to determine the likelihood that the match is appropriate. Consider the following description: "Steve is very shy and withdrawn, invariably helpful, but with little interest in people or the world of reality. A meek and tidy soul, he has a need for order and structure and a passion for detail" (Tversky & Kahneman, 1974), Suppose you are now asked to guess Steve's occupation. Is he a farmer, a circus clown, a librarian, a con artist, or a pediatrician? With adequate information about the number and characteristics of the people in these different occupations, one could conceivably estimate the likelihood of a meek clown, a shy con artist, and so on. This task, however, is likely to take a long time, and good information on which to form these judgments would undoubtedly be lacking In such cases, the representativeness heuristic provides a quick solution. One decides whether Steve is representative of (or similar to) the average person in each of the occupational categories and makes one's judgment about his occupation accordingly. Students given this task usually guessed that Steve was a librarian because the description of Steve is representative of attributes that are stereotypically associated with librarians (Tversky & Kahneman, 1974).

The representativeness heuristic, then, helps one to decide if a particular person or event is an example of a particular schema. However, this quite rapid method of identifying people and events is occasionally fallible because people sometimes fail to take into account other important qualifying information. For example, if Steve lives in a town with lots of farmers and only one librarian, the likelihood that he is a farmer and not a librarian is very high. The representativeness heuristic would not incorporate this qualifying information. As we noted earlier, people often ignore relevant statistical information that they ought to incorporate into their inferences. Under these kinds of circumstances then, use of the representativeness heuristic would probably produce an incorrect answer.

The Conjunction Error. The representativeness heuristic can also lead us to combine information that does not belong together, simply because the information seems as if it ought to go together. In one study, students were told that a fellow student was gregarious and literary. When asked how likely it was that he was an engineering major, they responded that it was very unlikely. However, when asked how likely it was that he would start out as an engineering major but switch to journalism, participants gave this possibility a much higher rating (Slovic, Fischhoff, & Lichtenstein, 1977). Presumably, they could readily imagine how a gregarious, literary person would decide journalism was for him and not engineering, but they could not imagine how such a person would remain an engineer. But note that the likelihood that any given student is an engineering major is much higher than the likelihood that a student beginning as an engineering major will switch to journalism. Thus, although starting out in engineering and switching to journalism seems more likely because journalism fits our ideas of what gregarious and literary people do, it is far less probable than the likelihood of staying in engineering. This error is called the **conjunction error.** It is an error because people believe the combination of two events (majoring in engineering and switching to journalism) is more likely than either of the events alone (majoring in engineering or majoring in journalism), which is incorrect reasoning (Gavanski & Roskos-Ewoldsen, 1991; see also Bar-Hillel & Neter, 1993).

The Availability Heuristic

How often does a person break a leg when skiing? How many college students are psychology majors? These are questions about the frequency of events or the likelihood that a particular event will happen. A common way that people answer such questions is to use examples that come to mind. If you can think of many college students who are psychology majors among your friends and acquaintances, you may assume that there are many psychology majors on campus. Or if you can think of several people who broke their legs in skiing accidents, you may assume that the chances of breaking your leg while skiing are rather high. Using the ease of remembering examples or the amount of information you can quickly remember as a guide to making an inference is called "using the availability heuristic" (Tversky & Kahneman, 1974).

As is the case with the representativeness heuristic, little cognitive work need be performed to accomplish this task. If you have no trouble thinking of psychology majors among your acquaintances, you will probably assume that a great many people in college are psychology majors; whereas if you have trouble bringing to mind examples of psychology majors, you may conclude that relatively few individuals are psychology majors (Rothman & Hardin, 1997).

Under many circumstances, use of the availability heuristic produces correct answers. After all, when examples of something can be easily brought to mind, it is usually because there are lots of them. Therefore, availability is often a good estimate of frequency. However, biasing factors can increase or decrease the availability of some kinds of phenomena or events without altering their actual overall frequency. For example, if you are a psychology major, many of your friends and acquaintances are likely to be psychology majors as well, and consequently you will have relatively little difficulty bringing examples of psychology majors to mind. Because of this bias, you are likely to overestimate the frequency of psychology majors. In contrast, another student who is a chemistry major and who spends most of her time with chemists or physicists would probably underestimate the number of psychology majors because she cannot bring to mind examples of many psychology majors.

The availability heuristic, then, enables you to answer questions concerning quantity and frequency on the basis of how quickly or easily you can retrieve examples from memory. The ease with which the process can be accomplished or the volume of information that can be retrieved quickly determines the answer (e.g., MacLeod & Campbell, 1992; Manis, Shedler, Jonides, & Nelson, 1993).

The Simulation Heuristic

Suppose you borrowed your father's car during a college vacation and smashed it up after a party you attended. How would you answer the question "What is Dad going to think when he finds out I've smashed up the car?" You may think through what you know about your father and his reaction to crises, run through this information in your mind, and generate several possibilities. The ease with which particular endings come to mind is used to judge what is likely to happen. Your father could refuse to pay your college tuition next term or he could ignore the whole thing, but in your mind, it is easiest to imagine that he will strongly suggest that you find a job so that you can help pay for the car. This inferential technique is known as the "simulation heuristic" (Kahneman & Tversky, 1982).

The simulation heuristic may be used for a wide variety of tasks, including prediction ("What will Dad say?"), causality ("Was I driving badly or was the other guy driving badly?" Mandel & Lehman, 1996), and affective responses (Kahneman & Miller, 1986). On this latter point, consider the situation of a near miss:

> Mr. Crane and Mr. Tees were scheduled to leave the airport on different flights, at the same time. They traveled from town in the same limousine, were caught in a traffic jam, and arrived at the airport 30 minutes after the scheduled departure time of their flights.
>
> Mr. Crane is told his flight left on time. Mr. Tees is told that his flight was delayed, and left just 5 minutes ago.
>
> Who is more upset: Mr. Crane or Mr. Tees? (Kahneman & Tversky, 1982, p. 203)

Virtually everyone says, "Mr. Tees." Why? Presumably, one can imagine no way that Mr. Crane could have made his plane, whereas were it not for that one long light or the slow baggage handler or the illegally parked car or the error in the posted departure gate, Mr. Tees would have made it. Thus, the simulation heuristic and its ability to generate "if only" conditions can be used to understand the psychology of near misses and the frustration, regret, grief, or indignation they may produce (Bar-Hillel & Neter, 1996). The contrast between the exceptional circumstance and the normal situation intensifies the emotional reaction to the unusual situation.

Counterfactual Reasoning. Abnormal or exceptional events lead people to imagine alternatives that are normal and consequently dissimilar to the actual outcome (Kahneman & Miller, 1986). This process is called **counterfactual reasoning.** For example, after you have done badly on a test, you may hold the counterfactual thought, "If only I had studied, I would have passed the test." As this example suggests, people are most likely to generate counterfactual thoughts when they have experienced unexpected or negative outcomes (Markman & Tetlock, 2000). When such an outcome is preceded by abnormal or unusual events, people are especially likely to undo the event mentally through counterfactual reasoning. For example, if the reason you failed to study was that you had to take your roommate to the hospital, you might be more likely to think "if only" than if you simply ran out of time.

When they construct their "if only" thoughts, people typically focus on only certain kinds of events or actions. They do not, for example, introduce unlikely antecedent events, called "uphill changes." Thus, for example, in thinking through how you might have studied more, the idea that the day could have been extended by 10 additional hours is not likely to occur to you, because it is an impossibility. On the other hand, you might think, "If only I had studied earlier" or "If only I hadn't had to take my roommate to the hospital." These changes are termed "downhill changes" because they delete unlikely antecedent events (e.g., the fact that your roommate had to be taken to the emergency room). For example, role-playing jurors deciding how much compensation an individual was entitled to after he was injured during a store robbery believed that he was entitled to more compensation when the store was presented as one in which he had never shopped before than when it was described as a routine stop for him (Miller & McFarland, 1986).

Why do people engage in counterfactual reasoning? Are they simply trying to make themselves miserable? After all, when something unexpected or negative takes place, imagining how it could have been otherwise is hardly going to change the situation. Research suggests that counterfactual thoughts about what might have been may serve two functions. First, under some circumstances, counterfactual thoughts may help people feel better. For example, when people have been through a stressful event, they often imagine how much worse it could have been (Taylor, Wood, & Lichtman, 1983). An automobile accident victim may focus less on the damage done to her car than on the fact that she could have been killed if the car had hit her driver's-side door. Imagining how much worse things could have been makes one feel better about the unpleasant situation that exists.

Counterfactual thoughts may also serve a preparatory function for the future. If you realize your car battery wouldn't have died if you hadn't left the inside light on, you probably won't do that again. When imagining how easily you could have avoided the problem produces negative affect, the motivation to change and improve—an emotional wake-up call—is increased (McMullen & Markman, 2000). And when there isn't anything we can do mentally to change the outcome or prepare for the future, we embrace a counterfactual explanation that puts us in the best light ("I could have really bombed the test. At least, I studied a little") (Tetlock, 1998). Not surprisingly, this tendency to come up with self-enhancing counterfactual thoughts is particularly true of people with high self-esteem, especially when they are in a bad mood (Sanna, Turley-Ames, & Meier, 1999). People who think well of themselves may use counterfactual reasoning to repair a bad mood.

Mental Simulation. Simulating how events may happen provides a window on the future by helping people envision possibilities and develop plans for bringing those possibilities about (Taylor, Pham, Rivkin, & Armor, 1998). But people can focus on different aspects of the future. They may envision the future as filled with bountiful possibilities, what some call "wishful thinking" or "fantasy" (Oettingen, Pak, & Schnetter, 2001). Or they might focus on the steps they need to take in order to achieve a future that is desired. Which type of mental simulation about the future helps people to achieve their goals?

If you are an avid reader of self-help books, you know that this advice-filled genre urges people to actively envision the state they hope to achieve in the future. Yet research suggests that this idea is badly misleading. In a study that tested this point, Pham and Taylor (1999) asked college students who were studying for an exam a few days away to envision either their satisfaction and celebration in achieving a good grade on the exam or to envision themselves studying in such a way as would produce a good grade on the exam. That is, one group focused on the outcome to be achieved, whereas the other group focused on the process for achieving it. Those students who had focused on the steps they would need to undertake to get a good grade in fact improved their grade substantially over a control group that practiced neither mental simulation, and those students who focused on the outcome they wanted to achieve had lower scores on the exam than the control group.

Clearly, if you want to use mental simulation to further your goals, it is best not to engage in wishful thinking and fantasy, but to focus your simulations clearly on what you will need to do to get there.

The Anchoring and Adjustment Heuristic

Imagine that someone asks you to guess how many people attended the UCLA-USC football game last night in the Los Angeles Coliseum. You have absolutely no idea, but you do know that last week's game in the Coliseum drew a crowd of 55,000. Assuming that the UCLA-USC contest drew a much bigger crowd, you might guess that 70,000 people attended. In this case, you have no information about the specific event in question, but you use information about a similar event as a reference point, or "anchor." You then adjust reference information to reach a conclusion (Tversky & Kahneman, 1974). In fact, when people are attempting to form judgments from ambiguous information, they will often reduce ambiguity by starting with the beginning reference point, or anchor, and then adjusting it. Social judgments are no exception, because information about social situations is often ambiguous; anchors can be helpful when one is trying to interpret the meaning of ambiguous information and behavior (Mussweiler, Strack, & Pfeiffer, 2000).

A common anchor used in social perception is the self. For example, suppose someone asks you whether Ellen, a classmate of yours, is smart. It may be easiest for you to answer this question by trying to decide whether or not Ellen is smarter than you. If she seems to be smarter than you are, you may decide that she is very smart. But if she seems to be not as quick as you are, you may decide that she is not very bright. Your judgment about Ellen's intelligence, then, is based not on her absolute standing on an IQ test or some other objective information, but on whether she seems brighter or less bright than you (Markus, Smith, & Moreland, 1985). The anchoring heuristic, then, provides people with a departure point for a judgment task that might otherwise be ambiguous. In social judgment tasks, the self seems to be a common anchor. For a description of the various heuristic strategies, see Table 3.1.

Which Schemas Are Used?

Suppose you observe two people feverishly searching a room. How do you decide what they are doing? In other words, how do you select which schemas to apply to the situation? Sometimes appropriate schemas are suggested by the nature of the information itself. For example, if you know the two people in question are roommates who keep gerbils and you see an empty cage, you may guess that they are trying to find their missing gerbils. Under other circumstances, information in the environment may not immediately suggest what schemas to invoke. Are the two searchers looking for something that they have lost? Are they burglars? Are they undercover police officers con-

Table 3.1

Some Heuristic Strategies for Making Judgments Under Uncertainty

Heuristic	Definition	Example
Representativeness	Representativeness is a judgment of how relevant A is to B; high relevance yields high estimates that A originates from B.	Deciding that George (A) must be an engineer because he looks and acts like your stereotype of engineers (B)
Availability	Availability is the estimate of how frequent or likely a given instance or occurrence is, based on how easily or quickly an association or examples come to mind.	Estimating the divorce rate on the basis of how quickly you can think of examples of divorced friends
Simulation	Simulation is the ease with which a hypothetical scenario can be constructed.	Getting angry because of a frustrating event on the basis of how easily you can imagine the situation occurring otherwise
Anchoring and adjustment	Anchoring and adjustment make up the process of estimating some value by starting with some initial value and then adjusting it to the new instance.	Judging how hard a friend studies by how hard you yourself study

ducting a drug bust? In this section, we consider the factors that influence which schemas people use to interpret information.

Natural Contours

The most obvious and probably also the most powerful determinant of which schema is used is the structure of the information itself. That is, schemas follow the natural contours of the information we receive. For example, if you are watching a football game, you will employ your schemas for football games, football players, and cheerleaders to interpret what is happening on the field. The information in the environment makes it obvious which schemas to use, and you would not invoke your schemas for cocktail parties, tennis games, or final examinations to interpret what is going on (cf. Gavanski & Hui, 1992).

But we do not take in all the environmental information when we form an inference. Rather, we absorb meaningful, structured chunks of it. For example, in a baseball game, we would notice the pitch, the batter's swing, and the outfielder catching the ball and recognize that the batter was out. The chunking process is imposed on the flow of behavior partly by the perceiver's own experiences and expectations. And the chunks partly reflect the real changes within the behavioral sequence (Newtson, 1976).

Salience

Environmental salience is another factor that influences which schemas people use to interpret information. Sometimes our interpretation of other people's behavior is influenced by what information about them is made salient by the environment. For example, if Linda is the only woman in a group that is otherwise composed of men, her gender will be particularly salient and therefore her behavior may be interpreted according to a gender schema for women (Taylor, Fiske, Close, Anderson, & Ruderman, 1977). For example, her request for help from a newcomer to the group might be interpreted as a sign of dependence, a trait sometimes associated with women. However, if Linda is in a group composed of several men and several women, her behavior toward the newcomer might not be interpreted in gender-related terms. Instead, a schema for "newcomers" might be invoked, and her gesture might simply be interpreted as an effort to make the newcomer feel at home. Salience, then, can influence the processing of information in the environment by determining which schemas will be invoked to interpret information that may be subject to multiple interpretations.

People perceive behavior in coherent, meaningful chunks of action, marked by breakpoints. For example, in a football game, a completed pass would form a natural unit, marked at the beginning by the throw and at the end by the successful reception.

Primacy

Often, which schema is used to analyze a person or a situation is determined very early by information present in the situation. For example, when introduced to someone with the words, "This is Susan, she's running for student body president," one is inclined to think of Susan and her subsequent behavior in terms of whether she would be a good student body president and to consider her behavior as determined at least in part by the fact that she is running for office. One reason **primacy** is so important is that when people have an organizing structure from the very outset, it influences the interpretation of information as that information is taken in. The effects of that influence are more powerful than if the schema is applied afterward (see Fiske & Taylor, 1991, for a review).

Priming

When a schema has been used recently, it is likely to be used again to interpret new information (Bargh, 1994). Suppose you have just come from a classroom discussion in which the professor castigated the class for its lack of commitment to intellectual pursuits. Walking across campus, you meet Stan, who enthusiastically tells you that he has just been appointed to the cheering squad. How do you interpret his enthusiasm? In the context of the prior lecture, you may regard his behavior as shallow and unintellectual. In contrast, if you had just come from a discussion of the importance of being a well-rounded college student, you might interpret his behavior as a sign of extracurricular interests. This tendency for recently used schemas to be used in unrelated subsequent situations is called the **priming effect.**

A study that demonstrates this point was conducted by Higgins, Rholes, and Jones (1977). Participants were first exposed to trait words designed to invoke either the positive schema of adventurousness (such as "brave") or the negative schema of recklessness (such as "foolish," "careless"). In a second study, ostensibly unrelated to the first task, participants read about Donald, who shot rapids, drove in a demolition derby, and planned to learn skydiving. People who had previously been exposed to the positive schema of adventurousness evaluated Donald more positively than did people who had been primed with the negative schema of recklessness. This priming effect did not occur when the primed schemas were not applicable to the description of Donald (such as "neat" or "shy").

Essentially, then, activating a schema puts it at the top of the mental heap, making it easily accessible for interpreting new information (Wyer & Srull, 1981). However, an important qualification is that previously activated schemas are invoked to explain new information only when the schema can meaningfully be applied to the new information. When new information is irrelevant to the primed schemas, those schemas are not used to interpret it (Higgins & Bargh, 1987).

Importance

Which schemas are used to interpret information from the environment and how many schemas are used can also be influenced by the importance of the information being processed. When the circumstances for making inferences are relatively trivial, people may make schematic inferences relatively quickly, with little thought. They may, for example, invoke a schema on the basis of which information is most salient. However, when the outcome of an inference is important, or when a person is accountable for the inference, that person may spend more time studying the situation and invoke more schemas, which yield more complex inferences (Chaiken, 1980; Tetlock & Boettger, 1989). For example, if asked your impression of a classmate, you may answer relatively quickly that he or she seems pleasant if your judgment of the person has no particular importance to you. However, if you were trying to decide whether to ask this classmate on a date, you would probably spend more time thinking through what you know about the person to decide whether he or she is fun to be with, attractive, pleasant, and attracted to you. Your inferences might consequently be more complex and based on more than one schema.

Individual Differences

Not everyone interprets the same information the same way. One reason is that different people have different schemas. For example, one person might describe other people primarily in terms of their sense of humor or warmth, whereas someone else might consider these characteristics relatively unimportant and instead might be concerned with another person's diligence and religiousness.

People also differ in their needs for structure, that is, the degree to which they need to create and use schemas to simplify previous experience (Neuberg, Judice, & West, 1997). Generally speaking, those with a high need for structure are more likely to rely on cognitive schemas than those who have a low need for structure (Bar-Tal, Kishon-Rabin, & Tabak, 1997).

A related construct, need for closure, which is the desire to achieve a firm answer to a question and an aversion to ambiguity, also leads people to make use of schemas as opposed to a more piecemeal consideration of available information (Chiu, Morris, Hong, & Menon, 2000; Kruglanski et al., 1997).

Goals

Which schemas are brought to bear on information in the environment is also based on the goals a social perceiver has in a particular situation (Hastie, Park, & Weber, 1984; Wyer & Srull, 1986). As we have seen, schemas are not simply passive reflections of the information in the environment. The person must actively organize the information into a more abstract, cognitive structure. One way in which this organizing cognitive activity is triggered is through an individual's goals (e.g., Trzebinski & Richards, 1986). When we have a particular goal in a situation, such as trying to remember what someone says or trying to form an impression of someone, we organize information in a way that fits our particular goals.

When Are Schemas Used?

Schemas are important because they help people make sense of experience quickly. If we approached every situation as if for the first time, it would be impossible for us to function in our everyday lives. Schemas, then, represent our social learning, the social categories that we use to assign meaning to the people we meet and the situations we encounter.

But as we also noted earlier in the chapter, there are liabilities to schematic processing. Sometimes we make assumptions about people and situations on the basis of our schemas that turn out not to be true. If we could pay more attention to the information at hand instead of jumping to conclusions on the basis of our schemas, we could avoid certain mistakes. For example, categorizing another person as loud-mouthed, opinionated, arrogant, and conservative may not matter much under most circumstances, but if the person happens to be the father of the woman you are hoping to date, you might want to pay closer attention to his qualities and opinions.

Dual Processing of Information

The distinction between the rapid, heuristically based use of schemas and the careful, systematic, piecemeal construction of inferences from evidence illustrates an important issue throughout social psychology: People have at least two quite different ways in which they can form inferences. This has been called the **dual-process model** of inference. According to this model, people may process information in a relatively effortless heuristic mode by using schemas, or in a more cognitively demanding, systematic mode, by drawing on more of the evidence in the specific situation. Under which conditions do we pay more attention to our schemas and somewhat less to the evidence at hand, and under what circumstances do we do the reverse?

Outcome Dependency. One condition that leads to less frequent use of schemas and more attention to the information is outcome dependency. When your outcomes depend on someone else's actions, you pay more attention to the other person (Berscheid, Graziano, Monson, & Dermer, 1976; Rush & Russell, 1988) and to schema-inconsistent information, apparently because it is potentially informative (Erber & Fiske, 1984). When people's outcomes are involved, they probe for more information about others (Darley, Fleming, Hilton, & Swann, 1988). For example, competitors remember more about members of a group with which they are in competition than do those not in competition with that group (Judd & Park, 1988).

Accountability. Accountability and/or the need to be accurate is another condition that leads people to pay more attention to data and less attention to their schemas. When people have to justify their decisions to other people and accountability is therefore high, they tend to go beyond the schema to look more closely at the data (Tetlock & Boettger, 1989; Pennington & Schlenker, 1999). Asked if a particular nerdy person is smart, you may draw on your schema that tells you that nerds usually are smart. However, if it is up to you to decide whether to admit him to your debating team, you will probably want more information than your stereotype about nerds will provide. Consequently, you will pay closer attention to his actual behavior and will focus less on the ways in which he matches your schema for nerds (Lerner & Tetlock, 1999).

Time Pressure. Conversely, other facts favor schema use over careful consideration of the data. For example, when people are forming impressions or making decisions under time pressure, they tend to use their schemas more. In one study, male and female participants were asked to judge the suitability of male and female candidates for particular jobs. When the decisions were made under time pressure, male participants as well as female participants with conservative attitudes toward women tended to discriminate against the female job applicants. In the absence of time pressure, however, discrimination toward the female applicants was less strong. Under time pressure, then, the participants resorted to their stereotypes about men and women in jobs to make the judgments, whereas when they had time to consider the evidence and found that the female applicants were as well qualified as the male applicants, their degree of discrimination against the female candidates was considerably less (Bechtold, Naccarato, & Zanna, 1986).

We also fall back on our schemas when all the available information seems to fit the schema well and when we are not particularly motivated to examine the data more thoroughly. However, when we are told that a task is important or when some of the information is incongruent with the schema, we are more likely to engage in systematic processing of the data (Maheswaran & Chaiken, 1991).

To summarize, then, when there are pressures in the situation to be accurate, people tend to look at data more closely, sometimes rejecting easy, schematically based conclusions. They may attend to more of the information and pay particular attention to schema-inconsistent information. Conditions that seem to favor this kind of data-driven processing are outcome dependency, accountability, and other situational cues that suggest a need to be accurate. In contrast, other circumstances favor more schematically based processing. In particular, any pressure to form a quick or coherent judgment that can be communicated easily to others may favor the use of schemas (Fiske & Taylor, 1991).

Schemas in Action

The use of schemas for processing information is important not only because it helps people to form judgments and make decisions, but also because it provides guidelines for interactions with others.

Confirmatory Hypothesis Testing

We learn about other people in many ways. We may hear about them before we meet them, or we may have hints about the kind of people they are on the basis of their initial behavior. Regardless of how we form an impression of another person, we may relatively quickly develop ideas about what the person is like. As we interact with the person, how do these ideas (or schemas) influence our behavior?

How does this process work? Suppose you learned that Susan, an attractive young woman in your psychology class, is with the cheering squad for the school; you quickly form an image of her as an outgoing, athletic, and enthusiastic person. In talking with her, you might ask her about the various sports she has played, the parties she has been to this year, what she thinks of the games she has attended, and so on. All this information tends to confirm your view of her as an extroverted, athletic, fun-loving person. However, after seeing her for several weeks, you might discover that she is actually rather shy and introverted, that she's not particularly athletic, and that she is not a cheerleader at all but rather coordinates uniform purchases and bus transportation to out-of-town games. You might wonder how you came to be so deceived. Looking back on the situation, however, reveals that Susan may have done nothing at all to deceive you. Rather, you deceived yourself by selectively seeking information that supported your beliefs. Many college students have played some kind of sport in high school or attended at least a couple of parties. Because you asked Susan about these kinds of activities, that is the information she gave you, and it augmented your image of her as an outgoing, athletic person (Swann, Giuliano, & Wegner, 1982). This process has been called **confirmatory hypothesis testing,** and it has been demonstrated under a broad range of circumstances. For example, Snyder and Swann (1978) told college student participants that they would be interviewing another student. Half were told to find out if the other was an extrovert (i.e., outgoing and sociable), and half were told to find out if the other was an introvert (i.e., shy and retiring). All participants were then given a set of questions assessing introversion and extroversion, and they were told to pick out a set of questions to ask the other student. Students who were told to find out if the person was an extrovert preferentially selected extroversion questions (e.g., "What would you do if you wanted to liven things up at a party?"), and those who were told to find out if the person was an introvert picked introversion questions, which, in turn, made the target students appear especially extroverted or introverted, respectively, simply because they answered the questions they were asked (see also Davies, 1997; McDonald & Hirt, 1997).

Considerable research suggests that people behave toward others in ways that tend to confirm the beliefs they hold about those others (Garcia-Marques, Sherman, & Palma-Oliveira, 2001). Perceivers employ interaction strategies to elicit information from others that preferentially supports these schemas (Snyder & Gangestad, 1981).

Although a number of studies have found evidence for confirmatory hypothesis testing, there are conditions under which we are less likely to confirm a hypothesis selectively through leading questions. Holding an opposite hypothesis or having a need for valid information reduces the degree to which people selectively confirm hypotheses (Devine, Hirt, & Gehrke, 1990). For example, when people expect to have to work with a target in the future, they ask better questions and are less likely to engage in question-asking techniques that selectively confirm their expectations (Darley, Fleming, Hilton, & Swann, 1988). And when they have more than one hypothesis in mind, they will test for these alternative hypotheses as well (McDonald, 1990).

Self-Fulfilling Prophecies. Sometimes a prior schema we have about an individual will not only influence the kind of information we seek from the person and the subsequent inferences we draw but will also affect the other person's actual behaviors and self-impressions. When a perceiver's false expectations about another person lead that person to adopt those expected attributes and behaviors, this is called a **self-fulfilling prophecy** (see Figure 3–3). For example, Snyder, Tanke, and Berscheid (1977) gave male college students a folder of information about a woman on campus that included a picture that represented the woman as either highly attractive or unattractive. In actuality, the photos were fake and were randomly assigned to women regardless of their true looks. Each student was then asked to phone the woman whose folder he had read and chat for 10 minutes. Tape recordings were made of the conversations. The men who believed they were talking to attractive women behaved more warmly on the phone than did the men who called supposedly unattractive women. Even more remarkable, the women who had been miscast as highly attractive were perceived by other students who judged the tapes to be more friendly, likable, and sociable in their interactions with the men than those who were miscast as unattractive (see also Neuberg, Judice, Virdin, & Carrillo, 1993). These kinds of self-fulfilling prophecies have been widely demonstrated (see Jussim, 1989, for a review).

When Expectations Challenge Self-Conceptions. The implication of the discussion thus far is that schemas are so powerful, they not only influence how information in the environment is interpreted but also help push the environment to become consistent

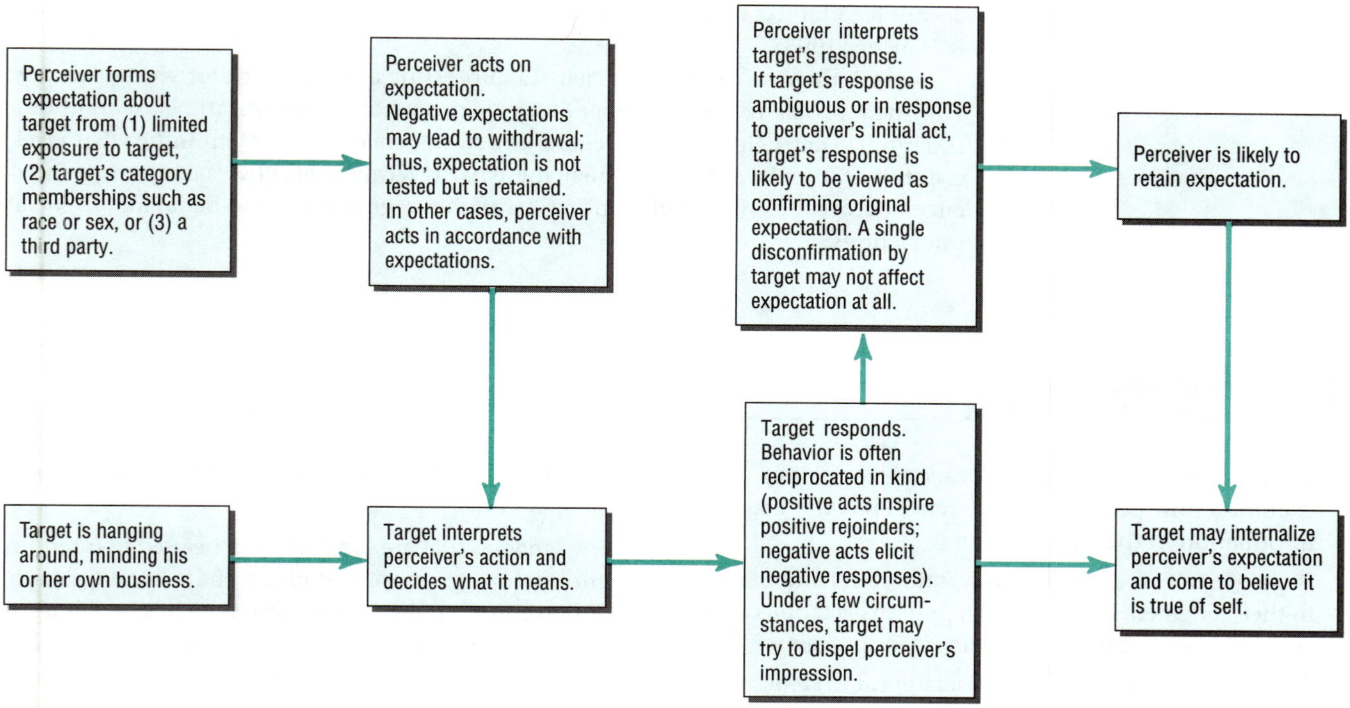

Figure 3–3 **The Development of a Self-Fulfilling Prophecy.**

Source: Adapted from Darley and Fazio (1980).

with the schema. Obviously, this is not always the case. For example, sometimes people hold beliefs about others that those others feel are untrue about themselves. Consequently, those others may be motivated to disconfirm what they feel is an incorrect belief (Smith, Neuberg, Judice, & Biesanz, 1997). For example, if a professor whose opinion you value saw you commit a foolish prank with some of your friends, you might be highly motivated to correct the professor's low opinion of you.

Under these circumstances, whose viewpoint will triumph? The perceiver's misconceptions or the target's beliefs about himself or herself? Research by Swann and Ely (1984) attempted to address this question by considering the certainty of the perceiver's expectations and the target's self-conceptions. Perceivers first formed relatively certain or uncertain expectations about targets that were inconsistent with the target's self-conceptions. Thus, for example, some perceivers were led to believe that the target was extroverted (when the target perceived herself to be introverted), whereas other perceivers were led to believe the target was introverted (when the target considered herself extroverted). The perceivers then interacted with targets who possessed either relatively certain or uncertain self-conceptions about their introversion or extroversion. The results indicated that the target's self-concept was a stronger determinant of the perceiver's ultimate opinion of the target than was the perceiver's expectation. That is, after they had interacted together, the perceivers' impressions of the targets were more in line with the targets' self-concepts than with the perceivers' initial expectations. Only when targets were uncertain about their introversion or extroversion and perceivers were certain about their expectations did behavioral confirmation occur. That is, when perceivers were certain and targets were uncertain about their attributes, the perceivers' expectations tended to prevail. The general point, then, is that perceivers' expectations may have some effect on a target's behavior. But they do not lead targets to act in ways that are counter to their self-concepts (e.g., Snyder & Haugen, 1995).

Overall, then, schemas and schematic processing are important for several reasons. They help people to organize their past experiences in ways that can be useful in new situations. They help in the processing of new information by determining what is relevant, by filling in gaps, by influencing what is recalled, and by making some inferences automatic. And they can act as effective guidelines for behavior in social interactions.

Summary

1. Social cognition is the branch of social psychology that examines how people form inferences based on social information in the environment.
2. Social perceivers are prone to certain errors and biases in their judgments. In particular, prior expectations and theories weigh heavily in the judgment process.
3. These predictable errors and biases appear to stem from the fact that people need to make judgments relatively quickly and efficiently to process the volume of information they encounter.
4. Cognitive structures called schemas help us organize information about the world. Schemas make information processing more efficient and speedy, aid recall, fill in missing information, and provide expectations. However, they sometimes lead to erroneous inferences or may lead us to reject good but inconsistent evidence.
5. Heuristics are shortcuts that help relate information in the environment to schemas. Heuristics reduce complex or ambiguous problems to more simple, judgmental operations.
6. The schemas that are most likely to be used to interpret information are those that match the natural contours of that information. In addition, which schemas a social perceiver uses is influenced by salience, social roles, goals, primacy, priming, the importance of the judgment context, and individual differences.
7. People sometimes attend more to the evidence than to their schemas, especially if they need to be very accurate, if they will be held accountable for their judgments, or if their future outcomes depend on their judgments.
8. Schemas not only help people form judgments and make decisions but also provide guidelines for interactions with others. In some cases, schemas may be so powerful that they bring about self-fulfilling prophecies.

Critical Thinking

1. What are some of the errors and pitfalls that occur when people are trying to understand the social environment? How costly or problematic are these errors?
2. Pick some social role, such as police officer or professor, or a situation, such as a football game, and think about your schema for this role or event. What kinds of general information does your schema include? How would having this schema help you understand a particular situation or person better? How might it interfere with your understanding of a specific instance?
3. Heuristics are shortcuts that reduce a complex problem to a simple one. Some important heuristics that most people use were described in the chapter, but all of us invent our own heuristics for solving problems. Can you think of a situation or problem you commonly encounter and a heuristic that you have developed for managing it efficiently?
4. Much of the time, we use schemas and heuristics to process social information very rapidly. Other times, however, we are more thoughtful and pay attention to the specific information at hand. When are we more likely to use careful, systematic processing, and when do we fall back on our more rapid, heuristic processing?

Key Terms

case history information, 70
confirmatory hypothesis testing, 94
conjunction error, 85
counterfactual reasoning, 86
covariation, 72
dual-process model, 92
exemplars, 81
heuristics, 84
illusory correlation, 72
mood-congruent memory, 74
planning fallacy, 77
primacy, 90
priming effect, 90
schema, 80
scripts, 80
self-fulfilling prophecy, 94
social cognition, 67
statistical information, 70

In the News

Do Academy Award Winners Live Longer Than Losers?

Do winners live longer than losers? So it would seem. A recent, highly publicized article in the *Annals of Internal Medicine* discovered that actors and actresses who had won Academy Awards lived nearly 4 years longer than their peers who had not.

Physician Donald Redelmeier and his associate Sheldon Singh looked at the birth dates and death dates of all actors and actresses ever nominated for an Academy Award, and for each, they identified another cast member of the same sex in the same film who was born in roughly the same time period. Compared to the less recognized performers, who died on average around 75.8 years, the nominees lived to be nearly 80 years old. Winning an Academy Award was associated with a large gain in life expectancy for both actors and actresses. Performers who had been nominated but who did not win lived about as long as those who had not been nominated, and multiple nominations did not improve one's chances for survival unless they were also accompanied by wins. Movie stars who won multiple Academy Awards lived on average nearly 6 years longer than their peers (Redelmeier & Singh, 2001).

What accounts for these effects? One possibility is that those who won an award had to mind their behavior a little better than those who didn't. Movie stars receive a lot of media scrutiny and need to avoid disgraceful behaviors or bad health habits that would undermine their reputation. Perhaps their winning led to cleaner living and thus to a longer life.

Alternatively, movie stars have more control over their life, more ability, perhaps, to avoid stress, more resources, more admirers, and special privileges. These factors, too, may contribute to greater longevity. Or it may be that basking in the acclaim of others is conducive to a physiological and neuroendocrine state that helps to stave off illness. Or perhaps social support, resilience, or even ambition itself may contribute to longevity through as yet unidentified physiological pathways. So far, the reasons are unknown.

Nonetheless, as we'll shortly see, the kind of self-enhancement that comes from high self-esteem and the esteem of others is a central issue in the study of the self. How one experiences oneself, what one considers to be one's most distinguishing qualities, and how they may be similar to or different from the ways others think of one self are important aspects of identity. This chapter considers the nature of the self, how we know our own characteristics, and how we use our self-conceptions to guide our selection of activities, the development of our personal beliefs, and our interactions with other people.

CHAPTER 4

THE SELF: LEARNING ABOUT THE SELF

Focus of This Chapter

What Is the Self?

The self is first and foremost the collection of beliefs that we hold about ourselves. What are our important characteristics? What are we good at? What do we do poorly at? What kinds of situations do we prefer or avoid? One person may think of herself as a black woman who plans to become a sociology professor. Another might think of himself as not very academically inclined but good at most sports. A third person may think of herself primarily in terms of a future goal, such as the desire to become the biggest real estate mogul in the Midwest. The set of beliefs we hold about who we are is called the **self-concept.**

Often we have a clear idea of who we are, whereas we other times hold self-doubts and confusion and feel we are buffeted by external pressures and evaluations by others. This distinction refers to self-concept clarity, and to having a sense of self that is clearly and confidently defined, providing a coherent sense of direction (Campbell, 1990; Kernis, Paradise, Whitaker, Wheatman, & Goldman, 2000).

Self-esteem is the evaluation we make of ourselves. That is, we are concerned not only with what we are like, but also with how we value these qualities. Table 4.1 shows some of the items from a commonly used measure of self-esteem (Rosenberg, 1965). As you can see, the items measure the general value that people place on themselves—whether they are fundamentally good or bad people, talented or not, and so on. People with high self-esteem have a clear sense of what their personal qualities are, think well of themselves, set appropriate goals, use feedback in a self-enhancing manner, and cope successfully with difficult situations.

People with low self-esteem, on the other hand, have less clear self-conceptions, think poorly of themselves, often select unrealistic goals or shy away from goals altogether, tend to be pessimistic about the future, have more adverse emotional and behavioral reactions to criticism or other kinds of negative feedback, are more concerned about their social impact on other people, and are more vulnerable to depression when

Table 4.1

Self-Esteem Scale

Indicate whether each item is true (T) or false (F) for you.

___1. I feel that I have a number of good qualities.

___2. I feel I do not have much to be proud of.

___3. At times I think I am no good at all.

___4. I feel I am a person of worth, at least on an equal basis with others.

___5. All in all, I feel that I am a failure.

___6. On the whole, I am satisfied with myself.

If you answered "true" on items 1, 4, and 6, you scored high on self-esteem. If you answered "true" to items, 2, 3, and 5, you scored low on self-esteem. The entire scale includes 10 items.

Source: Adapted from M. Rosenberg, *Society and the adolescent self-image.* Copyright © 1965 by Princeton University Press. © renewed.

they encounter setbacks or stress (Heatherton & Vohs, 2000; Kernis et al, 1998; Kernis et al, 2000; Leary, Tambor, Terdal, & Downs, 1995; Setterlund & Niedenthal, 1993).

In addition to our overall sense of self-esteem, we hold specific evaluations of our abilities in particular areas. Joan may think well of herself generally but may know that she is not very diplomatic and not very talented artistically. David may generally think poorly of himself but know that he is very organized and a good pianist. The importance and value we attach to these more specific self-views also influence global feelings of self-worth.

For the most part, researchers have studied people's explicit sense of self-esteem, that is, the concrete positive or negative evaluations they make of themselves. But more recent research suggests the importance of implicit self-esteem as well (Greenwald & Banaji, 1995; Greenwald & Farnham, 2000). Implicit self-esteem refers to the less conscious evaluations we make of ourselves. Studies of implicit self-esteem sometimes reveal things that studies of explicit self-esteem do not. For example, as we will see, one strong cultural difference is that Asians, especially the Japanese, are much less likely to answer explicit self-esteem scales in a self-enhancing manner. Instead, they report relatively modest self-esteem. However, in a test of implicit self-esteem (Kitayama & Karasawa, 1997), Japanese students were found to hold a preference for alphabetical letters contained in their own names over letters that were not in their names. They were also found to prefer numbers that corresponded to the month or the day of their birthdays over numbers that did not appear in their birthdays. These measures of implicit self-esteem, then, suggested a self-enhancing quality that the students did not acknowledge more directly.

How does a sense of self develop? One of the most influential theories of how the self develops was put forth by Erik Erikson (1963), who argued for a stage theory of ego development. He maintained that although identity formation is a lifelong task (Whitborne, Zuschlag, Elliot, & Waterman, 1992), it is of critical importance during adolescence and young adulthood. This time, when identity begins to come together, marks the transition between childhood and adulthood. Erikson (1963) believed that the goal of this process is "the ability to experience one's self as something that has continuity and sameness, and to act accordingly" (p. 38). Once the young adult has acquired a firm sense of identity, he or she has a basis for making job or career plans and for establishing intimate relationships.

Although Erikson was no doubt correct in his assessment of adolescence and young adulthood as pivotal times for developing a sense of self, it would be false to claim that the sense of self develops and is maintained only or primarily during this time. The sense of self begins in infancy with the recognition that one is a separate individual (Butterworth, 1992; Pervin, 1992a, 1992b). Very young children have fairly clear conceptions of their personal qualities and what they do or don't do well. Moreover, many changes occur in middle and late adulthood that may influence the self-conceptions that people hold. Thus, although psychologists continue to believe that Erikson was essentially right when he argued that issues of identity are especially important in adolescence and young adulthood, it is also clearly the case that the development of a personal sense of self is a lifelong process that begins in childhood and never truly ends (Waterman & Archer, 1990).

Where Does Self-Knowledge Come From?

Knowledge of the self comes from many sources. Some of it may seem to be spontaneous; a realization that something is true of one self without any certainty of where that knowledge comes from. More commonly, however, we can identify the origins of our beliefs about ourselves in specific experiences.

Socialization

Much of our self-knowledge comes from **socialization.** During childhood we are treated in particular ways by parents, teachers, and friends, and we participate in religious, ethnic, or cultural activities that later come to be significant aspects of ourselves. From attending synagogue at an early age, taking Hebrew lessons, and eventually participating in a bar mitzvah, a Jewish boy may come to regard being Jewish as an important part of his identity. A child whose parents take her to art exhibits and concerts every weekend may come to think of herself as a cultured person. Socialization forms the core of our early experience, and the regularity of those experiences may eventually come to be internalized as important aspects of the self-concept.

Reflected Appraisal

We also learn about ourselves through the reactions that other people have to us. C. H. Cooley (1902) developed the concept of the "looking-glass self," which maintains that

Much self-knowledge comes from socialization. By participating in activities that are important to our families, we come to regard these activities as important to ourselves as well.

people perceive themselves as others perceive and respond to them. Our perceptions of how other people react to us are called **reflected appraisals.**

In a humorous example of the importance of reflected appraisal, Baldwin, Carrell, and Lopez (1990) recruited Catholic students for a study during which the students encountered a picture of the scowling face of either the pope or an unfamiliar other person and were later asked to evaluate some of their own personal qualities. Practicing Catholics who were exposed to the picture of the scowling pope evaluated themselves more harshly than both the nonpracticing Catholics who were exposed to the same picture of the pope and the Catholics who were exposed to the picture of the unfamiliar other person. Apparently, the picture of the scowling pope was enough to shake the self-images of these students.

Feedback from Others

Sometimes people give us explicit feedback about our qualities. This process often begins in socialization, when our parents tell us not to be so shy, that we are good at playing the piano, that math is not our strong point, or that we are good readers. Generally speaking, there is a strong relationship between how parents think about their children's abilities and children's own self-conceptions about these same dimensions (Felson & Reed, 1986).

In later childhood and early adolescence, feedback from peers may be more important. All of us can remember being picked early or late when captains were choosing members for athletic teams, and we measured our popularity in terms of how quickly we were picked to be in someone's carpool for a field trip (see Leary, Haupt, Strausser, & Chokel, 1998). Adolescence brings with it additional sources of direct feedback, such as whether one is asked out on dates by many people or few, or whether the people that one asks out accept or decline. Also, students get direct feedback from teachers about their academic abilities in the form of comments and grades (Jussim, Soffin, Brown, Ley, & Kohlhepp, 1992).

Research has suggested that, on the whole, people prefer objective feedback (such as test scores) about their personal attributes (Festinger, 1954). Objective feedback is regarded as less biased and more fair than personal opinion. But the opinions of others also count. In particular, when those opinions are shared by a large number of people, we may come to believe that they are true.

Self-Perception

As we saw in Chapter 3, Volume 1, people also infer their personal qualities from observing their own behavior. That is, in the process of observing ourselves, we see ourselves consistently preferring certain activities over others, certain foods over others, or certain people over others. From observing these regularities, we may gain self-knowledge.

However, as Daryl Bem's (1967, 1972) **self-perception theory** also suggests, this source of self-knowledge may be useful primarily for aspects of the self that are not particularly central or important. For example, you do not need to observe yourself avoiding anchovies on your pizza to know that you do not like anchovies. You do not need to observe yourself ordering flowers for your mother on Mother's Day to know that you love your mother. Many important aspects of the self have clear internal referents in the form of enduring beliefs, attitudes, and affective preferences. And so it is likely that self-perception as a source of self-knowledge applies primarily to more incidental than to important aspects of the self.

Labeling Arousal States

Often we infer our internal states and personal qualities from our own physiological arousal. We respond to things that we perceive—a threatening dog, an attractive prospective partner—and recognize our emotions by considering our mental and physiological reactions. But many emotional reactions are biochemically similar. We can distinguish high arousal from low arousal, but often not specific emotions.

Stanley Schachter (1964) suggested that perceptions of our own emotions depend on (1) the degree of physiological arousal we have and (2) the cognitive label we apply, such as angry or happy. To arrive at a cognitive label, we review our own behavior and the situation. For example, if we feel physiologically aroused and are laughing at a comedy show on television, we might infer that we are happy. If we are snarling at someone for shoving us on a crowded street, we might infer that we are angry. Like Bem's theory of self-perception, this point of view emphasizes the ambiguity of internal states and proposes that self-perception depends at least somewhat on perceptions of overt behavior and of the external environment.

High degrees of physiological arousal give rise to a search for an appropriate attribution. If a plausible attribution is available for the arousal, it will be accepted. If no such attribution exists, the person will search the environment for something that could have caused the arousal. To illustrate this point, Schachter and Singer (1962) conducted a now classic experiment. One group of undergraduate students was injected with epinephrine. Half were told its true side effects (e.g., rapid breathing, flushing, increased heart rate), and half were told to expect effects that are not, in fact, produced by epinephrine (e.g., dizziness, slight headache). A control group of participants was given no drug. Participants were then placed in a room with a confederate of the experimenter and were instructed to fill out some papers. After a brief time (during which the epinephrine took effect in those who had received it), the confederate began to act in either a euphoric manner (engaging in silly antics and making paper airplanes) or in an angry manner (ripping up the papers and stomping around the room).

Schachter and Singer reasoned that if physiological experience is indeed subject to various interpretations, then those participants who had been misinformed about the side effects of epinephrine and who later found themselves in a state of arousal would be searching for an explanation for their state. For these participants, the behavior of the confederate could act as a salient cue to explain their arousal, suggesting to those participants in the euphoric condition that they were also euphoric and to those in the angry condition that they were angry. Participants who had been informed about the true side effects of epinephrine, in contrast, already had an adequate explanation for their arousal state and could remain amused or annoyed by the confederate without acquiring his mood. Participants in the control condition would have no arousal state to explain and also should not catch the mood of the confederate. Generally speaking, this is what Schachter and Singer found. The procedure and results of this experiment are shown in Table 4.2.

Table 4.2

The Schachter-Singer Experiment

	Sequence				
	Step 1	**Step 2**	**Step 3**	**Step 4**	**Step 5**
Condition	**Given Arousing Drug**	**Told It Would Be Arousing**	**Confederate's Behavior**	**Presumed Attribution for Own Arousal (Unmeasured)**	**Own Behavior (Measured)**
No explanation	Yes	No	Euphoric or angry in all cases}	Situational	Euphoric or angry
Informed	Yes	Yes		Drug	Calm
No arousal	No	No		None	Calm

Source: Adapted from Schachter and Singer (1962).

In this case, then, people inferred their own emotions: first, from their arousal, and second, from the cognitive label or attribution that was provided by the environment. When the experimenter provided a label (the drug), participants acted as if they were experiencing no emotion, but when they had no explanation for their arousal state, they took their cues about their emotional states from the social environment.

Usually our arousal states are not so ambiguous. We usually know what is causing our emotional states. However, Schachter's two-factor theory of emotion (physiological arousal plus label) provides a cogent understanding of those circumstances under which our emotional states are ambiguous and we must infer them from what goes on around us.

Environmental Distinctiveness

The environment provides us with other cues about our personal qualities. In particular, the self-concept is heavily influenced by factors that make us distinctive. For example, McGuire and his associates (McGuire & McGuire, 1982; McGuire & Padawer-Singer, 1976) asked students to "tell us about yourself" and found that students often mentioned aspects of themselves that make them distinctive. For example, a boy is more likely to mention his gender if he is the only boy in his family. If he has three sisters, none of the young women is as likely to mention the fact that she is a girl.

We also mention things about ourselves that make us distinctive in the particular situation. So, for example, an African-American woman is more likely to mention that she is African American if there are relatively few African Americans in a group, whereas she is more likely to mention the fact that she is a woman if she is in a group composed predominantly of men. When we are in a group of other people like ourselves, we tend to think of ourselves in terms of our personal identity, that is, the characteristics that distinguish us from those who are otherwise similar to us. Thus, a college student athlete in a room filled with other college students is likely to think of himself in terms of his athletic ability. However, when we are in a situation with several different groups—such as college students and their parents—we tend to think of ourselves in terms of our category membership (e.g., college student) (Turner, Oakes, Haslam, & McGarty, 1994), a tendency especially true of people from cultures such as Japan that foster a norm of relatedness to others, as we see below (Kanagawa, Cross, & Markus, 2000).

Comparisons with Self and Others

Some of the time when we want to evaluate ourselves on a particular dimension or quality, information is not readily available. For example, if you want to know if you are a graceful dancer, there is no test you can take to find that out. You could conceivably consult an expert, but perhaps an expert isn't available. You could ask other people if you are a graceful dancer, but you might be shy about doing so. Consequently, sometimes we assess our personal qualities by comparing ourselves to other people. You know if you are a good dancer in part by observing those around you and noting whether you seem to be dancing more gracefully than those other people. This process is termed **social comparison.** Social comparison processes are discussed in more detail later in this chapter.

Often we evaluate our current situation in terms of our past. Our personal storehouse of memories, for example, lets us know how much progress we have made on particular skills or lets us assess our current qualities. Have we grown more or less tolerant with age? Are we more or less skilled at tennis than we were a year ago? These temporal comparisons are a common source of self-knowledge, particularly about how one has changed (Taylor, Neter, & Wayment, 1995; Wilson & Ross, 2000). A caveat, however, is that such comparisons are often biased, since it is easy to distort one's prior position on an attribute when trying to gauge progress. In effect, an individual says, "I was so bad at it before; I've made a lot of progress" (Conway & Ross, 1984).

Table 4.3

Four Identity Orientations Based on Degree of Identification with One's Ethnic Group and the Majority Group

	Identification with Ethnic Group	
Identification with Majority Group	**Strong**	**Weak**
Strong	Integrated Acculturated Bicultural	Assimilated
Weak	Separated Ethnically identified Ethnically embedded Dissociated	Marginal

Source: Phinney (1990).

Social Identity

Social identity is the "part of an individual's self-concept which derives from [his or her] membership in a social group (or groups) together with the value and emotional significance attached to that membership" (Tajfel, 1981, p. 248; see also Turner et al., 1994). These groups include your family and other personal relationships; your work; your religious, political, ethnic, or community group; and other groups that highlight or reinforce important aspects of the self (Deaux, Reid, Mizrahi, & Ethier, 1995). In childhood, the groups in which one participates often occur as a part of socialization. We are born into a particular family, a particular ethnic group, and sometimes a particular religious group. As we get older, the attributes we value in ourselves lead us to choose social groups that reflect and reinforce those values. Self-concept and social identity mutually determine and shape each other (see Bettencourt & Dorr, 1997; Luhtanen & Crocker, 1992).

Much of the research on social identity has focused specifically on **ethnic identity.** Ethnic identity is the part of an individual's self-knowledge that concerns his or her membership in a particular ethnic group. Developing a sense of self can raise particular issues for minority group members. During the adolescent and young adult years, when people are forming their sense of themselves, reconciling ethnic background with mainstream culture can be difficult for African Americans, Asian Americans, Native Americans, those from Hispanic backgrounds, and other ethnic minority members (Sellers, Rowley, Chavous, Shelton, & Smith, 1997; Spencer & Markstrom-Adams, 1990). This process becomes more difficult when it is coupled with change, such as occurs when a student changes schools or enters college (Ethier & Deaux, 1994).

As Table 4.3 suggests, some adolescents may identify with both mainstream culture and their ethnic group, creating what is called a "bicultural" or "integrated identity" (Phinney, 1990; Ryder, Alden, & Paulhus, 2000). Others may maintain a strong ethnic identity but have few ties to the majority culture, maintaining a separated identity. Individuals who give up their ethnic heritage in favor of mainstream culture are said to be assimilated. Finally, some adolescents and young adults develop only weak ties to both their ethnic culture and the mainstream culture and feel marginal, like outsiders in both cultures (LaFromboise, Coleman, & Gerton, 1993; Phinney, 1990, 1991; Rowley, Sellers, Chavous, & Smith, 1998).

Research shows that these distinctions are important because they predict the amount of contact that individuals will have with their ethnic group and with the larger society. For example, Dona (1991) found that Central American refugees in

Canada who were assimilated spent less time with other Central Americans than did those who were integrated or those who maintained a separated ethnic identification (see also Gurin, Hurtado, & Peng, 1994). In turn, individuals who were integrated had more contact with Canadian society than individuals who maintained a separate identity (Dona, 1991).

An interesting aspect of ethnic identity and of social identities more generally is that they can lead to self-stereotyping. Self-stereotyping involves perceiving oneself as a member of a particular group and consequently behaving in line with this social identity (Turner, Hogg, Oakes, Reicher, & Wetherell, 1987). Sometimes this means that people assume the negative as well as the positive attributes of the group with which they identify. For example, a professor may think of herself as smart, but also as absent-minded. When negative aspects of a social identity are salient or threatened, people are especially likely to identify with the positive aspects of their social identity, that is, to self-stereotype only on positive dimensions (Biernat, Vescio, & Green, 1996).

Ethnic identity is an important part of self-knowledge that comes from membership in a particular ethnic group and participation in the group's valued activities.

In a review of research on ethnic identity, Phinney (1991) found that a strong ethnic identity is typically related to high self-esteem, but only when accompanied by a positive mainstream orientation (see also Sanchez & Fernandez, 1993). Among individuals who hold a strong ethnic identity without some adaptation to the mainstream culture, self-esteem can be more problematic. Similarly, other research suggests that individuals may be able to gain competence within two cultures without losing cultural identity and without having to choose one culture over the other. This notion of **bicultural competence** has been related to successful functioning in both one's culture of origin and the new culture (LaFromboise et al., 1993).

What leads people to become highly identified with their ethnic or racial group? A study of African American college students found that those students whose parents were members of predominantly black organizations, who had taken black studies courses, and who had experienced racism or racial prejudice were more likely to include their African-American background as a strong feature of their self-concept (Baldwin, Brown, & Rackley, 1990; Thompson, 1990, 1991). Thus, participation in ethnically related activities and being treated in particular ways because of one's ethnic or racial background foster a sense of ethnic identity.

Culture and the Self

Cross-cultural research suggests that conceptions of the self vary greatly, depending on the culture one lives in (Rhee, Uleman, Lee, & Roman, 1995; Triandis, McCusker, & Hui, 1990). In a thoughtful investigation of this point, Markus and Kitayama (1991) explicitly contrasted American culture with Japanese culture to illustrate the substantial differences in self-conceptions that may exist between Western cultures and Eastern cultures.

In America, there is a strong emphasis on individuality and how one can best distinguish oneself from others by discovering and making use of one's unique talents. This **independent self** is "a bounded, unique, more or less integrated motivational and cognitive universe, a dynamic center of awareness, emotion, judgment, action, organized into a distinctive whole and set contrastively, both against other such wholes and against a social and natural background" (Geertz, 1974, p. 48). Not only do Westerners construe the self as an independently functioning unit, they actually define independence as a fundamental task of socialization. Westerners teach their children how to be independent (Kitayama, 1992).

The **interdependent self** of many Eastern, southern European, and Latin cultures consists of seeing oneself as part of an encompassing social relationship and realizing that one's behavior is determined and dependent on what one perceives to be the thoughts, feelings, and actions of others in the relationship (Markus & Kitayama, 1991). The self becomes meaningful and complete largely within the context of a social relationship, rather than through independent, autonomous action. Although the inter-

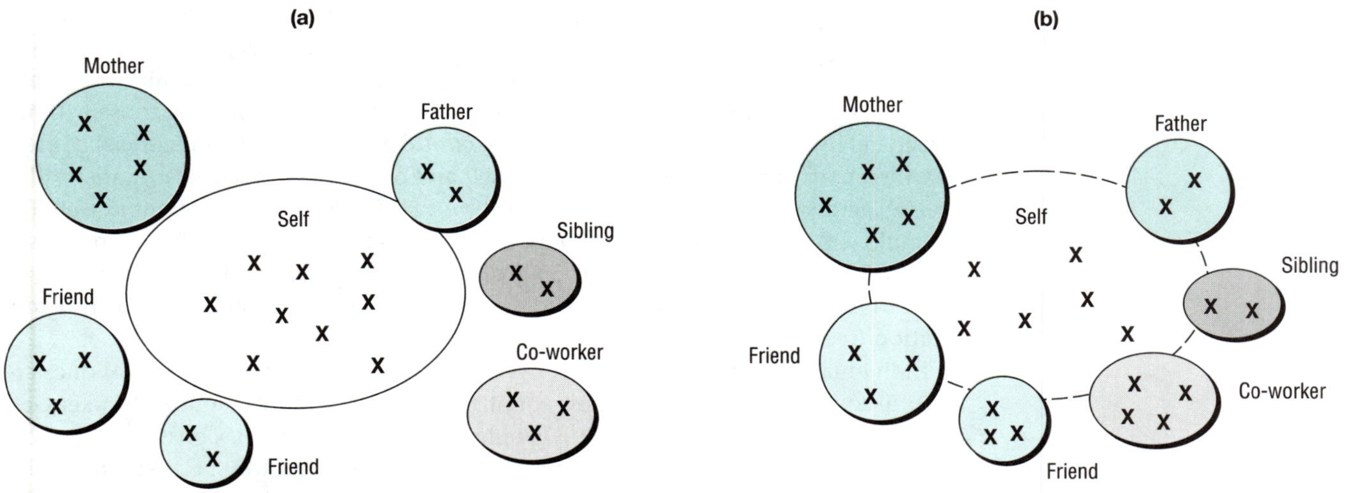

Figure 4–1 Conceptual Representations of the Self.
(a) Independent Construal; (b) Interdependent Construal.

Source: H. R. Markus and S. Kitayama (1991). Culture and the self: Implications for cognition, emotion, and motivation, *Psychological Review, 98,* 224–253. Copyright © 1991 by the American Psychological Association. Reprinted with permission.

dependent self is regarded as possessing a set of internal qualities, such as abilities or opinions, these attributes are thought to be situation-specific and unstable, rather than as defining characteristics of the self (Bochner, 1994; Cousins, 1989). Thus, the interdependent self is not a bounded whole but changes its structure with the nature of the social context. In interdependent cultures, so fundamental is the emphasis on blending in that those attributes that uniquely differentiate one person from another are not regarded as particularly representative of the self. So, for example, although people from the United States would regard great musical talent in a child as a distinctive quality of that particular child, the Japanese might not.

The Western viewpoint regards the self as composed of individual attributes, such as ambition, good humor, or extroversion (Trafimow, Triandis, & Goto, 1991). These attributes are considered distinctively one's own, even when they are shared with others. A student, for example, may regard herself as creative, but this judgment is independent of judgments she might make about her roommate's creativity. Even if she regards both herself and her roommate as creative, her creativity is independent of her roommate's, not shared. In contrast, the collectivist view of the interdependent self regards the individual not in terms of distinctive qualities, but in terms of those that are shared. Because people are regarded as fundamentally connected to each other, they are thought to have attributes in common rather than attributes that they uniquely possess (Bochner, 1994; Trafimow et al., 1991). Thus, two students might be creative interdependently and not independently. These different culture-based views of the self are illustrated in Figure 4–1.

Markus and Kitayama (1991, 1994) suggest that this conception of self as independent versus interdependent is a fundamentally important aspect of an individual's self-system. It influences how people think about their own personal characteristics, how people relate to others, what emotions are experienced in different situations, and what motivates people to engage in action. Moreover, this cultural conception of the self becomes rooted in the ideas, values, and social scripts of a culture, further shaping individual experience and the expression of the self (Han & Shavitt, 1994; Markus & Kitayama, 1994). Table 4.4 shows items from a scale that assesses independence and interdependence. Which are you?

Culture, Cognition, and Emotion. Different construals of the self have potentially important cognitive consequences. For example, those with an independent sense of self see themselves as distinctive. Although they may regard other people as like them, they do not regard themselves as similar to other people. In contrast, among those with interdependent selves, the self and others are considered part of a specific social context in which both are embedded. Thus, both self and others are construed as quite similar.

The factors underlying personal motivation to achieve may be different as well. For example, Americans tend to strive for personal achievement, whereas the Japanese tend to strive for the achievement of group goals. Personal choice enhances motivation for those in the United States, whereas it has a lesser effect on Asian students' intrinsic motivation (Iyengar & Lepper, 1999).

Individualistic (or agentic) motives versus interdependent (or communal) ones are even used to organize information about the social world in memory (Woike, Gershkovich, Piorkowski, & Polo, 1999). People with independent self-construals are more likely to ignore the context in the inferences they draw about the social environment, whereas those with interdependent self-construals process social stimuli by paying attention to their relation to the context (Kuhnen, Hannover, Schubert, 2001). For example, whereas North Americans often describe events in terms of the specific actors involved and their personal qualities, those with collectivist orientations are more likely to refer to the social groups to which those others belong (Menon, Morris, Chiu, & Hong, 1999).

People with independent versus interdependent selves may experience fundamentally different kinds of emotions. Those with an independent sense of self, as found in U.S. culture, frequently experience ego-focused emotions, such as the experience of pride ("I did well") or frustration ("I was treated unfairly"). In contrast, cultures with interdependent conceptions of self tend to experience other-focused emotions. As an example, Markus and Kitayama use *amae,* the Japanese word for the sense of being lovingly cared for and dependent on another's indulgence. *Amae* is the formation and maintenance of a mutually reciprocal interdependent relationship with another person. There

Table 4.4

The Measurement of Independent and Interdependent Self-Construals

Indicate the extent to which you agree or disagree with each of the items below, on the following scale:

1	2	3	4	5	6	7
Strongly disagree						Strongly agree

___1. I have respect for authority figures with whom I interact.

___2. I am comfortable with being singled out for praise or rewards.

___3. My happiness depends on the happiness of those around me.

___4. Speaking up in class is not a problem for me.

___5. I should take into consideration my parents' advice when making education/career plans.

___6. My personal identity independent of others is very important to me.

If you answered "agree" on items 1, 3, and 5, you scored high in interdependence, whereas if you answered "agreed" on items 2, 4, and 6, you scored high in independence. Note that the entire scale is longer than the excerpt above.

Source: T. M. Singelis, *Personality and Social Psychology Bulletin, 20* (5), pp. 580–591, copyright © 1994 by Sage Publications, Inc. Reprinted by permission of Sage Publications, Inc.

Cultural Highlight: Motivation and the Self

What motivates you to strive and succeed? People in the United States usually believe that motivation is internal, rooted in the individual need to achieve and even in the need to surpass others. In interdependent cultures, however, motivation is experienced in receptivity to others, in the desire to adjust to their needs and demands, and in the ability to restrain one's own inner needs or desires. Although there is striving to excel and accomplish tasks, it is not in the service of self-promotion, but in the service of demonstrating and furthering one's interdependence.

Consider what happened in a U.S. plant located in Japan when Japanese women who were hired to wire electronic products were paid on a piece-rate system that rewarded those who produced more over those who produced less. About 2 months after the plant opening, the head foreladies approached the plant manager. "Honorable plant manager," they said humbly as they bowed,

> we are embarrassed to be so forward, but we must speak to you, because all of the girls have threatened to quit work this Friday. Why can't our plant have the same compensation system as other Japanese companies? When you hire a new girl, her starting wage should be fixed by her age. An 18-year-old should be paid more than a 16-year-old. Every year on her birthday, she should receive an automatic increase in pay. The idea that any one of us can be more productive than another must be wrong, because none of us in final assembly could make a thing unless all of the other people in the plant had done their jobs right first. To single one person out as being more productive is wrong and is also personally humiliating to us. (Ouchi, 1981, p. 41)

The company changed its compensation system to the Japanese model. Clearly, then, we cannot make assumptions about what motivates people to work hard and do well by using the assumptions of our own culture. We must understand what motivates members of other cultures and, in so doing, may discover that those others' hard work and striving are in service of very different goals.

is no equivalent for *amae* in the English language. The differences between independent and interdependent self-conceptions are summarized in Table 4.5.

Similarly, self-esteem is likely to vary, depending on the sense of self that a person holds (Crocker, Luhtanen, Blaine, & Broadnax, 1994). Recall from Table 4.1 the kinds of items that assess self-esteem, such as "I feel I am a person of worth." Members of cultures with an independent sense of self are more likely to endorse such items than are members of cultures where the self is viewed interdependently (Markus & Kitayama, 1991; Yik, Bond, & Paulhus, 1998). More generally, the importance one attaches to self-esteem and its implications for life satisfaction vary between independent and interdependent countries. Evidence for this assertion was reported by Diener and Diener (1995). In a study of 31 countries, they found that the relation between self-esteem and life satisfaction was lower in interdependent or collectivist countries, whereas in independent countries, individuals with high self-esteem reported high life satisfaction as well (Diener & Diener, 1995; see also Crocker et al., 1994). In collectivist cultures, social norms (such as social approval) are better predictors of life satisfaction, whereas individual emotions are stronger predictors of life satisfaction in individualistic cultures (Suh, Diener, Oishi, & Triandis, 1998). So different are these patterns that some have questioned how psychologists measure self-esteem, arguing that important components of self-esteem in interdependent cultures are missing from traditional Western definitions.

Despite differences between independent and interdependent cultures in willingness to endorse items on self-esteem scales, people in interdependent cultures who score high in self-esteem show many of the same effects as those from independent cultures who score high in self-esteem. For example, even in interdependent cultures, those who see themselves especially positively have higher levels of self-esteem (Yik et al., 1998). Members of interdependent cultures who have more independent self-construals look similar to those from independent cultures, for example, and show self-protective responses

Table 4.5

Summary of Key Differences between an Independent and an Interdependent Perception of Self

Feature Compared	Independent	Interdependent
Definition	Separate from social context	Connected with social context
Structure	Bounded, unitary, stable	Flexible, variable
Important features	Internal, private (abilities, thoughts, feelings)	External, public (statuses, roles, relationships)
Tasks	Be unique Express self Realize internal attributes Promote own goals Be direct: say what's on your mind	Belong, fit in Occupy one's proper place Engage in appropriate action Promote others' goals Be indirect: read other's mind
Role of others	*Self-evaluation:* others important for social comparison, reflected appraisal	*Self-definition:* self defined by relationships with others in specific contexts
Basis of self-esteem[a]	Ability to express self; validate internal attributes	Ability to adjust, restrain self, maintain harmony with social context

[a]Esteeming the self may be primarily a Western phenomenon, and the concept of self-esteem should perhaps be replaced by self-satisfaction, or by a term that reflects the realization that one is fulfilling the culturally mandated task.

Source: H. R. Markus and S. Kitayama. (1991). Culture and the self: Implications for cognition, emotion, and motivation. *Psychological Review, 98,* 224–253.

to negative feedback. Moreover, as already noted, measures of implicit self-esteem suggest that even in interdependent cultures, there is some tendency to self-enhance indirectly, as by overvaluing the letters in one's name (Kitayama & Karasawa, 1997).

Aspects of Self-Knowledge

What form does our self-knowledge take? That is, how are the beliefs that we hold about ourselves represented cognitively?

Self-Schemas

In Chapter 2, Volume 1, we considered the concept of a schema. A schema is an organized, structured set of cognitions about some concept or stimulus. Just as people hold schemas about the nature of other people and events, they also hold schemas about themselves. **Self-schemas** describe the dimensions along which you think about yourself. You may, for example, be very concerned about maintaining and displaying your independence. You might refuse to take money from your parents for college, might do your own laundry, might not ask your roommate for help with your math, and the like. Or you might consider yourself more dependent and think a lot about ensuring security for yourself by surrounding yourself with people you can depend on, like your brother, girlfriend, doctor, minister, and so on. In either case, you have a strong self-schema concerning the independence-dependence dimension. On the other hand, you may not think of yourself very much in connection with that dimension, in which case you are not thinking schematically in those terms. You would be described as aschematic on the dimension of independence-dependence.

People are schematic on dimensions that are important to them, on which they think of themselves as extreme, and on which they are certain that the opposite is not true. If independence is important to you and you think of yourself as extremely independent and not at all dependent, this belief implies that you have accumulated considerable knowledge about yourself on that domain. For example, you are certain that you would never ask anyone for help setting up your stereo, even at the potential cost of damage to it or yourself. When you hold a schema for yourself on a particular dimension, it helps you to identify situations as relevant to that dimension. For example, if you think of yourself as independent, you are likely to see that the purchase of a new stereo system with complex instructions for installation requires independent behavior. Moreover, the recognition that situations are schema-relevant sets guidelines for your own behavior (Kendzierski & Whitaker, 1997). You are likely to recognize not only that the situation calls for independent behavior, but that you will be the one to wade through the instructions and set up the stereo.

Not all self-schemas are positive. People also hold well-articulated, highly organized beliefs about themselves regarding negative qualities (Malle & Horowitz, 1995). For example, someone who thinks of himself as overweight will quickly notice that eating situations are relevant to him; he might plan what he will eat and may count the calories that he consumes. Being weight-schematic also means that he is likely to notice weight-relevant behaviors in others. Thus, for example, he may more quickly notice and infer that someone who has only cottage cheese and peaches for lunch is on a diet than would someone who is not so concerned with weight (Sedikides & Skowronski, 1993; Wurf & Markus, 1983).

People hold self-conceptions not only about their current qualities, but also about traits that may become self-descriptive at some time in the future (Markus & Nurius, 1986). These are called **possible selves.** Some of these involve goals or roles to which people aspire, such as the 5-year-old's desire to be a firefighter or the student's expectation of becoming a doctor. Most possible selves tend to be positive. That is, people think of themselves in the future primarily in good terms (Markus & Nurius, 1986). However, some possible selves represent fears concerning what one might become in the future, such as the suspicion that one's enthusiastic consumption of alcohol on certain occasions could eventually lead to alcoholism. Contemplating feared selves can, not surprisingly, induce anxiety and guilt (Carver, Lawrence, & Scheier, 1999).

Possible selves function in much the same way as self-schemas. They help people to articulate their goals and develop behaviors that will enable them to fulfill those goals. In a study by Ruvolo and Markus (1992), participants were told to imagine themselves being successful at work, lucky at work, failing at work despite clear effort, or failing because of bad luck. Subsequently, participants worked on a task that measured persistence. Those participants who were asked to envision themselves as successful because of their own efforts worked longer on the task than did participants who envisioned themselves as failing or as succeeding due to luck, presumably because they had a vision of the successful possible self firmly in mind. Thus, possible selves provide focus and organization for the pursuit of goals. They help people to gather appropriate self-knowledge and develop plans that enable them to rehearse the actions they need to undertake in pursuit of their goals (Markus & Ruvolo, 1989).

Self-schemas, including possible selves, then, have many important functions regarding self-knowledge and the self in action. Knowing about our personal qualities enables us to identify quickly whether situations are relevant to us or not. Self-schemas help us to remember schema-relevant information. They help us to make inferences about the meaning of our past behavior and to make decisions and judgments that guide our future behavior.

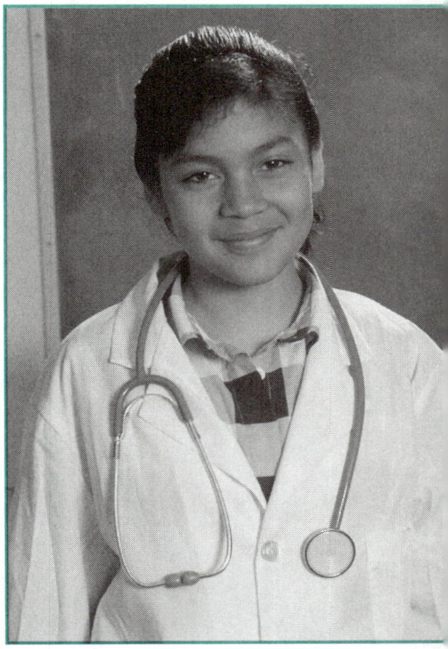

Possible selves are goals or roles to which people aspire that are currently not self-descriptive but may become so.

Self-Discrepancies

Other aspects of the self that influence our thoughts and behavior concern discrepancies between how we actually are and how we ideally want to be or think we ought to be. Psychologist Tory Higgins (1987, 1989) suggests that these **self-discrepancies** produce strong emotions. When we perceive a discrepancy between our personal qualities and what we would ideally like to be **(ideal self),** we experience disappointment, dissatisfaction, or sadness (what are called "dejection-related emotions"), as well as a reduction in self-esteem (Moretti & Higgins, 1990). Discrepancies between our actual self and what we think we ought to be **(ought self)** produce agitation-related emotions such as fear or anxiety (e.g. Boldero & Francis, 2000). Although the actual content of beliefs about the self shifts over time, the use of the ideal self versus the ought self and the impact of discrepancies on well-being remain relatively stable (Strauman, 1996).

To test these points, Higgins, Klein, and Strauman (1985) asked college students to fill out a questionnaire that assessed their self-perceptions, including how they would ideally like to be and how they felt they ought to be. The first time, the participants filled the questionnaire out for themselves. At a later time, they filled it out from the standpoint of their father, mother, and closest friend. They also rated the extent to which each of the personal attributes they rated was relevant or meaningful to them.

Discrepancies between the actual self and the ideal self did indeed produce dejection-related emotions (Higgins & Bargh, 1987) and loss of self-esteem (Higgins, Shah, & Friedman, 1997; Moretti & Higgins, 1990). For example, wanting to be editor of the school newspaper but failing to attain that position produced disappointment and sadness. Perceived discrepancies between one's actual self and a friend's or parent's ideal self produced anxiety. For example, perceiving that one was not going to be the successful entrepreneur of one's father's dream produced anxiety but not sadness. The more important the personal attribute was to the respondent, the greater the emotion experienced (see also Higgins, 1999).

Self-discrepancy theory postulates that concerns about the ideal or the ought self emerge from temperament and from early socialization. That is, we are predisposed, and may be taught as well, to think in terms of becoming our ideal self or meeting the standards of others. Generally speaking, people who are more concerned with becoming their ideal self recall having been raised by their parents in a warm and supportive way, whereas those who are more concerned about the opinions of others report a parenting style marked more by rejection (Manian, Strauman, & Denney, 1998). Cultural differences also affect whether the ideal or the ought self governs self-regulatory behavior. Specifically, people with an independent sense of self are more likely to be motivated by discrepancies between themselves and their ideal selves, whereas people raised with an interdependent self are more attentive to the concerns or demands of others.

Self-Regulation

How do we take all of this information we have about ourselves and employ it in our daily life? **Self-regulation** refers to the ways in which people control and direct their own actions. As we have seen, people have enormous quantities of information about themselves, including their personal characteristics and desires and their conceptions of themselves in the future. They formulate goals and pursue them, drawing on their social and self-regulatory skills (Sheldon & Kasser, 1998). In this section, we deal explicitly with how conceptions of the self regulate thought, emotion, and action in social situations. The ability of human beings to control, override, and interrupt their responses is a significant, important, energy-consuming aspect of the self (Muraven, Tice, & Baumeister, 1998). To understand self-regulation, we begin with the working self-concept.

The Working Self-Concept

Which aspect of the self influences our thoughts and ongoing behavior depends in large part on what aspect of the self-concept is relevant to a particular situation. The aspect of the self-concept that is accessed for a particular situation is called the **working self-concept.** In a classroom situation, the academic self is likely to be the dominant determinant of our thoughts and feelings, whereas if we are reminded about a party coming up on Friday, the social self may be accessed. The working self-concept is important because it draws on our overall self-concept but guides social behavior in specific situations and is, in turn, modified by what goes on in the situation (McGuire & McGuire, 1996).

The working self-concept can sometimes be at odds with the stable self-concept. Think about a time when you had an argument with a friend and snapped at her. Afterward, you probably didn't feel very good about yourself, and she probably didn't think much of you either. Yet you probably have a stable sense of yourself as a nice person who is easy to get along with. After that particular incident, you may not have thought well of yourself for at least several hours or perhaps even a few days. Over time, however, your stable self-concept won out, and you again thought of yourself as pleasant and easy to get along with, even though occasionally you are not this way at all. As this example implies, changes in self-esteem may fluctuate with these day-to-day activities as well (Nezlek & Plesko, 2001). These fluctuations in feelings about the self seem to depend most heavily on whether needs to feel competent, in control, and tied in with others are satisfied during daily activities (Reis, Sheldon, Gable, Roscoe, & Ryan, 2000).

Changes in the working self-concept produce changes in the permanent self-concept only when the working self-concept is stable over time. For example, while in college, you may not think of yourself as particularly authoritative. Yet, on graduation, if you get a job supervising several other people in a bank and you do this day in and day out for months or even years, you may come to think of yourself as authoritative, and that view may become an important part of your stable self-concept. It was not so before, but it became so because you are now consistently in a situation that requires an authoritative manner. The working self-concept, in this case, became part of the stable self-concept.

Self-Complexity

Another aspect of the self that is important for self-regulation involves **self-complexity.** Some people think of themselves in one or two predominant ways, whereas others think of themselves in terms of a variety of qualities. One college student may think of herself primarily as a student, focusing her attention and beliefs about herself on how well she does in her courses. Another may think of herself in more complex ways, as a student, a daughter, a girlfriend, a member of the track team, and a part-time employee (Linville, 1985; Woolfolk, Novalany, Gara, Allen, & Polino, 1995).

Linville (1985) suggests that people with simple self-conceptions are buoyed by success in their particular area of importance but are very vulnerable to failure. So, for example, the student who is focused primarily on her grades and who receives a bad grade may feel very upset and depressed because of it. People who are more complex, however, may be buoyed by success but have other aspects of themselves that buffer them in the case of failures or setbacks. The student who has an academic setback but has a complex self may temporarily turn her attention away from her schoolwork to prepare for a track meet and thus cope somewhat more successfully with the academic setback. Thus, positive self-complexity can act as a buffer against stressful life events and may help prevent people from becoming depressed or ill in response to setbacks (Showers & Ryff, 1996).

Considerable research has demonstrated the importance of self-complexity for buffering people against setbacks, with one caveat: Only positive complex self-representations achieve this function. Negative complex self-representations, by contrast, represent a risk factor for depression and predict poorer recovery from depression (Woolfolk et al., 1995). It stands to reason that thinking about oneself as inadequate or as likely to do poorly in a variety of domains is not going to buffer a person against failures or setbacks.

Self-Efficacy and Personal Control

Other aspects of the self that influence self-regulation include **self-efficacy** beliefs, that is, the expectations that we hold about our abilities to accomplish certain tasks (Bandura, 1986). Whether or not we will undertake a particular activity, attempt to do a particular task, or strive to meet a particular goal depends on whether we believe we will be efficacious in performing those actions. The smoker will not stop smoking unless she believes she can do it, however much she may want to stop. Faced with a challenging paper, the student who believes he has the ability to do a good job will be more likely to start it and persist at it than the student who has doubts about his ability to complete it successfully. Psychologists believe that early experiences with success and failure lead people to develop fairly stable conceptions of their self-efficacy in different life domains (Bandura, 1986).

It is important to realize that self-efficacy beliefs are highly specific, control-related perceptions of one's ability to perform a particular behavior. They are not general feelings of control. So, for example, if you want to know if someone will work hard to try out for the tennis team, you need to know his self-efficacy beliefs specifically related to making the tennis team, not his general feelings about himself as an effective person.

Behavioral Activation and Inhibition

Self-regulation involves fundamental decisions about what people and activities to approach and which ones to avoid. Psychologists have argued that people have two quite independent motivational systems that control these tasks: an appetitive system, referred to as the "behavioral activation system" (BAS) and an aversive system, or "behavioral inhibition system" (BIS). When BAS is activated, people tend to approach people or activities in the environment; when BIS is activated, people are more likely to avoid people and acitivites.

One way to think about this distinction is as an individual difference. Some people are more BAS-oriented and some people are more BIS-oriented. For the most part, people who experience a lot of positive events and positive affect have a strong behavioral activation system, whereas people whose experience is dominated by negative affect have a stronger behavioral inhibition system. Daily experience influences the activation of these systems as well. If good things are happening to you, you are more likely to be in an activation state (BAS) than in an inhibited state (BIS) (Gable, Reis, & Elliot, 2000).

Earlier we discussed people's concerns with discrepancies from their own ideal self versus their concerns with other's expectations for them. This distinction may map onto the difference between BAS (activation or goal promotion) and BIS (inhibition or

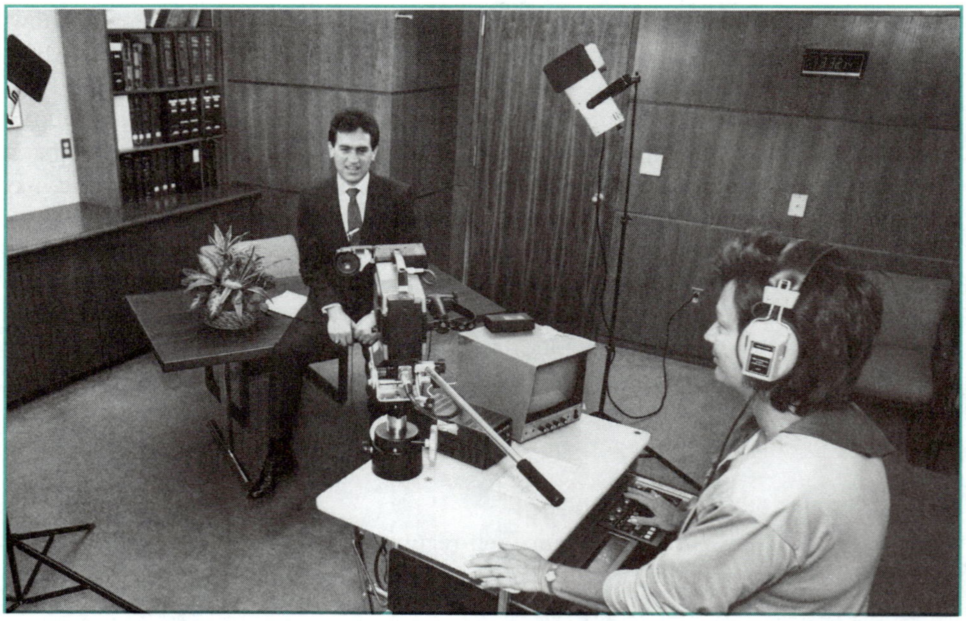

Certain experiences, such as being filmed, put us in a state of self-awareness. Self-awareness causes people to compare and evaluate themselves according to available standards.

prevention) (Shah & Higgins, 2001). Discrepancies from one's ideal facilitate efforts toward attaining the ideal (activation), whereas anticipatory concerns over not meeting the expectancies of others represent a prevention orientation (Forster, Higgins, & Idson, 1998).

Self-Awareness

Self-regulation is also influenced by our direction of attention, specifically, whether attention is directed inward toward the self or outward toward the environment (Duval & Wicklund, 1972). Usually our attention is focused outward toward the environment, but sometimes our attention is focused inward on ourselves. Certain experiences in the world automatically focus attention inward, such as catching sight of ourselves in the mirror, having our picture taken, or, more subtly, being evaluated by others, or even simply being in a minority in a group situation. We begin to think of ourselves not as a moving actor in the environment, but as the object of our own and others' attention. This state is called **self-awareness** (Duval & Wicklund, 1972; Wicklund & Frey, 1980).

In general, self-awareness leads people to evaluate their behavior against a standard and to set an adjustment process in motion for meeting the standard. Suppose, for example, that you go out to an elegant restaurant and you are seated facing your date but also, to your irritation, you are looking directly into a mirror on the wall behind you. Try as you might, each time you look up, you catch sight of your own face. You notice your windblown hair, the awkward way you smile, and the unattractive way you chew. Feeling utterly foolish by the time the main course arrives, you flee to the bathroom to comb your hair, vowing that if you still look as bad when you return, you will change tables (Duval, Duval, & Mulilis, 1992; Sedikides, 1992).

Self-attention causes people to compare themselves to standards, such as those for physical appearance, intellectual performance, athletic prowess, or moral integrity (Macrae, Bodenhausen, & Milne, 1998). We attempt to conform to the standard, evaluate our behavior against that standard, decide that it either matches the standard or does not, and continue adjusting and comparing until we meet the standard or give up. This process is called "feedback," and the theory is called the **cybernetic theory of self-regulation.**

People also differ in the degrees to which they attend to public or to private aspects of themselves. This distinction has been called "public" versus "private self-consciousness" (Fenigstein, Scheier, & Buss, 1975). People high in **public self-consciousness** are concerned with autonomy and issues of identity (Schlenker & Weigold, 1990). They are concerned with what other people think about them, the way they look, and how they appear to others. Those high in **private self-consciousness** try to analyze themselves, think about themselves a great deal, and are more attentive to their inner feelings. People high in private self-consciousness seem to have better articulated self-schemas, and they are more aware of their internal dispositions (Shrum & McCarty, 1992). When the public self is made especially salient, people tend to place more weight on their personal attitudes, but when their attention is diverted outward, they are more likely to place weight on social norms (Ybarra & Trafimow, 1998). Public and private forms of self-consciousness are not opposites. People can be high in both, low in both, or high in one or the other.

Public and private forms of self-consciousness have implications for behavior. When publicly self-conscious people become self-aware, they may try to adjust their behavior to conform to external standards, such as the values or attitudes of others, especially if they are also low in private self-consciousness (Doherty & Schlenker, 1991). In contrast, when privately self-conscious people become self-aware, they may be more attentive to internal goals and beliefs and thus try harder to meet personal standards (Froming & Carver, 1981; Nasby, 1989; Scheier & Carver, 1980). Which are you? Or are you high in both? Answer the questions in Table 4.6 to find out.

Table 4.6

Self-Consciousness Scale

Indicate whether you generally agree (A) or disagree (D) with each of the following items.

___1. I'm always trying to figure myself out.

___2. I'm concerned about my style of doing things.

___3. Generally, I'm not very aware of myself.

___4. I reflect about myself a lot.

___5. I'm concerned about the way I present myself.

___6. I'm self-conscious about the way I look.

___7. I never scrutinize myself.

___8. I'm generally attentive to my inner feelings.

___9. I usually worry about making a good impression.

If you answered "agree" on items 1, 4, and 8 and "disagree" on items 3 and 7, you scored high on the private self-conciousness scale. If you answered "agree" to items 2, 5, 6, and 9, you scored high on the public self-conciousness scale. Note that the entire scale is considerably longer than the excerpt above.

Source: Adapted from Fenigstein, Scheier, and Buss (1975).

Motivation and the Self

So far, this chapter has considered the working self-concept, self-efficacy expectations, and focus of attention as determinants of how people regulate their activities in the environment. It is also important to know the motivations that drive self-regulation. Generally speaking, people seek an accurate, stable, and positive self-conception and will seek out situations or behave in ways that further those aspects of the self (Jussim, Yen, & Aiello, 1995; Sedikides & Strube, 1995).

The Need for an Accurate Self-Concept

To make our future outcomes predictable and controllable, we need to have a fairly accurate assessment of our abilities. Psychologist Yaacov Trope (1975, 1983) has argued that in the absence of factors that might induce people to save face or strive to succeed, people tend to pick tasks that will be most informative about their abilities, tasks that he called "diagnostic." For example, if you, a college student, want to know if you are a good dancer, you are unlikely to go to a children's dancing class or to a ballroom competition. You will do extremely well in the first setting and incredibly poorly in the second (unless you have been trained in competitive ballroom dancing). The situation most diagnostic for your dancing ability is a college dance or party.

Overall, Trope's work suggests that having an accurate sense of self is an important determinant in the selection of a task, especially when our knowledge of our ability is uncertain (Sorrentino & Roney, 1986). Accurate self-assessment enables us to anticipate and control our future performance (Trope & Bassok, 1982). Research suggests that we are most likely to seek accurate self-relevant information when we anticipate that the news will be good, but we also show a desire for self-assessment when we anticipate that the news may be bad (Brown, 1990).

The Need for a Consistent Self-Concept

Related to the need for accuracy is the need to have a sense of self that is consistent. We do not want to think of ourselves as changing dramatically from situation to situation;

rather, we need to believe that we have certain intrinsic qualities that remain relatively stable over time (Swann, 1983). People, then, tend to seek out and interpret situations that confirm their already-existing self-conceptions, and they avoid or resist situations and feedback that are at odds with their existing self-conceptions. This process is termed **self-verification.** Imagine, for example, that a seminar has just ended and a classmate comes up to you and says, "Boy, you don't talk much in class, do you?" Perhaps you didn't talk in class that particular day, but you may think of yourself as someone who usually does. You may find that during the very next class, you talk even more than you usually do in order to convince your classmate, as well as yourself, that your conception of yourself as an active class participant is a correct one.

People choose signs and symbols in their clothing and appearance to make statements about who they are. This process is called self-verification.

A series of studies by Swann and Read (1981b) suggests that this need to see ourselves as consistent is quite pervasive. In one study, college students were led to believe that other college students' evaluations of them would be either consistent or inconsistent with their own self-image. When given a chance to see those evaluations, the students spent more time perusing consistent than inconsistent feedback. This was true even when the consistent attributes were ones on which people perceived themselves negatively (see Swann & Schroeder, 1995). When interacting with others, people use behavioral strategies that confirm their self-conceptions. That is, they deliberately act in ways that confirm the existing self-image (McNulty & Swann, 1994), especially when they are certain of their self-views (Pelham & Swann, 1994). This tendency is especially strong when people believe that others have incorrect beliefs about them. The earlier example of volunteering more in class to counteract a classmate's false impression illustrates this point.

This need to see the self in a consistent manner extends to several other strategies of self-regulation. We selectively interact with others who see us as we do ourselves (Swann & Pelham, 1990; Swann, Stein-Seroussi, & Giesler, 1992). We choose signs and symbols in our clothing and appearance that say things about who we are (Swann, 1983). Thus, if you want people to think of you as an athlete, you are more likely to wear your athletic jersey than a T-shirt to class. We remember feedback that is consistent with our self-attributes better than we remember incongruent feedback (Story, 1998).

The previous discussion implies that people spend much of their time seeking out situations and ways of behaving in accordance with their existing self-concept. In fact, this picture is probably not accurate. Most of the time, people are able to maintain their views of themselves without any active or conscious effort. Maintaining a consistent sense of self is part of the process of interacting with family, friends, and coworkers in familiar settings, performing familiar tasks. However, when people receive discrepant feedback from others, they may then be motivated to focus active attention on the threat to a consistent self-conception and thus enact efforts to dispel the incorrect view.

Self-Improvement

In addition to the desire for an accurate sense of self, people are motivated by the desire to improve. The educational process, for example, assumes that people will strive to enhance their ability to master fundamental learning tasks. Many people aim to improve their performance in sports and other leisure activities rather than to maintain a static level of ability. Once we are employed, we want to improve our job skills so we can maintain or enhance our standing in our work organization. Many self-regulatory activities serve this need to improve (Kasser & Ryan, 1996).

What kinds of information and situations do we seek when our goal is self-improvement? Earlier, this chapter discussed Markus's concept of possible selves, the visions that people have of themselves in the future. Markus argues that by clearly articulating visions of ourselves in desired activities, we are able to set appropriate goals, make progress toward achieving those goals, and chart how well we are doing with respect to those goals. For example, the would-be college professor can chart and plan her personal progress better if she has a clear view of how she will perform in this future role.

Thus, possible selves give explicit vision to the goals we set for ourselves in the future and help us to attain them.

Self-improvement may also be facilitated by social contact with other people. Specifically, comparing the self with someone who possesses a desired skill or attribute can enable a person to improve (Taylor & Lobel, 1989). This process is called "upward comparison." For example, a college football player may keep pictures of his favorite professional players on his wall to inspire him and remind him of the steps he needs to take to reach the same level of success. People who embody the attributes or skills we wish to attain can motivate us and can also be a source of specific information that is helpful for improvement.

Although social psychologists have not yet exhaustively explored the area of self-improvement—namely, the conditions under which we seek to improve ourselves, the attributes on which we wish to improve, and the sources of information and inspiration we turn to—they have begun to understand the issue.

Self-Enhancement

Clearly, we need to have accurate information about our abilities and opinions. Without some degree of accuracy and consistency in our self-image, we would be vulnerable to a host of faulty judgments and decisions. We also need to set goals, acquire new skills and information, and generally improve on the abilities and skills that are important to us. Yet our self-regulatory activities are also heavily determined by the need to feel good about ourselves and to maintain self-esteem. These **self-enhancement** needs appear to be important, perhaps even preeminent, most of the time (Sedikides, 1993), and they become especially important following situations of threat, failure, or blows to self-esteem (Beauregard & Dunning, 1998; Krueger, 1998; Wills, 1981).

One way that people satisfy their self-enhancement needs is by holding self-perceptions that are falsely positive and somewhat exaggerated with respect to their actual abilities, talents, and social skills (Taylor & Brown, 1988). Taylor and Brown have called these **positive illusions.** There are at least three types of positive illusions: People see themselves more positively than is true; they believe they have more control over the events around them than is actually the case; and they are unrealistically optimistic about the future. For example, when students are asked to describe how accurately positive and negative personality adjectives describe themselves and others, most evaluate themselves more favorably than they evaluate others (Alicke, Klotz, Breitenbecher, Yurak, & Vredenburg, 1995). We remember positive information about ourselves, but negative information often slips conveniently from mind (Sedikides & Green, 2000). We respond to threats by bolstering our self-perceptions in other life domains (Boney-McCoy, Gibbons, & Gerrard, 1999). If pressed, most of us would have more difficulty reconstructing circumstances when we have failed than circumstances when we have succeeded (Story, 1998). We believe we are more likely than others to engage in selfless, kind, and generous acts (Epley & Dunning, 2000). Also, we often remember our performance as more positive than it actually was (Crary, 1966). We believe we are happier than most other people (Klar & Giladi, 1999).

As we saw in Chapter 3, Volume 1, people are more likely to attribute positive than negative outcomes to themselves (Miller & Ross, 1975). We credit the volleyball win to our own spectacular plays, but we attribute the loss to "a bad day" or "poor team coordination." When we do acknowledge our negative qualities, we often regard them as less important or consequential than our positive qualities (e.g., Campbell, 1986; Harackiewicz, Sansone, & Manderlink, 1985). Although we may dimly recognize that we have no talent in some areas of our lives (such as athletics), we keep those negative self-perceptions from mind by avoiding thinking about them, avoiding situations that would bring them to the fore (Showers, 1992), or by remaining oblivious to just how bad we are (Kruger & Dunning, 1999). Alternatively, we may develop unique definitions of talents and shortcomings, so that we value more highly the things we do well than the things we do poorly (Dunning & Cohen, 1992; Dunning & McElwee, 1995).

Are there conditions when people are more accurate or balanced in their self-appraisals? It appears that when people are about to receive feedback from others they are reasonably realistic, even pessimistic about the news they will get (Taylor & Shepperd, 1998). When people are in the process of deciding between alternative courses of action or setting goals, they are fairly accurate and honest with themselves. But once they move on to the task of implementing those goals, their positive illusions become more evident (Taylor & Gollwitzer, 1995). As these findings imply, viewing oneself in an unrealistically favorable light is more feasible about the future than about the present (Robinson & Ryff, 1999). Evidence also suggests that people who are low in self-esteem or moderately depressed may be more evenhanded in their self-perceptions. They tend to recall both positive and negative information, their self-perceptions are more congruent with others' evaluations of them, and they are less likely to show the self-serving attributional bias of taking credit for good but not bad outcomes (Taylor & Brown, 1988). People are also more modest in their self-appraisals when they expect that others will have accurate information about their abilities, when their self-descriptions can be relatively easily verified, or when they expect to receive self-relevant feedback (Armor & Taylor, 1998; Shepperd, Ouellette, & Fernandez, 1996). In summary, people are much more likely to be self-aggrandizing when they won't get caught up in their little white lies than when disconfirming evidence is likely to be forthcoming.

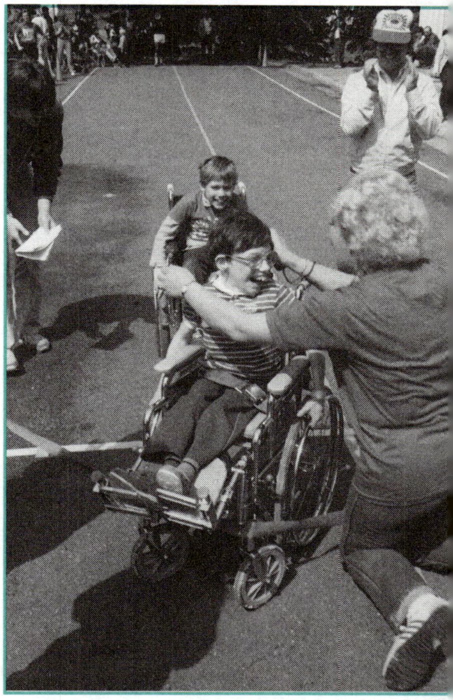
Sometimes just feeling good about ourselves (self-enhancement) is important.

Why are most people so apparently self-enhancing in their self-perceptions, and moreover, why do these self-enhancing perceptions exist if they do not conform to reality? Taylor and Brown (1988) argued that self-enhancing positive illusions are adaptive. Unrealistic optimism about the future and a false sense of personal control may help us feel better about ourselves (Regan, Snyder, & Kassin, 1995) and persist longer in trying to achieve our goals. When we feel good about ourselves, we are happy, our social interactions go more smoothly, and we are more likely to help others. Feeling good about ourselves keeps us motivated and engaged in productive and creative work. Who, for example, would continue to work on a major project if he or she anticipated that it would be unsuccessful? Believing that we are talented and that our efforts will be successful keeps us going. In short, then, our self-enhancing self-perceptions may foster many of the tasks that are regarded as evidence of successful life adjustment: a sense of personal well-being, pleasant social interactions, and the ability to engage in creative, productive work (see Brown & Dutton, 1995). Positive self-regard is thought to foster good social relationships as well; however, it appears that this relation has an upward limit. People who are noticeably self-enhancing can alienate their peers, as we will see shortly in our consideration of self-presentational skills (Colvin, Block, & Funder, 1995; Paulus, 1998).

The need to feel good about oneself is often caricatured as blatant self-aggrandizement or self-deception. Yet feeling good about ourselves—not feeling threatened or undermined—is important in other aspects of personal and social life. For example, when people are feeling less threatened, they are, perhaps paradoxically, more receptive to negative information about themselves. On a day when you get a good grade in one course, you may be more ready to hear a more qualified assessment in another course, for example. And when people are feeling good about themselves, they are less likely to be negative about other people (Ybarra, 1999).

Whether people are primarily motivated to be accurate in their self-assessments, or self-enhancing, has been a particular area of controversy, and the answer seems to depend, in part, on the circumstances in which feedback is sought (Brown & Dutton, 1995; Dunning, 1995; Roney & Sorrentino, 1995; Taylor, Neter, & Wayment, 1995). People in an intuitive frame of mind self-enhance, whereas those in a more analytical, rational mode of mind seek consistent or accurate information. The salience of these motives also appears to vary culturally. People from Western cultures, such as the United States, are more likely to self-enhance, whereas those from interdependent cultures, such as the Japanese, may be more concerned with self-improvement and therefore more likely to engage in self-criticism (Kitayama, Markus, Matsumoto, & Norasakkunkit, 1997).

Of the motives that guide self-regulation, self-enhancement has been the most studied; several specific theories that address important aspects of self-enhancement are presented in the following discussion.

Self-Affirmation. Psychologists believe that self-enhancement needs become especially important under conditions of threat. When people have received some blow to their self-worth brought about by a failure at some important task, they may try to emphasize or otherwise recruit positive features of themselves in order to compensate for the setback. For example, the attractive male student who fails an exam may seek out female classmates who will flatter his ego. Or the college student who is not making friends easily may proudly display high school sports trophies. **Self-affirmation** theory, developed by Claude Steele (1988), explicitly predicts that people will cope with specific threats to their self-worth by affirming unrelated aspects of themselves (Aronson, Blanton, & Cooper, 1995; Blanton, Cooper, Skurnik, & Aronson, 1997; Cohen, Aronson, & Steele, 2000; Koole, Smeets, van Knippenberg, & Dijksterhuis, 1999).

In an experiment that tests some of these points, Brown and Smart (1991) gave students who were either high in self-esteem or low in self-esteem a success or a failure experience through an alleged test of their intellectual ability. Subsequently, the students were asked to rate themselves on a series of trait adjectives. Half the items referred to social traits and attributes and half referred to traits and attributes that were related to the task on which the students had received feedback—namely, achievement-related traits and attributes. Participants high in self-esteem who had failed on the intellectual task exaggerated the positivity of their social qualities; this result is consistent with the predictions of self-affirmation theory. However, participants low in self-esteem actually did the reverse. They generalized the failure experience: Both their self-ratings of intellectual attributes and their self-perceptions about social activities were low. Although the predictions of self-affirmation theory appear to be true generally, they may be more true of individuals who are high in self-esteem than of those low in self-esteem (Steele, 1988; Wicklund & Gollwitzer, 1982). For example, high-self-esteem individuals are more likely to make spontaneous use of self-affirmation processes following a threat; that is, they are more likely to reaffirm their strengths and pay less attention to their weaknesses (Dodgson & Wood, 1998).

In addition to its specific arguments about the value of self-affirmation, the theory suggests an important aspect of self-enhancement more generally, namely, that some self-enhancement may be enough. An opportunity to reaffirm an important value or personal quality may undercut an otherwise potent threat to self. On the other hand, one's good qualities may reduce the need to draw on additional experiences (such as success) that might otherwise be an opportunity for enhancing the self (Lockwood & Kunda, 1999). When people have the opportunity to self-affirm, they may be less defensive and more accepting of potentially negative information (Sherman, Nelson, Steele, 2000).

Terror Management Theory. Nonetheless, threat is an important stimulus to the need to enhance the self, and there is, perhaps, no greater terror than death itself. A theory that draws on this important insight is terror management theory. The theory maintains that people are vulnerable to fears about their own mortality and seek ways to manage and minimize the anxiety that this vulnerability causes (Greenberg, Pyszczynski, & Solomon, 1986). Research consistent with this viewpoint shows, for example, that when death is made salient, people actively suppress death-related thoughts (Greenberg, Arndt, Schimel, Pyszczynski, & Solomon, 2001).

According to the theory, the terror of mortality is kept under control by at least two factors: a cultural worldview that makes sense of an otherwise threatening world and personal self-esteem that leads to the sense that one is an object of value in a meaningful universe.

On the first point, the theory maintains that subscribing to and living up to culturally approved standards of behavior protect people from the anxiety that their vulnerability would otherwise create (e.g. Greenberg, Solomon, Pyszcynski, Rosenblatt, Burling, Lyon, Simon, & Pinel, 1992) (Greenberg, Porteus, Simon, Pyszczynski, & Solomon, 1995). The act of following a social or cultural norm is, in essence, soothing or reassuring. The reverse is also true: When fears of death are engaged, the threat of mortality motivates allegiance to cultural beliefs (Arndt, Greenberg, Pyszczynski, & Solomon, 1997). The theory also predicts that people are most likely to act on their beliefs when mortality threat is made salient. For example, in one study, people were more likely to aggress against a person who challenged their worldview following a manipulation in which their mortality had been made salient; they were less likely to do so if no threat of mortality had been made (McGregor, Lieberman, Greenberg, Solomon, Arndt, Simon, & Pyszczynski, 1998).

High self-esteem is also thought to help people manage the terror of mortality by reaffirming their value and importance. Other self-enhancement theories stress the psychological benefits of enhancing the self. In contrast, from the standpoint of terror management theory, self-esteem is not so much an effort to enhance the self as an effort to protect it against the forces that threaten to destroy it.

Tesser's Self-Evaluation Maintenance Model. Abraham Tesser and his associates (see Tesser, 1988, for a review) have suggested another social mechanism whereby people facilitate and maintain their positive impressions of themselves, namely, how they deal with the performances of other people around them who threaten or enhance their own sense of self. For example, John's best friend, Mark, recently won a prestigious prize for writing a short story. How will John react? Will he be overjoyed and eager to tell others about his friend's success? Or might he instead feel envious of Mark's success and unhappy to be reminded that he is a less talented writer? More generally, when does the successful performance of another individual enhance our self-evaluation, and when does it threaten our sense of self-worth? Tesser (1988) has developed a **self-evaluation maintenance model** designed to answer this question.

Tesser's model focuses on the motive for self-enhancement. The performance of other people in our social environment can affect our self-evaluation, especially when we are psychologically close to them. In the model, perceived closeness can come from having a relationship with another person, such as being a friend or relative. But closeness can also be based on shared characteristics, such as race, gender, religion, or physical proximity. In general, the behavior of people who are close has greater impact on us than the behavior of people who are psychologically distant.

In addition, Tesser focuses on situations in which the other person performs relatively better than we do. The performance of others is less important to our self-evaluation when it is mediocre or poor. According to Tesser, the critical situation arises when a person we are close to performs well. In such situations, what determines our reaction? Do we take pride in the other person's accomplishments or do we compare ourselves negatively to that person? A key factor is whether the performance is relevant to our self-definition. If John aspires to be an award-winning creative writer, his knowledge that a close friend has outperformed him is likely to threaten his self-evaluation and lead to feelings of envy and discomfort (Morf & Rhodewalt, 1993). On the other hand, if John has no particular concern about his writing ability and sees creative writing as irrelevant to his sense of self, he should take pleasure in the success of a close friend, since it poses no threat to his self-evaluation (cf. Brown, Nowick, Lord, & Richards, 1992).

In more technical terms, the main ideas of the self-evaluation maintenance model can be summarized as follows:

1. *The comparison effect.* When another person outperforms us on a behavior that is relevant to our self-definition, the better his or her performance and the closer our relationship, the greater is the threat to our self-evaluation. We feel envious, frustrated, or even angry.
2. *The reflection effect.* When another person outperforms us on a behavior that is irrelevant to our self-definition, the better his or her performance and the closer our relationship, the more we can gain in self-evaluation. A process of reflection leads us to feel positive and to take pride in the other person's success.

It is important to note the crucial role of the personal relevance of the behavior in question. The very same factors—closeness and high performance—can lead to opposite effects, depending on whether the behavior is relevant or irrelevant to our self-definition. Emotional arousal also appears to be critical to self-evaluation maintenance. That is, when another person outperforms us on a behavior important to our self-definition, we attempt to maintain high self-evaluation only if we actually experience strong emotions in response to the other person's success. If emotional arousal does not occur or if it is misattributed to some neutral source, the dynamics of self-evaluation maintenance take place to a far lesser degree (Tesser, Pilkington, & McIntosh, 1989; see also Tesser & Collins, 1988).

Culture and Self-Enhancement. The phenomenon of self-enhancement may represent an insight about the self that is culturally bounded. Heine and Lehman (1999), for example, found that Japanese people were far more self-critical than their Western counterparts. The self-serving bias is another example. Recall from Chapter 2, Volume 1 that people tend to see themselves as the origin of actions that have good, not bad, consequences. Such attributions are thought to have self-enhancing qualities. We would expect to find that the self-serving bias is greatly lessened or even nonexistent in cultures such as that of Japan that have an interdependent sense of self. Indeed, some research suggests that this is the case. Takata (1987) found no self-enhancing bias among Japanese students, but the opposite: a bias in a self-effacing direction. When Japanese students outperformed another person, they tended to regard their success as situationally caused, whereas when they were outperformed by another, they were more likely to see that other person's qualities as responsible for her or his success (see Shikani, 1978). The more modest self-attributions and self-perceptions of the Japanese and others with an interdependent sense of self appear to be a consistent finding (Heine, Takata, & Lehman, 2000; Oishi, Wyer, & Colcombe, 2000).

Social Comparison Theory

Earlier we noted that comparisons with other people can be an important source of self-knowledge. When we want to know where we stand on a particular quality or ability and objective information is not available, we may compare ourselves with others. This strategy is the core of one of social psychology's most important theories, social comparison theory.

In 1954, Leon Festinger, a pioneer in modern social psychology, developed **social comparison theory.** Festinger believed that people are motivated to make accurate assessments of their level of ability and the correctness of their attitudes. To do this, they assess their own standing in comparison to that of others like themselves. As an illustration of the choice of similar others for comparison, Festinger suggested that beginning chess players prefer to compare themselves to other beginners rather than to master players. Festinger's theory of social comparison can be summarized in three statements:

1. People have a drive to evaluate their opinions and abilities accurately.
2. In the absence of direct physical standards, people evaluate themselves through comparisons with other people.
3. In general, people prefer to compare themselves to similar others.

Psychologists' current understanding of social comparison processes is considerably more complex than Festinger's original model (Goethals & Darley, 1987; Taylor & Lobel, 1989; Wood, 1989). The scope of social comparison theory has been broadened. It is now known that people make comparative judgments not only about their abilities and opinions, but also about their emotions, their personality, and their outcomes on such dimensions as salary and prestige. The process of social comparison affects many aspects of social life. For example, the belief that our current dating partner is more wonderful than anyone we have ever dated before or could be dating now has important implications for our satisfaction in and commitment to the relationship. The belief that our social or ethnic group is economically or socially disadvantaged compared to other groups in society can increase discontent and intergroup conflict (see Chapter 4, Volume 3).

The Goals of Social Comparison

Festinger's assertion that accuracy is the goal of social comparison has been challenged. It now appears that social comparisons can be made in the service of a variety of other personal goals and motives. These motives, not surprisingly, are the same ones that drive self-regulation more generally.

Accurate Self-Evaluation. As Festinger suggested, people sometimes desire truthful knowledge about themselves, even if the feedback is not favorable. For example, learning that you are the worst player on the volleyball team may spur you to greater effort or encourage you to change sports. On the whole, people feel more confident when the feedback is consistent with their standing on stable attributes (such as their ability or education) and less confident when it is derived from their standing on an unstable attribute (such as practice) (Arnkelsson & Smith, 2000).

Self-Enhancement. Rather than seeking truthful self-evaluation, people may seek comparisons that show them in a favorable light. A desire for self-enhancement can lead people to make **downward social comparisons** with others who are less fortunate, less successful, or less happy (Wood, Michela, & Giordano, 2000; Wills, 1981). For example, a student who is struggling to learn calculus may comfort himself with the observation that he's doing better than those students who are flunking the course. As this example suggests, one may compare one self with others doing poorly or to seek feedback on one's own strongest attributes, so as to maintain or restore a positive sense of self (Wood, Giordano-Beech, & Ducharme, 1999). Comparing oneself with a person who is worse off virtually guarantees that one will look better by comparison. Self-enhancement may also operate to mute the affects of an unfavorable social comparison. When one has compared oneself with another person and come off poorly, strategically emphasizing one's positive qualities may mute the affect of the social comparison (Mussweiler, Gabriel, & Bodenhausen, 2000).

Self-Improvement. As we noted earlier, people sometimes compare themselves with others who can serve as models of success. Contrary to what Festinger assumed, an aspiring chess player may compare her opening strategies to those of great masters to gain an assessment of her stage of learning, to learn from the insights of the masters, or to be inspired by their example (Buunk, Collins, Taylor, Van Yperen, & Dakof, 1990;

Gibbons, Blanton, Gerrard, Buunk, & Eggleston, 2000; Taylor & Lobel, 1989; Wood, 1989). That is, a desire for self-improvement can lead to **upward social comparisons** with people who are more successful.

The danger, of course, is that comparisons with much better performers can be discouraging and lead to feelings of incompetence (Wheeler & Miyake, 1992), jealousy, or shame. Yet studies suggest that people are able to extract the helpful information of upward social comparisons without suffering in self-esteem; in fact, even when comparing themselves with others who are performing well, they can maintain a view that they are better than most people on the attribute (Blanton, Buunk, Gibbons, & Kuyper, 1999). Whether upward comparisons are inspirational or discouraging also depends on the person's sense of whether the better-performing person's standard is achievable (Lockwood & Kunda, 1997). Achievable standards are inspirational, whereas unachievable success is discouraging.

Sense of Communion. Much social comparison research has stressed how people compare themselves to others on objective characteristics that invite evaluation. Typically, such comparisons result in contrast effects, whereby one sees one's own attributes as different from or distinctive relative to others (Stapel & Koomen, 2001). But people often compare their feelings or reactions with those of others in situations that may yield a sense of bonding (Stapel & Kooman, 2001). For example, if you're on a plane that suddenly begins to rock and lurch rather wildly before settling down, you may well compare your reactions with those of nearby passengers. Your purpose in so doing might be less a desire to evaluate your own response of fear than to experience a sense of solidarity and comfort with others who are sharing the experience.

In one study that illustrates the importance of bonding in social comparison, Locke and Nekich (2000) had undergraduate students record their spontaneous social comparisons for 1 week. They found that the students often compared their subjective responses to situations with the other people they were close to during these events; these comparisons often increased their sense of connectedness and similarity to others, rather than their sense of distinctiveness. Thus, social comparison need not result only from a desire to understand, enhance, or improve one's individual attributes; it may also stem from a need to bond with others.

The Comparison Process

Festinger focused on situations in which a person deliberately chooses to make a social comparison. Illustrations of such situations are easy to find. For example, after surviving a frightening earthquake, a person may actively seek to compare his reactions with those of others and spend hours talking with neighbors and friends about their experiences. At other times, however, social comparisons are not intentionally sought but forced on people by the situation (Wood, 1989). For example, when elementary school children play baseball, it is very clear who is good at the sport and who is not. Many children may not want to undergo this social comparison experience, but they find it an unavoidable part of their life at school (see McFarland & Buehler, 1995).

Unsolicited comparisons can have important effects on a person (Marsh, Kong, & Hau, 2000). This point was demonstrated in a classic experiment by Stanley Morse and Kenneth Gergen (1970). Participants in their study were undergraduate men who responded to an ad in the school newspaper offering two part-time jobs in "personality research." When each student arrived for his job interview, he was asked to fill out some questionnaires that included a measure of self-esteem. He was then exposed to another job applicant, who was brought into the same room to fill out the application materials. The experimental manipulation varied the appearance of the other job candidate (actually a confederate of the researchers).

Half the participants were confronted with "Mr. Dirty," a young man wearing ripped trousers, a smelly sweatshirt, and no socks. He seemed very disorganized and glanced around the room frequently while filling out the forms. In contrast, half the participants were randomly assigned to encounter "Mr. Clean," a well-groomed and confident young man who wore a dark suit and carried an attaché case. Later in the study, the participants' self-esteem was reassessed for what impact the exposure to Mr. Clean or Mr. Dirty had. As predicted, participants who had an opportunity for downward comparison with Mr. Dirty increased their self-esteem; based on the comparison, they felt better about themselves. Participants who had an opportunity for upward comparison with Mr. Clean suffered a drop in self-esteem; based on the comparison, they felt less good about themselves. The results show that unsolicited opportunities for social comparison can have important effects on our self-evaluation.

Festinger emphasized that people prefer to compare themselves to similar others. But just what dimensions of similarity are most important? Consider the case of a college student enrolled in a large history class who wants to evaluate how well she is doing. She might decide to compare herself with all the other students in the class. She could do this by finding out where she ranks in the class based on her grades. However, she might decide that this is not the best comparison because students taking the course differ widely in how many history courses they had in high school.

Instead, she might decide to compare herself only to other nonhistory majors who, like herself, have a limited background in the subject. In technical terms, this is a comparison based on **related-attributes similarity.** The basis of similarity is not her performance, but her background or preparation for the course, an attribute that should be related to performance (Goethals & Darley, 1987).

Or the student might want information about the range of performance in this course and may so be interested in comparing herself to the best and to the worst students in the group. People are especially likely to seek information about the best and the worst cases when the meaning of the underlying dimension is unclear to them. For example, if you are told you are moderately good at integrative orientation and you don't know what "integrative orientation" means, you will probably seek out information about the characteristics of those who are either very successful or very unsuccessful at this skill.

Social comparisons sometimes lead us to see ourselves either as similar to others (assimilation) or as quite different from those others (contrast effects). Several factors influence whether assimilation or contrast is more likely. When comparison information comes from another person, we tend to contrast that other with ourselves, whereas when we evaluate our own qualities, we are more likely to assimilate information about others into our own self-perceptions (Stapel & Koomen, 2000). Not surprisingly, when we compare ourselves with similar others we tend to assimilate the information the comparison yields to ourselves, whereas when we compare ourselves with someone who is highly dissimilar, we tend to contrast ourselves with the other person (Mussweiler, 2001).

Overall, social comparison processes can exert powerful effects on our lives and how we feel about ourselves. Social comparisons influence our self-evaluations, moods, and responses to others. They can boost our confidence and instill motivation and at other times lead us to feel quite incompetent and unsuccessful.

Self-Presentation

John is carefully preparing for an important job interview. He rehearses what he'll say about his work experience. He gets his hair trimmed and ponders which suit to wear and whether a vest would look too formal. He buys a new briefcase to carry his papers and makes a point of arriving early for his appointment. When he meets the interviewer, John remembers to give a strong handshake and smiles pleasantly. During the interview, John tries to look attentive and to answer questions thoroughly. In short, he makes every effort to present himself as an energetic, competent person who would be successful in the job.

A pervasive aspect of social interaction is the desire to manage the impression we make on others. The term **self-presentation** refers to our efforts to control the impression we convey. The fundamental goal of self-presentation is to structure the interaction so that we obtain a desired outcome. In John's case, the goal is to obtain a job offer.

Why is self-presentation important for understanding the self? There are several reasons. We often want people to view us positively—as an interesting, friendly, intelligent, and caring person. But sometimes we strive to convey other images instead (Kowalski & Leary, 1990). For example, the schoolyard bully might want to present himself as tough and intimidating. At other times, our goal may be to minimize a bad impression, for instance, by finding a plausible excuse for showing up late for an exam. Self-presentation helps us describe and understand the manifold and different presentations of ourselves that we may want to make to others. In addition, though, self-presentation influences self-knowledge. The ways in which we make ourselves known to others has an impact on our self-concept. When we perform behaviors publicly, they often have a greater impact on our self-concept than when we perform them privately (Tice, 1992). Through our own behavior and actions, we gain self-relevant knowledge.

Self-presentation is often a deliberate activity. In his job interview, John is quite conscious of his desire to present himself as hardworking and talented. However, in familiar situations, self-presentational activities can become automatic (Baumeister, Hutton, & Tice, 1989). With his friends, John may habitually present himself as a fun-loving guy who doesn't take work too seriously. When self-presentation in a particular setting becomes routine, people are not as conscious about impression management and can focus their attention on other aspects of the situation.

An important aspect of self-presentation is knowing one's audience. For a fashion-conscious teenager, the trendy clothes and hairstyles that are popular among peers may be considered outlandish by older relatives. The ability to "take the role of the other," to anticipate how others will perceive and react to our actions, is essential for successful impression management. Thus, one of the challenges of social interaction is being able to change our behavior from situation to situation, depending on our self-presentational goals and on the nature of the audience.

Making a Good Impression

Perhaps the most common motive in self-presentation is to make a good impression (Schlenker, 1980). How do people accomplish this objective? Several tactics of successful impression management have been identified (Fiske & Taylor, 1991). One strategy is to conform to the norms of the social situation. For example, at a dinner party, a person might tell interesting stories and jokes. In contrast, at a funeral, expressions of sadness and sympathy for the family are more appropriate. Another strategy is to match the behavior of other people. For example, if your new acquaintance boasts about her tennis prowess, you might do well to boast about your own accomplishments. But if she behaves modestly and downplays her expertise, a similar degree of modesty might create the most positive impression.

A useful distinction can be made between two additional strategies for creating a positive impression: self-promotion and ingratiation. **Self-promotion** refers to conveying positive information about the self, either through one's actions or by saying positive things about the self. In contrast, **ingratiation** or flattery refers to saying positive things about the listener. Jones and Pittman (1982) have suggested that these two tactics reflect different goals: Whereas the self-promoter wants to be seen as competent, the flatterer wants to be liked. In some situations, such as a job interview, the person may try to accomplish both goals simultaneously, coming across as both likeable and talented.

Self-promotion can be tricky. Telling about your accomplishments can enhance your self-presentation, but it can also backfire and create the impression that you are conceited or insecure (Cialdini & De Nicholas, 1989; Jones & Pittman, 1982). The reason is that observers often evaluate a person on more than one dimension at the same time. The blatant self-promoter may indeed convince others that he or she is competent but may also display conspicuous egotism.

An important factor in self-promotion is the context in which people talk about themselves. One study compared impressions of people who made positive statements about their intellectual ability under several different conditions (Holtgraves & Srull, 1989). People who mentioned their intellectual accomplishments were seen more favorably when these statements were made in response to specific questions. For instance, when a person was asked how he had done on his midterm, his answer that he had received a grade of 93 made a favorable impression. In contrast, people who went out of their way to say good things about their own ability without being asked and without others' providing similar information were perceived as less likeable, less considerate, and more egotistical. The context of the conversation made a crucial difference in how observers interpreted self-promoting statements.

Another tactic of positive impression management is the careful use of modesty (Cialdini & De Nicholas, 1989). For example, the female basketball star whose brilliant plays have just saved her team from losing the championship might describe her performance as "pretty good" and emphasize that she couldn't have done it without the work of the entire team. By understating her accomplishments, she will probably be seen as both likeable and competent. The trick, of course, is to know when modesty will be effective. There are two rules of thumb. First, modesty boosts a person's public image only when the performance has actually been successful. Modesty about a poor performance does not enhance one's image. Second, modesty works to boost one's public image only when the audience already knows the full extent of the person's success. The champion athlete can afford to be modest because her fame precedes her.

Self-presentation involves both verbal and nonverbal behavior. Chapter 3, Volume 1 described ways in which nonverbal behavior contributes to self-presentation. In general, self-presentations are most convincing when verbal and nonverbal messages are the same. A person who says he's "very happy" in a glum and depressed tone of voice is not very credible.

We engage in impression management not only by the things we ourselves do, but also by associating ourselves with people who are successful, powerful, or famous. Robert Cialdini and his coworkers have used the term "BIRGing" to refer to the tendency to "bask in the reflected glory" of others (Cialdini et al., 1976; Cialdini & De Nicholas, 1989). People enhance their individual self-presentation by highlighting their associations with successful others, even when these connections are quite trivial. If a person tells us he comes from the same hometown as the president, or that he once met Barbra Streisand, or that his friend won a million dollars in the lottery, he is trying to impress us by his indirect association with the rich and famous.

Ineffective Self-Presentation

Self-presentation is not always effective. Sometimes our actions do not show us in a positive light. For example, you may forget your mother's birthday or spill a bowl of soup in your lap at a restaurant. In such cases, the best you can do is to minimize our losses.

Embarrassment is a common and unpleasant emotion, experienced when there is a disruption in self-presentation (Parrott, Sabini, & Silver, 1988; Schlenker, 1980). This can involve minor lapses in impression management, for instance, when a waiter drops a tray of food or when you inadvertently call someone by the wrong name. Flaws in self-presentation can also involve more serious failures in performance, such as when a professional actor forgets his lines or a famous scientist is shown to have misinterpreted her data. The embarrassed person usually responds with efforts to resume the interrupted pattern of interaction. The person may apologize or give an excuse—and then attempt to pick up where he or she left off. Because embarrassing situations are uncomfortable for everyone present, others are motivated to help the embarrassed person save face.

One way to handle a less than stellar performance is to give excuses (Kernis & Grannemann, 1990; Snyder & Higgins, 1988). Consistent with attribution theory (Chapter 3, Volume 1), people often try to attribute their failures to external and uncontrollable causes. It is more gratifying to say you failed the test because it was unfair and all the other students also flunked (external, uncontrollable cause) than to admit that the test was easy and you were not able to master the material (low ability).

The importance of excuses is not limited to achievement settings. Failure to meet a social obligation, such as being late for an appointment, can also create impression management problems. You will probably make a better impression—and avoid arousing anger in the other person—if you blame your late arrival on a flat tire (external, uncontrollable cause) than if you say you forgot to set the alarm clock (carelessness) (Weiner, Amirkhan, Folkes, & Verette, 1987).

Self-Handicapping

A related but more desperate strategy for dealing with failure has been called **self-handicapping** (Baumeister & Scher, 1988; Berglas & Jones, 1978). People sometimes engage in actions that produce insurmountable obstacles to success so that when they experience the resulting inevitable failure, they can attribute it to the obstacle, not to their own lack of ability (see Figure 4–2). The student who stays up all night before the calculus exam can attribute his low grade to fatigue, not to his complete lack of ability to comprehend math; the golfer who rarely practices can attribute her afternoon in the woods and sand traps to lack of practice, not lack of ability; the alcoholic can attribute the loss of his job to his drinking, not to poor performance. In Harold Kelley's (1967) attribution framework, the ability attribution is discounted because another plausible cause is present: the handicap.

People may also protect their images of their own competence by claiming to have handicaps that prevent success even when those handicaps do not exist. Snyder and Higgins (1988) and others have shown that in evaluative situations that threaten failure, people may claim such symptoms as test anxiety, social anxiety, shyness, depression, or a history of traumatic incidents. Reporting such symptoms can also protect people from having to make ability attributions for their own failures: By announcing that you need new glasses after an embarrassing session on the tennis court, you can spare yourself both

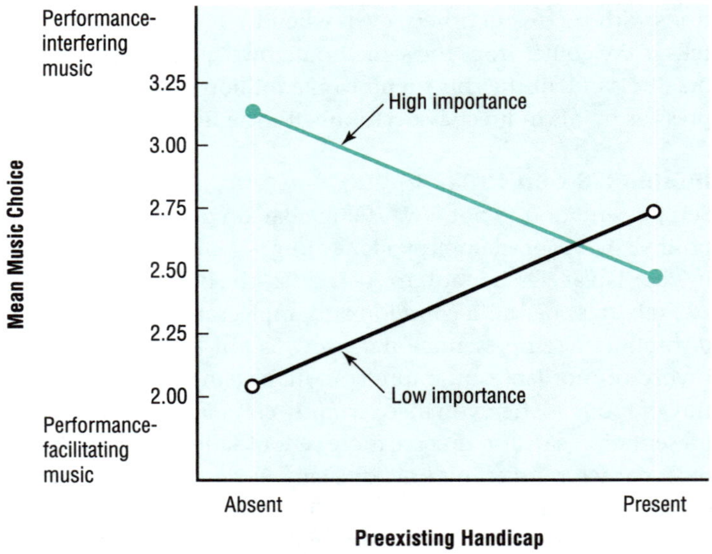

Figure 4–2
Subjects who expected to take an important test chose distracting music, apparently to have an advance explanation for their failure on the test. However, this effect occurred only when there was no preexisting distraction in the environment.

Source: Adapted from J. A. Shepperd, and R. M. Arkin. Determinants of self-handicapping: Task importance and the effects of preexisting handicaps on self-generated handicaps. Personality and Social Psychology Bulletin, 15, 101–112, copyright 1989, by Sage Publications, Inc. Reprinted by permission of Sage Publications, Inc.

self-censure and the criticism of others. As you might expect, using such excuses tends to reduce a person's negative affect over the failure, at least as long as no one else knows the truth about the situation (Mehlman & Snyder, 1985). Other people are not always easily persuaded by a person's self-handicapping strategies, however (Rhodewalt, Sanbonmatsu, Tschanz, Feick, & Waller, 1995).

There are two versions of the self-handicapping strategy. One is behavioral self-handicapping, by which people actively create genuine handicaps, such as fatigue, alcohol or drug abuse, lack of punctuality, inattention, and so on (e.g., Sharp & Getz, 1996); men are more like to practice this particular form of self-handicapping (Hirt, McCrea, & Kimble, 2000). The other is self-reported handicaps, by which people claim to be ill, anxious, shy, or the victim of traumatic incidents, when such states might excuse poor performance (Arkin & Baumgardner, 1985; Leary & Shepperd, 1986); it is a form of self-handicapping practiced by both genders. In both cases, as with self-serving attributional biases in general, the key motives are self-enhancement, or the need to boost one's ego, and self-protection, or the ego-defensive motive of avoiding a stable, uncontrollable, internal attribution for failure, such as an inherent lack of ability (Rhodewalt, Morf, Hazlett, & Fairchild, 1991; Tice, 1991).

Staying up all night before an exam may help you learn overlooked material, but it can also be a self-handicapping strategy: When you fail, you can attribute your low grade to fatigue and not have to question your ability.

An unfortunate implication of this analysis is that self-presentational pressures may sometimes cause people to lie—to others and to themselves—about the true reasons for their actions. At times, the desire to impress others favorably may conflict with a desire to be honest. Moreover, it is now clear that people who self-handicap to protect their self-esteem do themselves long-term damage. People who regularly engage in self-handicapping are more likely to use coping strategies of withdrawal and focusing on negative outcomes. As a result, they have poor study habits, do more poorly academically, and have poorer psychological adjustment (Zuckerman, Kieffer, & Knee, 1998). Self-handicapping may work in the short term, then, but it certainly is not a successful strategy for self-management in the long term.

A related strategy is sandbagging, that is, feigning inability or generating false predictions of lack of success. For example, a sandbagging poker player may bet as if he or she has a weak hand in the early betting round so as to draw others in. Sandbagging has clear benefits: It can reduce performance pressure by setting other people's expectations at a low level and also provide a low baseline against which subsequent performance can be compared. Almost anything looks better than the sandbagger's estimate (Gibson & Sachau, 2000). Carver, Sutton, and Scheier (2000) map approach and avoidance onto personality traits, with extroversion the exemplar of approach and neuroticism the exemplar of avoidance. On the whole, people with independent self-construals are more likely to adopt a promotion-focused self-regulatory focus, whereas those who have a predominantly interdependent sense of self are more likely to adopt a prevention focus (Lee, Acker, & Gardner, 2000). The reason is that in the independent self-construal, one is focused on one's own goals and successes, whereas when interdependent, one is motivated to reduce discrepancies between one's own behavior and what others think one should do.

Culture and the Self: A Comment

Early in this chapter, we noted some fundamental differences in self-conceptions, depending on cultural orientation. In particular, those from the United States and other Western cultures are often said to have an independent sense of self, whereas individuals from Eastern and Southern cultures are said to have a more interdependent sense of self. Because so much of the research that has explored the self has come from Western cultures, the coverage of the self in this chapter has disproportionately emphasized characteristics of the independent self. We have already noted several self-relevant phenomena that appear to vary significantly from independent to interdependent cultures. For example, self-enhancement is ubiquitous in Western cultures and uncommon in interdependent cultures. It seems reasonable to assume that many of the other processes we have studied in this chapter—self-affirmation (Steele, 1988), self-verification (Swann, 1983), self-consciousness (Fenigstein et al., 1975), self-control (Carver & Scheier, 1981), and self-handicapping (Jones & Berglas, 1978)—take a different form or are nonexistent in cultures that construe the self in interdependent terms (Simon, Pantaleo, & Mummedy, 1995). Psychologists are only beginning to understand the self and the cultural differences in the ways in which the self is experienced. Although research on the self has assumed a clearer direction and focus over recent decades, it nonetheless leaves many important issues to be explored.

Summary

1. The self is the collection of beliefs we hold about ourselves. The content of these beliefs is called the "self-concept." The evaluation we make of them is called "self-esteem."
2. Self-knowledge comes from early socialization, reflected appraisals of others, direct feedback from others, self-perception, environmental distinctiveness, social comparison processes, social identity, and culture.
3. Cultural analyses suggest that Westerners construe the self as independent, unique, important, and free-standing, whereas collectivist cultures construe the self as interdependent as part of an encompassing social relationship. This distinction is thought to profoundly influence self-relevant phenomena.
4. Beliefs about ourselves may be represented as self-schemas (which serve for the self the same functions that schemas serve more generally) and possible selves (images of ourselves in the future that represent what we may become). Discrepancies between our self-conceptions and our ideals or sense of what we ought to be produce strong emotions.
5. "Self-regulation" refers to how we control and direct our actions. It is influenced by the working self-concept, beliefs in our self-efficacy, our degree of self-complexity, and our focus of attention, called "self-awareness."
6. Several motivations drive self-regulation. People seek to have an accurate, consistent, and positive self-concept. They also seek information and situations that help them improve.
7. "Self-affirmation" refers to efforts to bolster our self-conceptions in one area after a threat to self-conceptions in another aspect of self. "Self-evaluation maintenance" refers to the processes we engage in when someone close to or distant from us outperforms us on a personally relevant or irrelevant task.
8. Often we compare our own attributes, opinions, and emotions with those of other people, a process called "social comparison." Typically, we prefer comparisons with someone similar, but sometimes we make upward comparisons to people who are better off than ourselves or downward comparisons with people who are doing more poorly than ourselves. Social comparison can aid in accurate or self-enhancing evaluations, and can also foster self-improvement.
9. Self-presentation concerns the efforts we make to control the impression we convey. As in theater, we construct our behavior in situations in order to make a desired impression, usually a positive one. Appropriate self-promotion and modesty are two strategies that often lead to positive impressions.
10. Poor impressions on others can be managed or controlled by making excuses or by self-handicapping, that is, engaging in actions or claiming to have problems that produce insurmountable obstacles to success.

Critical Thinking

1. Think through the sources of self-knowledge that were discussed in this chapter. Which have been important for you in developing your sense of self? In what ways?
2. People need to have an accurate self-concept, a consistent sense of self, targets for improving the self, and the ability to feel good about themselves and their accomplishments. Sometimes these four needs work together and other times they are at odds. How do we reconcile our need for a consistent self with our need to improve? How do we integrate our need for an accurate sense of self with the need to feel good about ourselves? Think through some of the circumstances that make one or the other of these needs particularly important and how conflict among these needs might be resolved.
3. Sometimes people present themselves in a manner that is consistent with how they actually see themselves, but other times self-presentational needs particular to a situation take over. What are some of the self-presentational needs that people have, and how do they manage the impressions that others form of them?
4. Analyses of culture and the self suggest that people from some cultures develop an independent sense of self, whereas those from other cultures develop an interdependent sense of self. But within any culture, people may be more or less independent or interdependent. How would you characterize yourself? Are you generally independent or interdependent? Is this sense of self consistent or inconsistent with the general values of the culture?

Key Terms

bicultural competence **106**
cybernetic theory of self-regulation **1115**
downward social comparisons **123**
ethnic identity **105**
ideal self **111**
independent self **106**
ingratiation **126**
interdependent self **106**
ought self **112**
positive illusions **118**
possible selves **111**
private self-consciousness **115**
public self-consciousness **115**
reflected appraisals **102**
related-attributes similarity **125**
self-affirmation **120**
self-awareness **115**
self-complexity **113**
self-concept **99**
self-discrepancies **111**
self-efficacy **113**
self-enhancement **118**
self-esteem **99**
self-evaluation maintenance model **121**
self-handicapping **128**
self-perception theory **102**
self-presentation **126**
self-promotion **126**
self-regulation **112**
self-schemas **110**
self-verification **117**
social comparison **104**
social comparison theory **122**
social identity **105**
socialization **101**
upward social comparisons **124**
working self-concept **112**

IN THE NEWS

Changing Attitudes Toward the Death Penalty

"A Changing Attitude toward the Death Penalty?" read a recent newspaper headline. For decades, people in the United States have been strong supporters of capital punishment. Yet recent statistics show that support for the death penalty has steadily declined from about 75 percent in 1996 to about 65 percent in 2000, and support for capital punishment continues to decline. When and why do people change strongly held attitudes?

Social psychologist Phoebe Ellsworth and attorney Samuel Gross have studied this shift in death penalty attitudes and argue that several factors account for this important change. A first reason has to do with the changing social climate concerning crime. Crime has been on the decrease for the last decade, which may create a context for shifting attitudes. As it comes to be seen as a less urgent or pressing problem, the public's enthusiasm for harsh punishment has waned.

Electric chair, Greensville Correctional Facility in Jarratt, Virginia.

More important, though, is that new information and new scripts about the death penalty have led people to change their minds. In particular, there is heightened awareness of cases in which innocent people have been sentenced to death and subsequently cleared, often by DNA evidence. Both real and fictional accounts of incompetent lawyers or police who ignore alternative leads have led people to question their belief in the infallibility of the judicial system and have made the idea of a wrongful conviction more salient.

Essentially, then, the changes in the political and psychological context of the death penalty have permitted some people to revise their strongly held attitude in favor of capital punishment to a strong attitude against it (Carpenter, 2001; Ellsworth & Gross, 2001). These changes in information and scripts concerning the death penalty provide a psychological "cover," so that people who once publicly took a stand in favor of the death penalty can now reverse their opinion without looking misinformed or wishy-washy.

CHAPTER

5

ATTITUDES AND ATTITUDE CHANGE

Focus of This Chapter

Defining Attitudes

Attitudes involve the categorization of a stimulus along an evaluative dimension, based on affective, behavioral, and cognitive information (the "ABCs" of attitudes). The **affective component** consists of the person's emotions and affect toward the object, especially positive or negative evaluations. The **behavioral component** consists of how the person tends to act regarding the object. The **cognitive component** consists of the thoughts the person has about that particular attitude object, including facts, knowledge, and beliefs. These three components of attitudes are not always highly related to each other, so it is important to consider all three aspects (Crites, Fabrigar, & Petty, 1994).

As an example, consider Evan's attitude toward safe sex, shown diagramatically in Figure 5–1. The focus of the attitude is the attitude object, which in this case is condom use. The attitude would typically be measured by asking Evan direct questions concerning safe sex, such as "Are you favorably or unfavorably inclined toward safe sex?" or "How important is the practice of safe sex to you?" or "Would you rate yourself as being for or against safe sex?" Surrounding the object are the various factors that are perceived as relevant to attitudes toward condoms. Some of these are impersonal factors, such as qualities of condoms. Other factors include people, such as Evan's parents, roommates, or friends, and their beliefs about safe sex and condom use. Others are personal states, such as Evan's feelings about condoms, and others are simply attributes of the object itself, such as its availability or cost. These clusters of cognitions and their links to the main attitude object constitute the cognitive component of an attitude.

The affective component consists of the positive or negative feelings associated with the attitude object. In Figure 5–1, positive and negative evaluations of the elements and central object are indicated by plus and minus signs, respectively. Evan's negative feelings about condoms may come from the awkwardness of purchasing them and later using them

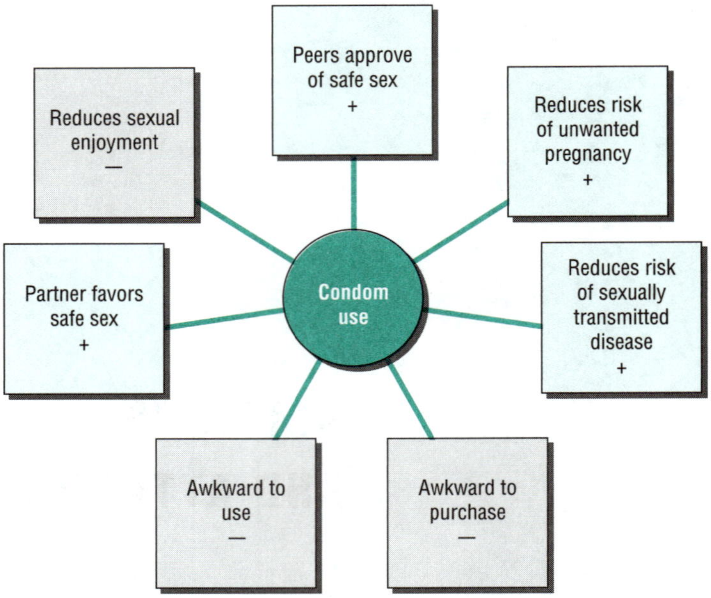

Figure 5–1 Evan's Attitude Toward Condom Use.
The core object is related to several other cognitions. The signs refer to the affective component of his overall attitude toward cognitions he associates with condom use. A positive sign (+) refers to a favorable affect and a negative (–) to an unfavorable affect.

and the concern that they may reduce sexual enjoyment. But there are also many positive links to condom use, such as the safety it provides, peer approval regarding the importance of safe sex, and the belief that one is doing the right thing.

Finally, there is a behavioral component. An attitude contains some tendency to behave in connection with the attitude object, in this case, whether or not Evan is willing to buy and use condoms.

The cognitive components of attitudes are often quite complex. Some of these beliefs are more or less important, and others are more or less amenable to persuasion by others. Thus, complexity is an essential feature of attitudes.

Even though attitudes tend to be cognitively complex, they are often evaluatively quite simple. As noted in Chapter 2, Volume 1, impressions of other people quickly tend to become evaluatively consistent, and the same is true of attitudes. Despite some of his negative evaluations of condoms, Evan's attitude toward condom use is fundamentally positive.

When cognitive complexity is coupled with evaluative simplicity, one implication is the fact that whereas an individual may alter the cognitions that go into the makeup of an attitude relatively easily, overall evaluations toward attitude objects are often difficult to change. For example, Evan may learn that some of his peers don't think much of condom use, but that may not change his overall evaluation that the use of condoms for safe sex is a good thing.

A final important aspect of attitudes is their links to decision making and behavior. Attitudes make it possible to access relevant information and related attitudes quickly because they provide important links among pieces of information held in memory (Judd, Drake, Downing, & Krosnick, 1991). Attitudes enable people to make decisions very quickly because they provide information for making choices (Sanbonmatsu & Fazio, 1990). The links to behavior are somewhat more tenuous. Sometimes behavior is controlled by attitudes and sometimes not. Evan may be in favor of condom use generally, but if there is a troop of 11-year-old Girl Scouts at the drugstore when he goes in to make his purchase, he may not actually purchase condoms, despite his generally positive attitude toward safe sex. Behavior can change attitudes, too. Suppose Evan's attitude toward safe sex was not positive, but more ambivalent. If he encountered a partner who insisted on safe sex, his attitudes might begin to shift in the direction of being more committed to safe sex. Relations between attitudes and behavior can go either way. Attitudes may control behavior, and behavior sometimes controls attitudes.

Theories of Attitudes

Many important attitudes are acquired in early childhood. We associate our country with the patriotic activities we experienced as children. In particular, we may imitate the attitudes of others who are strong, important people in our lives.

Several theories are helpful for understanding how attitudes are formed and how they can be changed. The learning approach regards attitudes as habits, like anything else that is learned. Principles that apply to other forms of learning also determine the formation of attitudes. Motivational approaches based on the principle of cognitive consistency assert that we seek consistency among our attitudes and between attitudes and behavior. It emphasizes the acceptance of attitudes that fit into our overall cognitive structure. Expectancy-value approaches to attitudes maintain that we adopt attitudes that maximize our gains. Each side of an issue has costs and benefits; expectancy-value approaches maintain that an individual will adopt the side on which the net gains are greater. The cognitive approach of cognitive response theory considers the conditions that lead us to argue against or passively accept a persuasive communication designed to change our attitudes. These approaches are not necessarily contradictory or inconsistent with each other.

Learning Theory

Learning theory began at Yale University with the work of Carl Hovland and associates during the 1950s (Hovland, Janis, & Kelley, 1953). The assumption behind this approach is that attitudes are acquired in much the same way as other habits. People learn information and facts about different attitude objects, and they also learn the feelings and values associated with those facts. A child learns that a dog is an animal, that most dogs are friendly, and that most are good pets. Finally, the child learns to like dogs. As can be seen, the child acquires both the cognitions and the affects associated with the attitude object. Moreover, she or he learns them through the same processes and mechanisms that control other kinds of learning.

Thus, basic learning processes should apply to the formation of attitudes. We acquire information and feelings by the process of **association.** For example, if a history teacher shows you a picture of a mean-looking military man in a storm trooper's uniform and says the word "Nazi" in a hostile voice, you form an association between negative feelings and the word "Nazi."

Learning can also occur through **reinforcement** and **punishment.** If you take a class in psychology and get an A in it and enjoy it, the act of taking psychology classes is reinforced, and you are likely to take more such courses in the future. If you take a course and get an F, you are more likely to stay away from similar courses in the future.

Attitudes can also be learned through **imitation.** People imitate others, especially when those others are strong, important people. Consequently, a major source of basic political and social attitudes in early life is the family. Children are likely to imitate the attitudes of their parents. In adolescence, they are more likely to imitate attitudes of their peers on many matters.

The learning approach to attitudes views people as primarily passive agents in the process of attitude formation and change. They are exposed to stimuli; they learn through association, reinforcement, or imitation; and this learning process determines the person's attitude. The final attitude contains all the associations, values, and other bits of information the individual has accumulated. Learning theory accounts of attitude change and persuasion emphasize two main methods whereby attitudes may be acquired or changed: message learning and transfer of affect.

Message learning is regarded as crucial to attitude change. If a person learns a message, change is likely to follow. This obvious point is nonetheless quite controversial. Learning a persuasive message is actually much less important in attitude change than we might expect. Most studies show only modest relationships between memory of the content of a persuasive communication and attitude change (McGuire, 1985; Moser, 1992). Although it is vital that a listener know what position is being advocated, beyond this basic requirement memory of the details of a message is not strongly related to its persuasiveness.

We acquire attitudes in part by association. A car paired with a beautiful woman, for example, leads us to believe that the car is a good one and that owning it will bring social rewards.

Learning theory also suggests that people are persuaded when they transfer an affect from one object to another that is associated with it. To understand **transfer of affect,** imagine a television commercial for an automobile. To persuade you to adopt a positive attitude toward the car, the advertiser associates the car with many other positive objects, such as beautiful women, handsome men, lovely children, or cute dogs in the background. Presumably, you will associate all these attractive features with the car, and your positive feelings toward the car will increase. In other words, people simply transfer the affect they feel about one object (happy family life) to another (the car).

Research has supported this transfer-of-affect idea in a wide variety of contexts (e.g., Krosnick, Jussim, & Lynn, 1992), although it appears to work better for material with which people are relatively unfamiliar and less well when people are already familiar with the attitude objects (Cacioppo, Marshall-Goodell, Tassinary, & Petty, 1992).

Cognitive Consistency

The second major theoretical framework for studying attitudes and persuasion is **cognitive consistency.** The cognitive consistency tradition depicts people as striving for coherence and meaning in their cognitions. Similarly, if their cognitions are already consistent and they are faced with a new cognition that might produce inconsistency, they strive to minimize that inconsistency. Several theories emphasize the importance of cognitive consistency.

Balance Theory. The earliest consistency theory is **balance theory** (Heider, 1958). Balance theory considers the consistency among the affects within a simple cognitive system held by a person. Balance theory is usually described in terms of a person, another person, and an attitude object. There are three relevant evaluations: (1) the first person's evaluation of the other person, (2) the first person's evaluation of the attitude object, and (3) the other person's evaluation of the attitude object. For example, consider Michelle's attitudes toward her teacher and toward legalized abortion. If we consider only simple positive-negative feelings, there are a limited number of combinations of these elements. These combinations are diagrammed in Figure 5–2, with the symbol P standing for Michelle (person), O for the teacher (other person), and X for legalized abortion (attitude object). The arrows indicate the targets of the feelings. A plus sign means a positive affect, and a minus sign means a negative one. The upper left triad shows that Michelle likes her teacher and that they both support legalized abortion.

Balanced relations between people fit; they go together; they make a sensible, coherent, meaningful picture. The main motive that drives people to achieve balance is their desire for harmonious, simple, coherent, and meaningful perceptions of social relationships. A balanced system is one in which you agree with a liked person or disagree with a disliked person. Imbalance exists when you disagree with a liked person or agree with a disliked person.

On the left side of Figure 5–2 are the four balanced situations—situations in which the relations among the elements are consistent with each other. When Michelle likes her teacher and both support abortion, the system is balanced. When Michelle likes her teacher and both oppose abortion, balance also exists: Neither supports abortion, and they are united in opposition to it. Nor is there a conflict if Michelle and her teacher disagree about abortion, but Michelle dislikes the teacher. The imbalanced systems occur when Michelle and her teacher like each other but disagree about abortion or dislike each other and agree about abortion. The inconsistency lies in the fact that we expect those

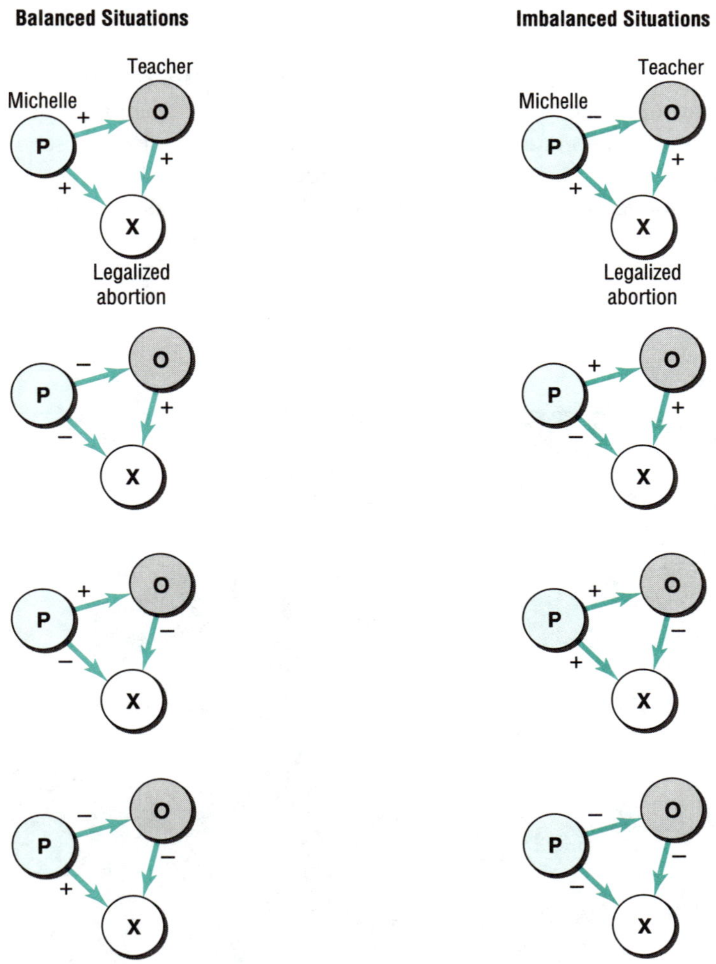

Figure 5–2 The Balance Model.
There are eight possible configurations of two people and one object. According to the model, the imbalanced structures tend to become balanced by a change in one or more elements.

we like to have attitudes similar to ours, and we expect those we dislike to have attitudes that are different from ours. In general, imbalance is present when the system has an odd number of negative relations.

Balance theory maintains that imbalanced configurations tend to change toward balanced ones. This assumption gives the model its importance. Imbalanced systems produce pressures toward attitude change and continue this pressure until they are balanced. That is, the systems on the right side of the figure eventually change into those on the left.

This attitude change can occur in many ways. Balance theory uses a least-effort principle to predict the direction of change. People tend to change as few affective relations as they can to produce a balanced system. Any of the relations may be altered to produce balance. For example, if Michelle supports abortion but her teacher does not and Michelle likes the teacher, balance could be produced in several ways. Michelle could decide that she really does dislike the teacher or that she actually opposes abortion. Alternatively, she might distort reality by misperceiving that the teacher really supports abortion. Which mechanism is chosen depends on the ease of using it and on the individual doing the changing. The important point is that various possibilities exist.

Research on balance theory has generally supported these predictions: People do adjust imbalanced systems toward balance, and in ways that minimize the number of changes that must be made (Abelson et al., 1968). People prefer balanced systems, and they remember balanced systems better (von Hecker, 1993). But balance pressures seem to be weaker when we dislike the other person than when we like him or her. We do not care very much whether we agree or disagree with someone we dislike; we simply end the relationship.

Cognitive Dissonance Theory

The most influential of the cognitive consistency theories is **cognitive dissonance theory,** proposed by Leon Festinger (1957). Like other cognitive consistency theories, cognitive dissonance theory assumes that there is a pressure to be consistent. Dissonance theory deals especially with inconsistencies between people's attitudes and their behavior.

Dissonance is defined as an aversive motivational state that results when some behavior we engage in is inconsistent with our attitudes. Dissonance appears to be most consistently aroused when the attitudes and behavior that are dissonant are important to the self (Aronson, 1968; Stone & Cooper, 2001).

Balanced relations occur when people achieve good form in their perceptions of each other. Mary likes Sara, Sara likes Elaine, and Elaine likes Mary. They go together, making a sensible, coherent, and meaningful picture.

Dissonance creates psychological tension (Elliot & Devine, 1994), and people feel pressure to reduce or remove it. Reducing it means restoring consistency, or consonance. There are three ways of achieving this consonance. One way is to revoke or change our behavior in some way, although often this is not feasible. Sometimes individuals trivialize the dissonance so that they do not have to change their attitudes (Simon, Greenberg, & Brehm, 1995). Most often, however, people resolve dissonance between their attitudes and their behavior by changing their attitudes. Dissonance theory explores these processes in several types of situations.

Dissonance Following a Decision. One action that almost always arouses dissonance is decision making. When we must decide between two or more alternatives, the final choice is virtually always inconsistent with at least some of our beliefs. After we make the decision, all the good aspects of the unchosen alternative and all the bad aspects of the chosen alternative are inconsistent with the decision.

We can reduce dissonance by improving our evaluation of the chosen alternative or by lowering our evaluation of the unchosen alternative. After making decisions, we tend to increase our liking for what we chose and to decrease our liking for what we did not choose. A study by Brehm (1956) demonstrated this tendency empirically. Female college students were shown eight products, such as a toaster, a stopwatch, and a radio, and were asked to indicate how much they would like to have each of them. They were then shown two of the products and asked to choose one. In the high-dissonance condition, Brehm gave the women a choice between a product they had ranked high and one they had ranked next best. In the low-dissonance condition, he gave the women a choice between a high-ranked product and one they ranked as far inferior. After they had made their decision, they were asked to rate all the objects again. On the second rating, there was a strong tendency for women in the high-dissonance condition to increase their evaluation of the item they had picked and to decrease their evaluation of the rejected item. In a no-dissonance control group, instead of choosing between two items and receiving their preference, the women were simply given one of the products they had rated favorably. When they rerated all the products, they showed no tendency to improve the evaluation of the object they owned. This condition demonstrates that the reevaluation in the high-dissonance condition was not simply due to pride of ownership; making the decision was the critical factor.

The tendency toward reevaluation is particularly strong when the two alternatives are initially rated as close in attractiveness. Brehm (1956) tested this notion also. When the women chose between two highly ranked products, they experienced more dissonance, and therefore, they reevaluated the products as more different from each other after having picked one than was true in the low-dissonance condition (See also Schultz, Leveillé, & Lepper, 1999).

Postdecisional dissonance can also be produced when we commit ourselves to a single course of action. This point was dramatically illustrated in a classic study of a doomsday group that predicted the world was going to end on a particular day and believed that they would be saved by a ship from outer space. In a book describing this unusual group, *When Prophecy Fails* (Festinger, Riecken, & Schachter, 1956), the authors observed the group members' reactions to their own prophecy and, more important, to its ultimate failure (i.e., the world did not end as they had expected). In the days and weeks after making their original prediction, group members sold many of their belongings and prepared for the end of the world. When the fateful day arrived and passed without the world being destroyed, they were initially greatly shaken. Their response, however, was not to give up their beliefs and return to normal life. They could not have reduced dissonance by accepting that nothing had come of all the effort they had put into their plans. Instead, they decided that the day had been put off and that the end of the world was still coming soon. Moreover, they began to argue that their efforts had actually postponed the end of the world, and they became very active in trying to recruit new supporters to their cause. Presumably this activity helped reduce their dissonance by justifying their original behavior.

Part of the appeal of cognitive dissonance theory is that it often makes counterintuitive predictions. In this case, common sense might have suggested that the group would give up after its prediction had failed so miserably. But dissonance theory predicts that this disproof would lead them not to abandon the theory, but to argue it even more forcefully. And that is just what happened.

Counterattitudinal Behavior. Cognitive dissonance theory has also been applied to the effects of counterattitudinal behavior, also called **attitude-discrepant behavior.** When a person holds a belief and performs an act that is inconsistent with it, dissonance is produced. Because it is difficult to take back the action itself, the dissonance typically is relieved by a change in attitude.

For example, some people enter law school because they believe they can help the poor and needy and improve society. Yet, when they go into legal practice, most find themselves doing repetitious and uninteresting work that has more to do with business contracts and tax advantages than with helping others. Many of these once idealistic individuals eventually justify and even enjoy what they do. They may come to believe that nothing much can be done to help the poor, and even that the poor do not deserve much help. Why the change?

Dissonance theory argues that they began engaging in attitude-discrepant behavior when they first took a job, because that was the condition of the job. To get paid, they had to spend long hours doing relatively uninspiring work. But this requirement created dissonance: Their behavior was inconsistent with their attitudes. With time, they adjusted their attitudes to become more consistent with their behavior.

Insufficient Justification. The most interesting prediction of dissonance theory concerns the level of incentive that is required to produce attitude change. On the one hand, there has to be enough incentive to make a person commit a counterattitudinal act. But if there is too much pressure on the individual or too much incentive to perform the discrepant act, there is no inconsistency, and very little dissonance is produced. This principle is called **"insufficient justification":** The less incentive one has for performing a counterattitudinal behavior, the more dissonance is experienced.

If you're asked to work on a political campaign and you put in long hours for a candidate about whom you have some misgivings, you should come to regard that candidate more positively. Else, why would you be working so hard? However, if you're paid well for your efforts, you may not grow more positive in your attitudes toward the candidate. When you ask yourself why you're putting in the long hours, the answer is easy: It's for the money.

Attitude change that is realized through this and similar methods is stronger, the more simple and clear-cut the attitude (Stalder & Baron, 1998), and therefore, it often involves significant attitudes that generalize to broad beliefs (Leippe & Eisenstadt, 1994). Thus, the phenomenon is by no means confined to laboratory studies of inconsequential attitudes.

Threats. In principle, negative incentives ought to work exactly the same way as positive incentives. One way to try to get people to perform disliked tasks is to threaten them with punishment. If you do not pay your income taxes or do your homework, you are penalized.

Greater threat should produce less dissonance and so less attitude change. In an experiment designed to test this idea, children were shown a group of toys and then were forbidden to play with a particularly desirable toy (Aronson & Carlsmith, 1963). They were threatened with either mild or severe punishment if they played with the forbidden toy. The children were then left alone in a room with the toys, and the amount of time they spent playing with the forbidden toy was assessed. After playing with the toys, they were asked how much they liked them, including the forbidden toy. Dissonance theory predicts that the children who were severely threatened would probably not play with the toy but would not devalue the toy either. After all, they know why they are not playing with it: They have been threatened with punishment. However, children who receive a mild threat do not have a sufficient justification for avoiding the toy, and consequently, when asked to rerate the toys, they might reevaluate the toy, deciding that it isn't all that attractive anyway. This outcome is, in fact, what the experimenters found. The children reduced their evaluation of the forbidden toy more under mild threat than under severe threat.

Choice. Another major contributor to dissonance is the feeling of choice about the behavior. Attitude-discrepant behavior creates dissonance only when the behavior is freely chosen (or at least the person feels it is freely chosen). If you're working on a campaign for a political issue because you're whole sorority is, and you don't feel you can get out of it, you shouldn't feel any dissonance over misgivings you might have about the issue.

Irrevocable Commitment. Another key to attitude change as a dissonance-reducing mechanism is the person's **commitment** to the decision or behavior. As long as we feel irreversibly committed to a course of action, dissonance promotes attitude change. But when we feel that we can change our decision if it works out badly, or that we can do it halfheartedly, or that we may not have to go through with it at all, dissonance will not be present and no attitude change may occur.

Foreseeable Consequences. For dissonance to occur, people need to believe that they could have foreseen the negative consequences of their decisions. If a classmate decides to walk to class on the left side of the street rather than the right side, and as she walks along a brick suddenly falls off a roof and lands on her foot, this is a misfortune. But she is not likely to experience dissonance. On the other hand, if she knew that there was some chance that she might be injured, perhaps because there was high-rise construction on that side of the street, dissonance would probably be aroused.

Responsibility for Consequences. The importance of perceived choice is that it brings with it perceived responsibility for all consequences, whether or not it is "logical" to feel responsible for them. If decision makers feel responsible for the consequences, dissonance occurs whether the consequences could reasonably have been foreseen or not. If they feel no responsibility for the outcome, there is no dissonance, regardless of how disastrous the results.

The critical question regarding unforeseen negative consequences is whether people believe that their prior behavior is responsible for bringing those consequences about. That is why perceived choice is so important. When we choose something that works out badly, we feel responsible for the outcome, and dissonance is created. Indeed, some psychologists now argue that perceived personal responsibility for aversive consequences is so important in producing attitude change that it does not matter whether the behavior is counterattitudinal or not. Even acts that are consistent with our attitudes are likely to produce attitude change (strengthening our prior attitudes) if they produce negative outcomes and we feel responsible for the acts (Scher & Cooper, 1989).

Effort. The more effort one expends in executing acts that have aversive consequences, the more dissonance is likely to be aroused. If you volunteer for the U.S. Marine Corps and basic training is exhausting, painful, and stressful, dissonance will probably be created: You are likely to persuade yourself that you made the right choice and love the

Marine Corps. The attitude change helps to justify the effort you have expended (or even expect to expend; see Wicklund, Cooper, & Linder, 1967).

In summary, the main preconditions for cognitive dissonance, and for the attitude change that results from taking decisive action, are minimum incentives, perceived choice, irrevocable commitment, foreseeable consequences, personal responsibility for those consequences, and great effort.

Self-Perception Theory

Cognitive dissonance theory originally inspired research on the effects of behavior on attitude change, and for a number of years, it provided the only theoretical interpretation of these findings. Bem (1967) then offered another interpretation: **self-perception theory.** As we saw in Chapter 2, Volume 1, Bem argued that often we do not really know what our attitudes are and simply infer them from our own behavior and the circumstances in which this behavior occurs. For example, you choose to eat oranges from a basket of seven kinds of fruit and somebody asks you how you feel about oranges. You say to yourself, "I just chose oranges. Nobody forced me to. Therefore, I must really like oranges." Accordingly, you tell the person you like oranges.

It is easy to see how this theory might apply to attitude-discrepant behavior. A participant is paid one dollar to tell someone that a particular task was very enjoyable. When the participant is subsequently asked how enjoyable he himself thought the task was, he says to himself, "I said that the task was enjoyable and I was paid only one dollar. One dollar is not enough to make me lie, so I must really think that the task is enjoyable." On the other hand, if given 20 dollars, the participant might say to himself, "The reason I said it was enjoyable was just to get the 20 dollars; I didn't really believe it." Thus, self-perception theory makes the same predictions as dissonance theory; the more people are paid to make a discrepant statement, the less they believe it.

Note that cognitive dissonance theory and self-perception theory make the same prediction, but for entirely different reasons. The traditional view of attitudes reflected in dissonance theory is that they are strong, enduring predispositions. When people engage in counterattitudinal behavior, they suffer from unpleasant tensions that can be relieved only by their giving up these cherished attitudes. Bem's self-perception theory suggests that our expressions of attitudes are, instead, rather casual verbal statements. We observe the conditions under which our behavior occurred and then report on our attitudes.

Most psychologists now assume that aspects of both dissonance theory and self-perception theory are correct. When people have had few experiences with respect to the attitude or when the attitudes involve vague, uninvolving, minor, or novel issues, they infer their attitudes from their self-perceptions of their behavior. When more controversial, engaging, and enduring issues are involved, dissonance theory is more likely to operate.

Consistency: A Caveat. Generally speaking, the perception that consistency is an important aspect of attitudes is beginning to wane. One reason is that consistency seems to be an important concern in Western cultures—that is, of people in the United States and western Europe—but not as much a concern as southern European and Eastern attitudes. For example, in their social interactions, Japanese people may express quite different attitudes depending on the situation they are in, because they believe it is appropriate to express agreement with others to ensure social harmony, rather than threaten social accord through disagreement. But even Westerners are able to tolerate substantial degrees of inconsistency among their attitudes, which do not appear to have the adverse effects that dissonance theory and other consistency theories have described. Consistency, then, may be more of a value than a fundamental cognitive principle, whose importance should vary directly with the value placed on it. Another example of the impact of values on attitudes appears in the "Cultural Highlight."

Cultural Highlight: CULTURE AND PERSUASION

Advertisers try to persuade people to buy products. Is there a set of universal principles that make people more likely to be persuaded by an appeal, or are there cultural differences in what is persuasive?

Research suggests that a core dimension of cultural variability, individualism versus collectivism, may influence the kinds of ads that are most persuasive. In individualistic cultures, individuals value independence and often subordinate group interest to their personal goals. Consequently, appeals to social relationships and social responsibility may be more common in advertisements in collectivist cultures.

To test these predictions, Han and Shavitt (1994) studied popular magazines in two countries, the United States and Korea. The United States is generally considered an individualistic culture, whereas Korea is thought to be collectivist in orientation. Two hundred product ads from each country were randomly selected from magazines and coded for appeals to individualism versus collectivism. Ads that were coded as reflecting an individualist orientation included appeals to individuality or independence, reflections of self-reliance or individual competition, emphasis on self-improvement or self-realization, and emphasis on the benefits of the product to the individual. In contrast, ads were rated as collectivist in orientation if they appealed to family integrity, focused on group well-being, expressed concerns for others or the support of society, focused on interdependent relationships with others, or focused on group goals. As expected, ads in the United States were significantly more likely to use individualistic appeals to induce people to buy products, whereas in Korea collectivist appeals were more likely to be used.

In a second study, students in Korea and the United States were recruited for a study on persuasion and were presented with ads that were either collectivist or individualistic in orientation. Individualistic ads featured such headlines as "She's got a style all her own," "Alive with pleasure," "You . . . only better," "A leader among leaders," and "Treat yourself to a breath-freshening experience." Collectivist ads featured such headlines as "We have a way of bringing people closer together," "Celebrating a half century of partnership," "Sharing is beautiful," and "Share the breath-freshening experience." Students in the United States were more persuaded by ads that emphasized individualistic benefits, whereas students in Korea tended to be more persuaded by ads that emphasized collectivist benefits.

Advertisers, then, seem to be on the right track. Not only do they develop ads that reflect the values of their particular culture, but their ads also tend to be more persuasive when they do.

Expectancy-Value Theory

People often respond to persuasive communications in terms of incentives, that is, the costs or benefits associated with particular attitude positions. According to this theory, attitude formation and change is a process of weighing the pros and cons of various possible attitudes and then adopting the best alternative. This approach is best illustrated in **expectancy-value theory** (Edwards, 1954).

Expectancy-value theory assumes that people adopt a position based on their thoughtful assessment of its pros and cons, that is, on the values of its possible effects. The theory adds the notion that people take into consideration not only the value but also the likelihood of a position's possible effects. People tend to adopt positions that will most likely lead to good effects and reject positions that will most likely lead to bad effects. Stated more formally, the theory assumes that in adopting attitudes, people try to maximize the subjective utility of the various expected outcomes, which is the product of (1) the value of a particular outcome and (2) the expectancy that this position will produce that outcome (see Shah & Higgins, 1997).

Suppose you are trying to decide whether to go to your friend's party tonight. The expectancy-value analysis is presented in Table 5.1. You would try to think of the various possible outcomes of going to the party (dance, drink beer, not study for tomorrow's midterm, meet someone new), the values of those outcomes (enjoy the dancing, drink beer, and meet someone new but get a hangover, and do poorly on the midterm), and the expectancy of those outcomes (certain to dance and to get a terrible grade, but unlikely to meet anyone new at a small party). Taking both expectancy and value into consideration, it's time to start studying: An inevitable terrible grade is not balanced by a little fun, dancing, and drinking.

Table 5.1

Go to the Party or Study? An Expectancy-Value Analysis

	Value	×	Expectancy	=	Subjective Utility
Choice 1—Go to Party					
Dance	+2	×	3	=	+6
Meet someone new	+3	×	1	=	+3
Drink beer	+1	×	3	=	+3
Get hangover	–3	×	2	=	–6
Do poorly on midterm	–3	×	3	=	–9
Total attitude					–3
Choice 2—Study					
Improve midterm grade	+3	×	3	=	+9
Be bored	–1	×	1	=	–1
No hangover	+2	×	3	=	+6
Total attitude					+14

Note: Value is on a +3 (very good) to –3 (very bad) scale; expectancy is on a 3 (certain to happen) to 0 (certain not to happen) scale; subjective utility is the product of value and expectancy.

In summary, expectancy-value theories look at the current balance of incentives and predict that under conditions of conflicting goals, people will adopt the position that maximizes their gains. The approach treats people as calculating, active, rational decision makers.

Dual Processing Theories

Recent research suggests the usefulness of a dual processing approach to attitude change. In Chapter 2, Volume 1, we considered a dual processing account of social perception and noted that under some circumstances, people engage in rapid, heuristically based inferential processing, whereas in other cases, they more systematically and deliberately process information relevant to their inferences. This same distinction—dual processing—applies to persuasion as well. Researchers working in the dual processing tradition (Cacioppo & Petty, 1979; Chaiken, 1980) have found that people process a persuasive message systematically when they have both the motivation and the ability to do so. At these times, we learn arguments, sift through them for the points that are relevant to us, and counterargue them if we disagree with them. At other times, however, we are seemingly lazy and not motivated to analyze the pros and cons of complex arguments.

Cognitive Response Theory. One dual processing approach to attitudes is **cognitive response theory,** which seeks to understand attitude change processes by understanding the thoughts that people generate in response to persuasive communications. The theory argues that people react to different aspects of a particular message with positive or negative thoughts (termed "cognitive responses"), which in turn influence whether the person will support the position or not (Romero, Agnew, & Insko, 1996).

Suppose you listen to a televised speech by a senator who advocates cutting government Medicare payments to the elderly and you say to yourself, "What about retired people on small pensions or people who can't support themselves, such as the disabled or the poor? Somebody has to support these people, and government programs are about the only way to do it." These negative cognitive responses mean that you are unlikely to adopt the senator's position. But if you say to yourself, "That's right. Taxes are too high, and those programs are probably paying for extravagant hospital costs for people who should pay their own medical bills anyway," you are likely to support the speaker's position. The key assumption of the cognitive response viewpoint is that people are active processors of information and generate cognitive responses to messages, rather than passive recipients of the messages they happen to be exposed to.

Cognitive response theory predicts that attitude change depends on how much and what kind of **counterarguing** a message triggers. If the message stimulates strong and effective counterarguing, resistance to change will follow. Conversely, persuasion can be produced by interference with the counterarguing process. If we cannot think of any good counterarguments and are distracted from thinking about them while we are listening to a message, we are more likely to accept the communication.

Petty and Cacioppo (1986) developed the **elaboration-likelihood model** of persuasion, which analyzes cognitive responses to persuasive communications. They proposed that under some circumstances, people are motivated to engage in thoughtful consideration of the pros and cons of an argument, whereas under other conditions, people draw their conclusions from peripheral cues that are associated with the communication but irrelevant to the merits of the arguments. These include the attractiveness and prestige of the source or the pleasantness of the context (e.g., a beautiful woman or a handsome man smoking the advertised brand of cigarette).

Petty and Cacioppo drew a distinction between central routes to persuasion and peripheral routes to persuasion. Detailed information processing and reviewing and evaluation of arguments characterize the central route to persuasion. People are more likely to use the central route to persuasion when they are involved in the issue, are concerned about being accurate, or recognize that others are attempting to change their attitudes, among other factors (see Table 5.2) (Nienhuis, Manstead, & Spears, 2001). People draw on more superficial peripheral cues without thoughtful consideration of the important arguments when they pursue the peripheral route to persuasion. People are more likely to process a message peripherally when they are uninvolved in the issue, distracted by the source or pleasantness of the context, or overloaded with other things to do (e.g. Brannon & Brock, 2001).

Table 5.2

When Does Systematic Processing Take Place and When Is Heuristic Processing Used?

Category of Independent Variable	Conditions Promoting Systematic Processing	Conditions Promoting Heuristic Processing
Source	Number of independent sources	Likeability Physical attractiveness Expertise
Message	Repetition Rhetorical questions/arguments Written message High discrepancy	Length of message Number of arguments Video message
Target	Issue involvement Need for cognition Prior information	Response involvement
Situation	Forewarning Intent to persuade	Audience response Pleasant mood music Attractive models/actors

In a similar vein, Shelly Chaiken (1980, 1987) has distinguished **systematic processing,** which involves careful review and consideration of arguments, from **heuristic processing,** which involves using simple decision rules, such as the idea that longer arguments are stronger. Several investigations have shown that when people are motivated to peruse arguments carefully, they show more systematic processing, but that when motivation is low, heuristic processing tends to rule (Darke, Chaiken, Bohner, Einwiller, Erb, & Hazlewood, 1998).

The dual processing distinction between central and peripheral processing has become a major one in attitude change research. It is of particular importance because it bears directly on the question of how rationally we respond to persuasion attempts. Does the perceiver respond to the quality and price of a product or only to the "hype" that advertising specialists surround it with? Does the voter respond to real issues and real qualities of the candidates or only to superficial images presented on television? The answer is that we do both under different circumstances (Chaiken & Maheswaran, 1994).

This is not to suggest, however that systematic processing always gives us the right answers and that peripheral or heuristic processing gives us wrong or simpleminded ones. Indeed, systematic processing can be heavily biased. Suppose, for example, the president is giving a speech on energy conservation, and your roommate remarks that he is just trying to support the interests of energy companies in his home state. You might process the president's message systematically, but with a negative lens, which might influence the conclusions you draw and how carefully you process the quality of the message and the arguments (Killeya & Johnson, 1998). At times, we bring defensive motivations, such as prior biases, to the processing of attitude messages. Under these circumstances, our processing may be systematic, but it is highly likely to be biased through motives that guide the search for and elaboration of attitudinally relevant information and arguments (e.g., Darke et al., 1998; Lundgren & Prislin, 1998). The distinction between peripheral and systematic processing is covered in Table 5.2 and will be elucidated further in the sections on persuasion that follow.

Persuasion

With this theoretical background in mind, we now turn directly to the important topic of persuasion. Persuasion is ubiquitous in our society. Advertisers attempt to convince us that their product is better than others. Politicians try to convince us that they deserve our vote. Citizens' groups attempt to influence our attitudes toward the environment, abortion, civil rights, and other heated topics of the day. When do people adhere to their original attitudes in the face of a persuasive communication, and when do they respond to a persuasive communication and change their attitudes? Figure 5–3 presents a model of the persuasion process, which will guide this discussion of the variables involved in successful persuasion.

The Communicator

The first thing we notice in a communication situation is the communicator, or the source. Some communicators are authoritative, such as a high school teacher or a scientist. Others may be humorous, such as the person wearing the elephant suit on television who urges us to buy a particular brand of peanuts. One of the most straightforward and reliable findings in attitude research is that the more favorably people evaluate the communicator, the more likely they are to evaluate the communication favorably and to modify their attitudes in the direction of the communication. This finding follows directly from the transfer-of-affect idea in learning approaches to attitudes. Evaluations of communicators, whether positive or negative, transfer to the positions they advocate. Several aspects of a communicator influence whether the communicator is evaluated favorably.

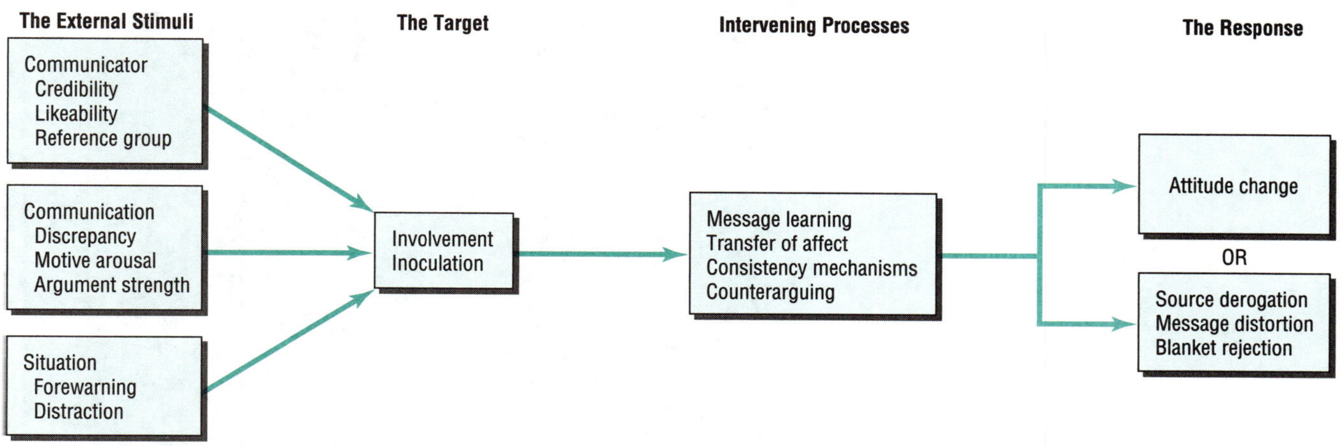

Figure 5–3 **Model of the Persuasion Process.**

Credibility. People are more persuaded by highly credible communicators than by those low in **credibility.** The first study of credibility to demonstrate this effect was a classic paper by Hovland and Weiss (1952). Participants heard communications on issues such as the advisability of selling antihistamines without a prescription. Each communication came from either a high- or a low-credibility source. The communication on antihistamines was said to come either from the *New England Journal of Medicine* or from a monthly mass-circulation pictorial magazine. The results indicated that communications attributed to high-credibility sources produced more attitude change than those from low-credibility sources. The importance of high credibility in a source has been demonstrated many times and is no longer controversial. Subsequent research suggested, however, that there are two separate components of credibility, namely, expertise and trustworthiness.

Expertise. Expert sources are typically more persuasive than nonexpert sources. In a typical study of this point, participants were told they were participating in a study on aesthetics and were asked to evaluate nine stanzas from obscure modern poems. They then read someone else's evaluation of the stanzas they had not liked very much. The communicator argued that the poem was better than the participant had indicated. The crucial variable was the source of the communication: For some participants, it was represented as the poet T. S. Eliot, whereas for others, it was represented as a student at Mississippi State Teachers College. After reading the communication, the participants reevaluated the poems. There was more change in response to the high-credibility communicator, namely, T. S. Eliot, than to the low-credibility communicator (Aronson, Turner, & Carlsmith, 1963).

Trustworthiness. Regardless of expertise, it is important that a communicator be perceived as unbiased and trustworthy. One way that communicators can encourage this perception is to argue for positions that seem to be contrary to their self-interest. Consider a situation in which a district attorney and a criminal are each making statements about whether law enforcement agencies should be strengthened. Normally, a district attorney is seen as better informed and more prestigious than a criminal, and therefore as more persuasive. In a study by Walster, Aronson, Abrahams, and Rottman (1966), this was exactly the outcome—as long as the speaker was advocating less power for law enforcement agencies. But what if the criminal takes a position against his own self-interest and argues in favor of strengthened law enforcement? In this case, the criminal becomes

Communicators who are perceived to be trustworthy and credible produce more attitude change in their audiences. Eleanor Roosevelt embodied these qualities.

quite persuasive and, indeed, even matches the persuasive power of the district attorney. Communicators are seen as especially trustworthy when they have little to gain from the particular stance they adopt, but as somewhat less trustworthy when they have incentives for making statements or when they stand to gain personally from persuading others of their position.

Another factor that enhances perceptions of trustworthiness is multiple sources. When several people say the same thing, they are more persuasive than when a single person makes the same argument, presumably because several individuals are perceived to be less subject to a personal, idiosyncratic bias (Harkins & Petty, 1981). Yet multiple sources have this advantage only when their judgments are regarded as truly independent of each other.

Liking. Because we try to make our cognitions consistent with our affect, it follows that we are likely to change our attitudes to agree with those of the people we like. In general, this has been shown to be true (e.g., Roskos-Ewoldsen & Fazio, 1992). Chaiken (1979), for example, showed that students who were rated by other students as physically attractive were also more persuasive communicators. Also, we tend to be influenced more by those who are similar to us than by those who are different (Brock, 1965). In a test of this point, Wood and Kallgren (1988) manipulated the likeability of a graduate student delivering a talk in the following way. He was described as having recently transferred to the participant's university, and then he either praised the faculty and student body in comparison to those at his old university or said that his previous school was better. Not surprisingly, he was liked better in the former case, and when he later gave a speech against environmental preservation, he produced more attitude change in his audience.

Reference Groups. We are also persuaded when a position is adopted by a group of people we like or identify with. Such groups are called **reference groups.** Diane Mackie (1987) told some participants that a majority (82 percent) of the students at their university supported the proposition that the United States should act to ensure a military balance in the Western Hemisphere. Others were told that 82 percent opposed the proposition. She then presented participants with speeches of equal strength on both sides; all participants received the same arguments. In four experiments, she found that the participants moved toward the side that their peers supported, whichever side that was.

Two reasons that reference groups are so effective in producing attitude change are liking and similarity (Holtz & Miller, 1985). If people admire a group, they want to be like the group's members. When the other members express a particular opinion, each member wants to hold a similar opinion. And consequently, people lean in the direction of changing their opinions to make them agree with those of their reference groups (Terry & Hogg, 1996).

Messages from in-groups are also more persuasive because they are processed differently from messages from out-groups. Mackie, Worth, and Asuncion (1990) found that communications from nonreference groups (out-groups) were processed at a very peripheral level and that participants were unpersuaded by either a strong or a weak message. Participants were, however, more persuaded by a strong message from the in-group than by a weak one, a finding suggesting more content-focused processing of the reference group's message. This effect was especially true when the issue was relevant to an individual's reference group.

In short, where a communication comes from—that is, the nature of the communicator—is clearly important in terms of how a message is evaluated. Attractive, likeable, credible, expert, trustworthy individuals are more persuasive than those who lack these attributes. Interestingly, however, it appears that communicator characteristics may be more important in audiovisual messages than in written messages. In audiovisual messages such as those on television, a great deal more information is available about the communicator, such as nonverbal information, appearance, and so on. In written communications, information about the communicator is less salient, and so message content tends to be relatively more important (Chaiken & Eagly, 1983).

Derogating the Source. Just as communicator characteristics can enhance the persuasiveness of a communication, they can also be used to discredit a communication. When faced with a communication that is inconsistent with our attitudes, we can reduce inconsistency by deciding that the source of the communication is unreliable or negative in some other way. This is called **source derogation.** Such an attack on the source of a communication is common in politics, informal debates, courtroom trials, and practically every kind of disagreement. The defense attorney in a trial tries to discredit the witness whose testimony is damaging to the defendant. The politician calls her opponent a communist or a liar or some other name when she finds it difficult to argue on the issues themselves.

Attacking the source of the communication is an effective way to reduce the pressure produced by a discrepant communication. It has the additional benefit of making all future arguments from the opponent much less powerful. When an opponent has been discredited, anything he or she says carries less weight. Consequently, when a source that is vulnerable to being discredited delivers a message, people sometimes scrutinize the message more closely to guard against either their own or others' unfair reactions (Petty, Fleming, & White, 1999).

The Communicator as a Peripheral Cue. As we have seen, characteristics of a communicator, such as whether he or she is trustworthy, expert, or likeable, are important determinants of whether we accept a persuasive communication. People who dislike or do not trust a communicator often reject the message by attacking the source. But sometimes a communicator's conclusion is accepted simply because it comes from an expert or from an otherwise favorably evaluated source, regardless of the arguments put forth. How can the communicator have these different effects?

The prediction from the elaboration likelihood model is that communicator characteristics are often used as simple **peripheral cues** to persuasion when we cannot or are not motivated to process arguments carefully. Under circumstances in which we are motivated to engage in little cognitive effort, we know we can rely on a trusted communicator's viewpoint, so we can avoid thinking the argument through ourselves. If we cannot remember any of the arguments presented very well, we also tend to rely on the source to determine our attitude in response to the communication (Wood & Kallgren, 1988). When do we not use communicator characteristics as peripheral cues? Generally speaking, when we have direct experience with an issue, we are less likely to use any kind of peripheral cue, including communicator expertise (Wu & Shaffer, 1987).

The Communication

In addition to the communicator, the communication itself is clearly important. The actual content of the message clearly influences whether people will accept it. Counterattitudinal communications about attitudes that are important to people, for example, are very likely not to be persuasive because people already know what their attitudes are. But beyond this basic point, a number of variables in the communication itself have important effects on the degree to which people are persuaded by it.

Discrepancy. A major factor that influences the degree to which we are persuaded by a communication is how discrepant that communication is from our own position. Generally speaking, the greater the **discrepancy,** the greater the potential pressure to change (Hovland & Pritzker, 1957). But extremely discrepant statements cause us to doubt the credibility of the source rather than to change our attitudes (e.g., Eagly & Telaak, 1972; Freedman, 1964). These two points predict a U-shaped relationship between discrepancy and attitude change, namely, that relatively little attitude change will occur with low-discrepant and high-discrepant communications, and that maximum attitude change will occur with moderately discrepant communications.

It follows that greater credibility is likely to allow communicators to advocate more discrepant opinions successfully because such opinions will not be rejected easily. In contrast, a low-credibility source makes rejection relatively easy; therefore, the maximum amount of attitude change tends to occur at lower levels of discrepancy. These predictions were confirmed in a study by Bochner and Insko (1966). They had a Nobel Prize winner (high credibility) or a YMCA instructor (lower credibility) give messages regarding the number of hours of sleep the average person requires per night. As predicted, there was more change in opinion regarding the necessary amount of sleep at moderate levels of discrepancy than at higher levels. In addition, as expected, the optimal level of discrepancy was greater for the high-credibility source. The YMCA instructor produced the most attitude change when he advocated 3 hours of sleep, but the high-credibility source achieved the maximum attitude change when he argued that only 1 hour was necessary.

Discrepancy affects how a message is perceived. When a discrepant position is quite close to that of an audience, they perceive it as closer than it really is. This process is called "assimilation." Exaggerating the closeness of a discrepant position makes it easy to reduce the small discrepancy or may eliminate the need for change by making the two positions essentially identical. On the other hand, when the source's position is very discrepant from that of the audience, it is perceived to be further away. This process is called **"contrast."** When the position is perceived to be extreme, it may be perceived as so extreme as to be ridiculous, and the communicator is easily discredited (Hovland, Harvey, & Sherif, 1957).

Strong versus Weak Arguments. Sometimes the arguments in a communication are strong and compelling, and sometimes they are weak and specious. For example, the evidence for the role of unsafe sex practices in spreading AIDS is very compelling. The evidence that Elvis is still alive is very weak.

One would think that strong arguments always produce more attitude change than weak ones, but that is not always the case. People respond more favorably to strong arguments in a persuasive communication primarily when they are motivated to pay close attention and are able to think carefully about the arguments. For example, when people are highly involved in a persuasive message, adding weak arguments to already strong ones actually dilutes the overall persuasiveness of a message (Friedrich, Fetherstonhaugh, Casey, & Gallagher, 1996). Under many circumstances, however, people do not give a message very detailed or careful thought; under those circumstances, the sheer number of arguments may be a more important factor than how strong the arguments are (Wanke, Bless, & Biller, 1996). Thus, the strength of arguments is not necessarily a crucial factor in how persuasive they are (Petty & Cacioppo, 1986); the effects of strong arguments depend on whether people are involved in an attitude issue and process arguments systematically or heuristically.

Repetition. Does repetition increase the persuasiveness of a message? Consider your reaction to seeing the same athlete in the same television commercial downing the same brand of beer at the same bar week after week. Does the repetition reinforce your association of that brand with the athlete, or do you simply tire of the commercial and tune it out?

Much research by Zajonc (1968) shows that familiarity based on repetition increases liking. With persuasive communications, however, repetition appears to increase attitude change only up to a point (Cacioppo & Petty, 1979). Why? It is easy to imagine that repetition might have two separate effects: It may increase one's opportunity to consider the content of a persuasive communication and therefore enhance the processing of the message, but it may also increase the chances of tedium and therefore produce a negative reaction. For example, when the overly familiar beer commercial comes on, your reaction might be "Oh, not again!"

The implication of this argument is that repetition helps strong arguments because people process them more completely. But it may hurt weak arguments because it exposes their flaws or simply makes them tedious (Cacioppo & Petty, 1985).

How can tedium be dealt with? Presumably, the content can be varied. Consistent with this argument, repetition of commercials for a particular product seems to increase effectiveness if the commercials are varied somewhat, but not if exactly the same commercial is used each time (Cacioppo & Petty, 1985).

Peripheral Cues and Message Characteristics. Under some circumstances, peripheral cues are very important in determining attitude change. When we have little motivation to think about the arguments in a message (e.g., when the issue has little importance to us), or when we are unable to process the arguments well (such as when we are uninformed or distracted), peripheral cues become very important in determining attitude change.

The number of arguments in a message and the length of those arguments are two such peripheral cues (Cacioppo & Petty, 1985). Presenting more arguments in a message increases attitude change when the issue is not very relevant to the person: That person is swayed not by the issue but by the number of arguments. Presenting more arguments increases attitude change toward strong and weak arguments alike, a finding indicating that little processing is going on. Similarly, longer messages have a more persuasive impact than short messages, but only among those who are uninformed, because they presumably give the actual messages little thought. Among the better-informed, strength of argument is a more important factor, presumably because people who are better informed are more motivated to pay attention to the nature of the arguments themselves (Wood, Kallgren, & Priesler, 1985).

A variety of factors, then, determine whether any given message will be persuasive. When people have the time and interest to pay attention to a message, strong arguments have a decided advantage. In the absence of strong arguments, peripheral cues, such as source characteristics or the sheer number of arguments, have more impact.

Matching the Persuasive Message to the Nature of the Attitude. A persuasive communication will be more so if it is matched to certain aspects of attitudes. For example, attitudes that are highly emotional may be more easily changed by persuasions that appeal to those emotions (Fabrigar & Petty, 1999). If the thought of the death penalty enrages you, then a message that enlists your anger should persuade you.

Attitudes are more strongly affected by messages that match the functional basis of the attitude. For example, if you support sports on campus because you think that it's a popular thing to do, a persuasive message that attacks this point (such as information suggesting that support for sports isn't so popular) would have a greater impact on your attitude than if your support of sports has to do with the physical health benefits of physical activity (Petty & Wegener, 1998).

Distorting the Message. Message factors may also be important in the rejection of a persuasive communication. Specifically, cognitive consistency theories maintain that inconsistency between our own position and that advocated in a message may be resolved by distortion or misperception of the communication to reduce the discrepancy between it and our own position. For example, the U.S. Surgeon General writes an article recommending that sexually active young adults practice safe sex because they may be at risk for AIDS. Young adults who do not want to practice safe sex may read this message and erroneously decide that the Surgeon General says not to worry too much about AIDS because the evidence about heterosexual transmission is not yet conclusive. They can do this by misperceiving the article when reading it, by distorting the article in memory, or perhaps by reading only part of the article and reconstructing the rest of it mentally. However accomplished, the result is the same: The message becomes considerably less discrepant. Sadly, in the case of AIDS, the price of distorting a health warning can be high indeed.

Blanket Rejection. The most primitive (and perhaps most common) mode of inconsistency resolution is simply to reject the communication altogether. Rather than refuting the arguments on logical grounds or weakening them by attacking their source, individuals simply reject arguments for no apparent reason. For example, a typical response by a smoker to a well-reasoned, logical attack on cigarette smoking is to say that the arguments are not good enough to make her stop. She does not answer them; she simply does not accept them. It often takes more than a good argument to convince people of something.

The Target

Target individuals—namely, the persons to be persuaded—vary in a number of respects that affect persuasion as well. Targets may be predisposed to agree with a message or to disagree with it. They may have personal motives that affect how willing they are to change in response to a persuasive message. This section begins with a consideration of the motives that a persuasive message may seek to arouse in the target. The learning approach to attitude change suggests that motive arousal leads to attitude change only in those circumstances in which accepting the message reduces arousal.

Aggression Arousal. In some persuasive messages, an effort is made to arouse aggression in the target. Aggression arousal should produce attitude change only when the communication urges an aggressive position. In a study by Weiss and Fine (1956), some participants underwent an annoying, frustrating experience that was designed to make them feel aggressive. Other participants had the opposite experience, a pleasant, satisfying one. Then both groups were exposed to a persuasive communication that either took a lenient attitude or a punitive stance toward juvenile delinquency. The experimenters hypothesized that participants who had been made to feel aggressive would accept the punitive communication because it would provide them with a way of expressing their aggression. The lenient message would be more likely to satisfy the relatively nonaggressive needs of the participants who had had the pleasant experience. The results were generally in line with these expectations. Personal frustrations, then, might make a person more vulnerable to persuasive communications that advocate military action, attacks on minorities, or harsh treatment of dissidents, but they probably would not increase susceptibility to such nonaggressive appeals as charity campaigns.

Fear Arousal. The case of fear is more complex. The learning-theory approach suggests that fear-arousing messages will be accepted if the communication offers fear-reducing recommendations. But the empirical evidence suggests that the level of fear must also be considered. Increasing fear usually increases the effectiveness of a persuasive communication. But when too much fear is aroused, the effects may be disruptive, causing people to be too frightened to act or leading them to ignore or reject the communication. At moderate levels, fear-arousing arguments can be more effective in producing attitude change than are arguments that cause little or no fear (Janis, 1967).

Whether persuasion is enhanced by fear appeals may depend on several additional factors. One is whether the message provides expectations of reassurance. If a message provides information about how to reduce fear, fear appeals are more effective. Another factor that may influence the processing of a fear appeal is the extent to which the message topic is relevant to the fear. Although high fear sometimes erodes attention and makes it difficult for people to learn important information, to the extent that a persuasive communication is directly relevant to the source of the fear, it may be noticed more and processed somewhat more carefully (Sengupta & Johar, 2001). However, the very relevance of the message coupled with the presence of high fear or anxiety may lead people to use heuristic cues in a message to bias their systematic processing (Sengupta & Johar, 2001). In short, when people are fearful, they may try to process a fear-relevant

Persuasive communications designed to arouse fear usually are effective. However, if the message arouses too much fear, the effects may be disruptive and may lead people to ignore or reject the communication.

message systematically but instead may seize on stray bits of information that bias their processing, precisely because they are fearful.

Many researchers now adopt an expectancy-value framework to understand the effect of fear on persuasion. This framework takes into account the nature of the feared event, the person's perceived vulnerability, and the perceived effectiveness of the recommended measures. This perspective (Leventhal, 1970) predicts that fear will increase attitude change when a person feels vulnerable to the feared event and when highly effective measures are recommended, but not when the person feels invulnerable or when there is little or no remedy. As we will see in Chapter 3, Volume 3, the expectancy-value account of the relation between fear and attitude change is often used in health communications to encourage people to change their behaviors, such as using condoms, adopting a low-fat diet, or stopping smoking.

Ego Involvement

Another factor related to the target and whether he or she will be persuaded by a communication relates to **ego involvement.** According to Sherif and Cantril (1947), attitudes that become highly entwined with the ego are highly resistant to change. Sherif and Cantril believed that ego involvement was more likely to occur when attitudes were linked to important reference groups, such as an individual's nation, religion, ethnicity, or social class. Later work has distinguished between several different kinds of ego involvement, however, with somewhat different dynamics. These include commitment, issue involvement, and response involvement.

Commitment. An important aspect of involvement is our commitment to our own initial attitude toward an issue. Resistance to a persuasive message depends in great part on the strength of this commitment.

Commitment may come from several sources. First, commitment increases when we engage in behavior on the basis of an attitude. A person who has just bought a new car, for example, is more committed to the belief that it is a fine car than he was before he bought it. Second, commitment is increased when we take a public stance on an attitude (Hovland, Campbell, & Brock, 1957). For example, someone who has just told all her friends that she thinks drinking is evil and dirty is more committed to this attitude than if she had kept her thoughts to herself. A third source of commitment is direct experience with an attitude object. When one has had direct experience with an issue, attitudes are typically more strongly held. Fourth, freely choosing an attitude position produces a greater feeling of commitment than being forced or nudged into a position.

Commitment to an initial attitude position shifts the amount of discrepancy necessary to create maximum attitude change. The more an individual is committed to an initial attitude, the less deviation he or she will tolerate in a persuasive communication before rejecting it (Freedman, 1964; Rhine & Severance, 1970).

In general, then, commitment reduces the amount of attitude change produced by a discrepant, persuasive communication. If changing an attitude means giving up more, suffering more, or changing more of our other attitudes or behaviors, commitment to the initial attitude position increases and makes it more difficult to change. We become more likely to use other modes of resolution instead.

Issue Involvement. A second type of ego involvement occurs when an issue has important consequences for the individual. This has been called "issue involvement" (or "personal relevance"), because we are involved in the issue rather than detached from it. Issue involvement is a key variable in elaboration likelihood theory (Petty & Cacioppo, 1986, 1990) because it motivates people to attend closely to the issue and to the relevant arguments. Consequently, when we are involved in an issue, strong arguments are more persuasive than weak ones (Petty & Cacioppo, 1990). For example, if you were told that your tuition might double next year, you would probably pay very close attention to the validity of the arguments for the increase. In contrast, if you heard that tuition was being increased at a college in Bulgaria, you might not scrutinize the arguments very carefully. An issue that is not personally relevant does not produce as much motivation to process the information. Under such conditions, people pay more attention to such peripheral cues as communicator expertise or the length or number of the arguments.

Response Involvement. Even when we are not very committed to our prior attitude or the issue is not personally relevant, our attitudinal response may nonetheless be very important because it will receive public scrutiny and bring social approval or disapproval. This kind of involvement is called "response involvement" (Zimbardo, 1960). The response-involved person is concerned primarily with whether others will approve, while the issue-involved person is more concerned with the quality of arguments because the issue is what matters.

These contrasting effects of issue and response involvement were compared by Leippe and Elkin (1987). They manipulated issue involvement by telling participants that their university was considering instituting comprehensive examinations. Some students were told that the exams would be put into effect the next year, thereby affecting them, whereas others were told that the exams would not be put into effect until some years later. Response involvement was manipulated by telling some participants that they would discuss the issue with another student and a professor, while others were not told of any such discussions.

Only the participants who were both highly issue-involved and weakly response-involved—those who expected to be personally affected by the issue but did not have to worry about what image they would present to others—scrutinized the arguments closely, as reflected in greater attitude change in response to the stronger arguments. With high response involvement—that is, when participants were preoccupied with their self-presentation—the strength of arguments was virtually ignored. Likewise, when the issue had no personal relevance, strength of argument had no effect.

Personality and Persuadibility. In addition to ego involvement, there are individual personality characteristics that may affect persuasion and the kinds of messages that may pursuade. Some of the variables that are studied in this context include authoritarianism/dogmatism, anxiety, locus of control, and self-esteem, among many others (Haugtvedt & Petty, 1992). Authoritarianism/dogmatism has received considerable research attention. It refers to a general inclination to have a closed mind, to be intolerant, and to be deferential to authority, independent of specific ideological or political beliefs. Individuals who are low in dogmatism tend to be persuaded by strong, but not by weak, arguments. Highly dogmatic individuals, in contrast, are persuaded by strong arguments only when the source is nonexpert. When the source is an expert one, highly dogmatic individuals respond to the authority of expertise and are equally persuaded by strong and weak arguments (DeBono & Klein, 1993). Dogmatism also influences the processes by which people respond to persuasive communications. For example, dogmatism is associated with more confident judgments as a result of generating more supportive and less contradictory evidence (Davies, 1998).

Another individual factor that influences persuasion is the need for closure. Need for closure is the desire to have a definite answer on a topic as opposed to remaining in a state of confusion or ambiguity. Participants who are high in need for closure are typically more resistant to persuasion than people low in need for closure because they don't like to change; those low in need for closure are more tolerant of the ambiguity that a persuasive communication creates and are more willing to change their attitudes. However, if a persuasive communication involves an issue on which people have relatively little information and they are distracted while listening to the persuasive communication, individuals with a high need for closure actually show more attitude change than those low in need for closure (Kruglanski, Webster, & Klem, 1993), presumably to escape the confusing state in which they find themselves.

The Situation

So far, this chapter has considered the communicator, the message, and the target as factors that influence attitudes and responses to persuasive communications. However, a persuasive communication is usually delivered within a broader situational context, in which other things are happening that also affect the degree to which persuasion succeeds.

Forewarning. If you are highly committed to a position and are told that you are about to be exposed to a discrepant communication, you are more likely to be able to resist the persuasive nature of that communication (Chen, Reardon, Rea, & Moore, 1992; Freedman & Sears, 1965).

Why? Most likely, our defenses and counterarguments are in some way exercised and therefore strengthened. When we hear that someone is going to try to change our attitude on an issue about which we care deeply, we may begin to counterargue the message, anticipating what the speaker is likely to say. Petty and Cacioppo (1977) showed that the delay period between called **forewarning** and exposure to a communication allows people to generate more counterarguments. For example, a forewarned person can convince herself that the communicator is unreliable, prejudiced, or misinformed.

What happens, however, if the attitude position espoused does not involve an issue about which one cares a great deal? When the listener is not very committed to a position, forewarning has the opposite effect; it actually facilitates attitude change. The warning seems to operate as a cue for the person to begin thinking about why the position to be advocated is a good one (Apsler & Sears, 1968).

Another kind of forewarning involves signaling the intent to persuade. We may not know the exact position a communicator is going to take, but we know that the communicator is going to try to persuade us of a position. When an issue is relevant and important to us and we are forewarned that someone intends to change our mind, we are likely to counterargue what we expect the arguments to be and thus show heightened resistance to attitude change.

Being forewarned about a person's intent to persuade usually makes people more skeptical about the message. Do you think the prospective customers will successfully resist the persuasive efforts of this salesman?

Distraction. People whose opinions are attacked usually try to resist changing their attitudes, particularly when they are committed to them. They counterargue, derogate the communicator, and generally marshal their forces to defend their position. An important implication is that the ability to resist persuasion is weakened by anything that makes it harder to counterargue the discrepant communication. In particular, distracting the attention of listeners may enable a persuasive message to get through.

Mild amounts of **distraction** do seem to enhance persuasion (Petty & Brock, 1981). Cognitive response analysis suggests why. Distraction tends to foster persuasion only when it interferes with an otherwise effective counterarguing process. Thus, distraction is more likely to lead to persuasion when the issue is a familiar one about which we have established our arguments than when the issue is one about which we do not have ready arguments. If we do not have arguments against an issue, distraction does not keep us from counterarguing. Distraction appears to work best when communications are very discrepant from our own attitude position and when we are very involved with the topic, presumably because these are the conditions that inspire the most vigorous counterarguing (Petty & Brock, 1981).

There are clear limits on the effects of distraction. Obviously, too much distraction prevents a persuasive message from being heard at all and reduces its effectiveness to zero. Advertisements in which the content of the message is very funny may have this paradoxical effect; the audience laughs so hard at the events in the ads that they may forget what the product is.

Inoculation. In the aftermath of the Korean War, psychologists became interested in reports of "brainwashing" of American prisoners of war (POWs) by the Chinese communists. A number of POWs had given public speeches that denounced the American government, and several said publicly that they wished to remain in China when the war was over rather than return to the United States. Psychologist William McGuire (1964) speculated that some soldiers might have been vulnerable to influence because their attitudes were assaulted on issues about which they were inexperienced and ignorant. Many soldiers, especially less educated ones, had never had to defend their beliefs about the United States against the kind of sophisticated Marxist arguments used by the Chinese.

McGuire (1964) hypothesized that an important source of resistance to change comes from past experience with an issue. He likened the target faced with a persuasive communication to someone who is attacked by a virus or a disease. The stronger the persuasive message (analogous to a virus), the more damage it does, but the stronger the person's defenses, the better able he or she is to resist persuasion (analogous to a disease).

There are two ways people can strengthen their defenses against disease. They can strengthen their bodies generally by taking vitamins or by exercising (which supports bodily defenses), or they can strengthen their defenses against a particular disease by building up antibodies (as through inoculation). For example, when people are given a mild case of smallpox that they are able to fight off, their bodies produce antibodies that, in the future, provide an effective and strong defense against more powerful exposure. McGuire argued that these two defenses—support and inoculation—are also applicable to persuasion attempts.

A study by McGuire and Papageorgis (1961) used both support and inoculation methods to build up defenses. They used three groups of participants: One group received support for their position, one group had their position attacked weakly and refuted the attack, and the third group experienced neither approach. Afterward, all three groups were subjected to a strong attack on their initial position. The supportive method helped participants resist persuasion slightly, but the inoculation method helped a great deal. Participants who received this preparation changed their attitudes much less than did participants in the other two groups.

One implication is that **supportive defenses** work best when a person simply needs to be taught specific arguments. The **inoculation defense** works better when people are stimulated to create their own defensive arguments. Consistent with this view, subsequent research has shown that supportive defenses are effective when subsequent attacks contain arguments similar to the content of the supporting arguments. But inoculation is effective even when an attack includes new arguments (McGuire, 1964).

Cognitive response theory provides a good explanation for inoculation effects. It suggests that when people refute a mild attack, they exercise all their defenses. They prepare arguments that support their own position, construct counterarguments against the opposite position, derogate the source of the opposing view, and so on, thus providing themselves with a stronger and better defended position.

Attitude Change over Time

So far we have focused on immediate responses to communications. For example, under what conditions does a televised speech, radio ad, or conversation with a friend immediately produce attitude change? In many cases, however, we want to know how attitudes change over time. For example, in order to assess the likely impact of a commercial, an advertiser may want to know the effects of repeated exposure to a message and whether the effects will last after the ad ends.

Spontaneous Attitude Change

Thinking about an attitude object tends to make the attitude more extreme. According to Tesser (1978), we review and rehearse our cognitions, and consistency pressures move them toward more evaluatively consistent clusters. For example, if you spend more than the usual amount of time thinking about your best friend, you will probably like her better. You might remember additional qualities or enjoyable experiences you have shared. And you might reinterpret some of your less pleasant memories to excuse your friend's behavior. However, if you think about your enemy more often, you will probably dislike her even more. You might lengthen your list of offenses and find negative motives for her apparently good and generous acts.

Basically, Tesser's hypothesis is that thinking about an issue produces more polarized attitudes because thinking allows people to generate more consistent attitudes. All this cognitive activity requires that the individual have a preconceived structure, or schema, concerning the person or issue. Without some schematic understanding of the issue, it is difficult for a person to generate new beliefs or to know how to reinterpret old ones, and so on.

The implication is that thought polarizes attitudes only when people have a schema about the issue and when their thoughts are specifically focused on that issue rather than on some other irrelevant or competing issue (Liberman & Chaiken, 1991). To test this implication, Chaiken and Yates (1985) studied two groups of people, some who already had a highly consistent knowledge structure about an issue (capital punishment) and others who did not. Every person wrote an essay either about this issue or about a different, irrelevant issue (censorship). Only the highly consistent participants who wrote an essay on capital punishment developed more extreme attitudes on that topic. No significant polarization occurred in any of the other conditions. To polarize attitudes, then, people's thoughts must be relevant to the issue, the people must have sufficient cognitive resources, and there must be no alternative issues competing for attention (Liberman & Chaiken, 1991).

Persistence of Attitude Change

Another question concerns the persistence of attitude change over time once it has been induced by a communication. Generally, memory of the details of an argument decays rapidly at first and then less rapidly. However, the persistence of attitude change does not necessarily depend on retention of the details of arguments. Other events that occur after the communication are of much greater significance.

One important factor that aids persistence is whether the recipient is later reminded of important cues, such as the credibility of the source. Kelman and Hovland (1953) manipulated source credibility and found the usual difference on an immediate posttest: The high-credibility source produced more attitude change. Three weeks afterward, the credibility difference was gone. The low-credibility source's message was, by then, just as effective. This rebound in the persuasiveness of the low-credibility source's message is called the **sleeper effect.** The original credibility difference can be reinstated, however, when a person is reminded of the original source of the message.

The reason for the sleeper effect is unknown, and it may be that as time goes on, the credibility of the source becomes increasingly dissociated from the message; that is, the recipient remembers the message but forgets who said it. An alternative interpretation is the differential decay hypothesis (Pratkanis, Greenwald, Leippe, & Baumgardner, 1988), which assumes that the impact of a discounting cue (such as a low-credibility source) on persuasion dissipates more quickly than does the impact of the message itself. Regardless of the reason, sleeper effects are commonly found. Attitude change may also be artificially suppressed by a forewarning about the communicator's intent; people tend to become stubborn when they believe the source is trying to persuade them. Over time, however, such people show increased attitude change, presumably as the discounting cue (persuasive intent) is forgotten (Watts & Holt, 1979).

Attitudes and Behavior

Much of the interest in attitudes comes from the assumption that they do affect behavior. Yet, in many instances, behavior does not follow from attitudes. The degree of influence of attitudes over behavior has become one of the most important controversies in attitude research.

In a classic study, La Piere (1934), a white professor, toured the United States with a young Chinese student and his wife. They stopped at 66 hotels and motels and ate at 184 restaurants. Although at the time there was rather strong prejudice against Asians in the United States, all but 1 of the hotels and motels gave them space, and they were never refused service at a restaurant. Some time later, a letter was sent to the same establishments asking whether they would accept Chinese people as guests. Of the 128 that replied, 92 percent said they would not. That is, the Chinese couple experienced nearly perfect service in actuality, but nearly universal discrimination in the subsequent letters. La Piere, and many psychologists after him, interpreted these findings as reflecting a major inconsistency between behavior and attitudes (Wicker, 1969).

Yet this conclusion has been widely criticized as underestimating attitude-behavior consistency. Indeed, later studies have shown much higher degrees of consistency between attitudes and behavior (Kraus, 1995). There is, however, variation across situations in precisely how consistent the relation is. In recent years, much research has gone into determining the conditions that yield greater or lesser degrees of consistency between attitudes and behavior. It now appears that stable attitudes, important attitudes, easily accessed attitudes, attitudes formed through direct experience, attitudes about which people are certain, and attitudes that show a high degree of consistency between cognition and affect are most likely to predict behavior (Kraus, 1995). Some of these characteristics are discussed next.

Strength of the Attitude

One important condition for high attitude-behavior consistency is that the attitude be a strong and clear one. Strong attitudes are typically stable, have personal implications,

Sometimes attitudes influence people's behavior, but other times they may not. In this picture, the demonstrator is clearly acting on behalf of her attitudes. Yet although many of the bystanders no doubt hold similar attitudes, they are not participating in the protest for other reasons.

and are held about personally important issues about which one feels extreme and certain. They are often formed through direct experience and become highly accessible as a result (Krosnick, Boninger, Chuang, Berent, & Carnot, 1993). When we see inconsistency between attitudes and behavior, it is almost always because the attitudes are weak or are held ambivalently.

Anything that contributes to a strong attitude also tends to increase attitude-behavior consistency. One contributing factor is the amount of information we have about the attitude object. For example, Kallgren and Wood (1986) found that environmental behaviors (agreeing to a home visit to hear about a recycling project or signing petitions to protect the environment) and attitudes about the environment were more consistent among students who knew the most about preservation of the environment.

Another factor that strengthens attitudes is rehearsing and practicing them. Attitude-behavior consistency is greater when people think about and express their attitudes, presumably because this helps to strengthen the attitude (Fazio, Chen, McDonel, & Sherman, 1982). Strong attitudes are often highly embedded attitudes; that is, they are tied to other beliefs that people hold. Embedded attitudes, therefore, should predict behavior well. Consistent with this point, Prislin and Oullette (1996) found that highly embedded attitudes about preservation of the environment were more strongly related to behavior than were less embedded attitudes.

Having direct personal experience with an issue encourages us to think and talk about it more than if the issue is remote to us. It follows that attitude-behavior consistency is greater when we have direct experience with the attitude object than when we only hear about it from someone else or read about it (Kraus, 1995). Regan and Fazio (1977) showed this effect with students at Cornell University during a severe housing shortage. Many first-year students had to spend the first few weeks of the fall semester in temporary housing—usually a cot in a dormitory lounge. Unlike students who were assigned immediately to permanent housing, they experienced the shortage personally. The researchers measured students' attitudes toward the crisis and their interest in possible behavioral actions, such as signing and distributing petitions or joining committees to study the crisis. Attitudes and behavior were closely related for the students with direct personal experience with the crisis. In contrast, behavior was not at all related to attitudes among students with only secondhand experience, such as those who only talked to friends or read about the crisis in the student paper.

Another source of attitude strength comes from having some vested or selfish interest in the issue. Sivacek and Crano (1982) found support for this idea by using the issue of the minimum drinking age. A ballot proposal in Michigan in 1978 would have raised the legal drinking age from 18 to 21. Presumably students under age 21 had more of a selfish interest in the issue than did older students. Indeed, attitudes toward the proposal were considerably more tightly correlated with behavior (volunteering to call voters) among those with a vested interest than among the disinterested.

A concept closely related to attitude strength is importance. Important attitudes are ones that reflect fundamental values, self-interest, and/or identification with individuals or groups that an individual values (i.e., reference groups or reference individuals) (Boninger, Krosnick, & Berent, 1995). Such attitudes are highly resistant to persuasion and also show a strong relationship to behavior (Zuwerink & Devine, 1996).

Stability of the Attitude

Stable attitudes that are easily remembered are more likely to predict behavior than attitudes that are less stable and not accessible in memory (Kraus, 1995). When people's attitudes are unstable, their current attitudes predict behavior more than the attitudes they held some months or years ago. You would not necessarily find a close relationship between a college student's evaluation of different careers and her career plans if her evaluations were measured when she was a first-year student and her plans were measured when she was a senior. Therefore, consistency between attitudes and behavior is at a maximum when they are measured at about the same time.

Longer time intervals diminish the attitude-behavior correlation because attitudes change. Also, people and situations change. For example, the fact that a 25-year-old woman says she does not want to have children will not necessarily reflect her behavior at age 30. The longer the interval between measuring the attitude and measuring the behavior, the more such unforeseen contingencies can arise. So, when assessing whether people do what they say, make sure you don't try to hold them to something they said 2 years ago. Things may have changed.

Accessibility of the Attitude

Attitudes that are more accessible in memory influence behavior more strongly (Kraus, 1995). A primary factor that determines whether an attitude is accessible in memory is how frequently it is expressed. For example, suppose your school eliminates grade curving, and you believe that the change in the grading system is unfair. If you have frequent opportunities to express this attitude, it is likely to affect your behavior toward a particular professor with whom you are discussing a grade; if you have less opportunity to express your attitude about the grading policy, you might talk with the professor without being influenced by the grading policy (Fazio, 1986, 1989).

Attitudes also become more extreme when they are expressed more frequently (Downing, Judd, & Brauer, 1992). Thus, if you have multiple opportunities to express your attitude toward the grading policy, you may come to feel more strongly about it in the process. Easily accessible attitudes also come to be viewed as important (Roese & Olson, 1994). That is, the more opportunities you have to express an attitude, the more you come to regard that attitude as important to you (Blascovich et al., 1993). Attitude accessibility also influences how people process persuasive messages. The more accessible the attitude, the more likely a person will be to elaborate the persuasive message as opposed to processing it heuristically (Fabrigar, Priester Petty, & Wegener, 1998).

Automatic Activation of Attitudes

Recent research suggests that attitudes are often activated automatically when the attitude object is present. Thus, much of our behavior may be guided by attitudes without our awareness or intention (Smith, Fazio, & Cejka, 1996; Bargh, Chaiken, Govender, & Pratto, 1992). This important observation means that we have a pervasive tendency to nonconsciously classify most, perhaps all, incoming stimuli as either good or bad. One result is that almost immediately, we develop a behavioral tendency to avoid negatively labeled stimuli and approach positive ones (Chen & Bargh, 1999).

Relevance of Attitudes to Behavior

Another obvious, but often ignored, point is that when attitudes are relevant to behavior, the two are more closely related. Attitudes vary quite a bit in their relevance to the act in question. La Piere's (1934) asking proprietors about their feelings toward Chinese people in general is plainly not as relevant as asking about their attitudes toward a particular couple. In general, behavior tends to be more consistent with attitudes that are specifically relevant to it than with very general attitudes that apply to a much larger class of potential behaviors.

Salience of the Attitude

In most situations, several different attitudes may be relevant to behavior. For example, cheating on college examinations might be determined by lax attitudes about honesty or by a strong desire to get into law school. A school superintendent's decision about whether to prevent a gay rights sympathizer from addressing a high school assembly might be dictated by her belief in free speech or by her personal attitudes toward homosexuality. The particular attitude that is salient is more likely to influence her behavior. Salience is particularly crucial when the attitude is not a very strong one. When an attitude is strongly held, presumably it does not have to be brought forcefully to the person's attention to be strongly related to behavior.

Affective versus Cognitive Aspects of an Attitude

Some attitudes depend heavily on cognitions to back them up, that is, beliefs about the nature of the attitude object. Other attitudes are more affectively based, dependent upon the positive or negative feelings or emotions that a person associates with an attitude object, so that making the affective component of the attitude (i.e., the feelings the attitude issue prompts) more salient increases the influence of the affective component over behavior, whereas making the cognitive component (i.e., the beliefs one holds about the attitude object) more salient makes the cognitive component the stronger determinant of behavior (Millar & Tesser, 1986). However, when the cognitive and affective components of an attitude are consistent with each other, it does not matter which is made more salient: Both will be highly correlated with the behavior when either is made salient (Millar & Tesser, 1989; see also Posavac, Sanbonmatsu, & Fazio, 1997).

Whether an attitude is affectively or cognitively based also influences susceptibility to persuasion. Specifically, when an attitude is based heavily on affect, persuasive appeals to emotion are more successful, whereas when attitudes depend more on the cognitions that support them, cognitively based persuasive appeals are more successful in bringing about persuasion (Fabrigar & Petty, 1999).

Reasoning About One's Attitudes

If one were trying to decide whether to take a particular summer job or choose a particular major, an obvious strategy might be to evaluate each of the various aspects of the decision and analyze one's evidence for the pros and cons of each alternative. Despite the intuitive appeal of such a strategy, it actually reduces the relation between attitude and behavior. In particular, Wilson and his colleagues (Wilson & Hodges, 1992) found that introspecting about the reasons one likes or dislikes some attitude object has a disruptive effect on those attitudes and reduces the influence of those attitudes on subsequent decisions. In essence, analyzing the reasons that underlie one's attitudes actually causes the attitudes themselves to change temporarily (Wilson & LaFleur, 1995; Wilson, Hodges, & LaFleur, 1995), especially if those attitudes have little cognitive support, that is, beliefs that buttress the attitude (Maio & Olson, 1998).

The reason this happens may be that people generally don't think a lot about their attitudes, and so, when they are induced to do so, they focus on particular aspects of the attitudes, and thus, those aspects become more salient. In so doing, they may fail to discriminate important from unimportant information or to properly perceive the relevance of particular information; the result is a poorer quality of decision (Tordesillas & Chaiken, 1999). Therefore, reasoning leads to increased inconsistency in the impact that attitudes have on other judgments and decisions.

Situational Pressures

Whenever people engage in overt behavior, they can be influenced both by their attitudes and by the situation. When situational pressures are strong, attitudes are not as strong determinants of behavior, especially weak attitudes, as when situational pressures are weak (Lavine, Huff, Wagner, & Sweeney, 1998). This effect is easy to see in the La Piere (1934) study. Well-dressed, respectable-looking people who are asking for rooms are hard to refuse, despite feelings of prejudice against their ethnic group. The external pressures are even stronger when the law requires that a room be given to anyone who wants one and can pay for it.

So strong is the effect of situational pressures on attitudes that people sometimes evolve completely different attitudes toward the same attitude object in different situations. As an example, Minard (1952) reported how white coal miners in the Pocahontas Coal Field of McDowell, West Virginia, treated black coworkers as equals in the mines, but as social inferiors when they encountered them in the outside world. Often, then, we form context-dependent attitudes toward a single social target that lead to discrepancies between our attitudes and our behavior, which may actually reflect multiple context-dependent attitudes (McConnell, Leibold, & Sherman, 1997).

The strongest influence on behavior is past behavior. People who have behaved in a certain way at, time usually do so again, and attitudes are only one input into this process. Accordingly, the sheer role of habit and knowledge of past behavior influence what a person will do in a given situation (Albarracin & Wyer, 2000).

Overall, then, sometimes attitudes are strongly related to behavior, and sometimes they are not. Some factors that are important are shown in Table 5.3.

The Reasoned Action Model

Perhaps the most influential effort to generate and test a general theory of attitude-behavior links is Fishbein and Ajzen's (1975; Ajzen & Fishbein, 1980) theory of reasoned action. This theory is an attempt to specify the factors that determine attitude-behavior consistency. It begins with the assumption that we behave in accord with our conscious intentions, which are based, in turn, on our rational calculations about the potential effects of our behavior and about how other people will feel about it. The **reasoned action model** is diagrammed in Figure 5–4.

The central point of the theory of reasoned action is that a person's behavior can be predicted from **behavioral intentions.** If a woman says that she intends to use birth control pills to avoid pregnancy, she is more likely to do so than is someone who does not intend to. Behavioral intentions can themselves be predicted from two main variables: the person's attitude toward the behavior (does she think taking the Pill is

Table 5.3

Conditions That Contribute to High Attitude-Behavior Consistency

Attitude is strong.
Unconflicted attitude
Consistent affective and cognitive components
Information about attitude object
Direct personal experience with attitude object
Attitude is stable over time.
Attitude is relevant to the behavior.
Attitude is salient.
No conflicting situational pressures are present.

a positive step for her?) and subjective **social norms** (her perception of what others think she should do: Does her partner want her to? What about her church? Her mother?). A person's attitude toward his or her own behavior is predicted by the expectancy-value framework: The desirability of each possible outcome is weighted by the likelihood of that outcome (for example, avoiding pregnancy is extremely important to this woman, and the Pill is almost certain to prevent pregnancy; the Pill can have mildly unpleasant side effects, but not for everyone who takes it). Subjective social norms are predicted by the perceived expectations of significant others weighted by the motivation to conform to those expectations (for example, her husband may strongly want her to take the Pill, and she wants to please him; her church strongly opposes it, but she thinks its views are outdated and no longer cares about them).

The reasoned action model appeals to many social psychologists both because it makes people seem reasonable and because it places attitudes in a central place in determining behavior. It also has the value of great simplicity: It explains a wide range of behaviors using a small number of variables. Consequently, the model has been widely used. A simple example is a study by Manstead Proffitt, and Smart (1983) that predicted whether pregnant women would breast-feed or bottle-feed their babies. In prenatal questionnaires, the researchers measured behavioral intentions (Did the woman intend to breast-feed?), attitudes toward the behavior (Did she believe that breast-feeding establishes a closer mother-baby bond, and how important is that bond?), and subjective social norms (What did the woman's partner, mother, closest female friend, and doc-

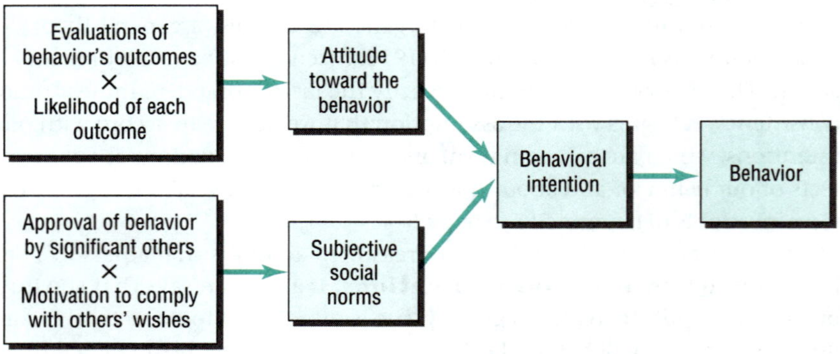

Figure 5–4 The Reasoned Action Model of Factors that Determine a Person's Behavior.

tor prefer, and how motivated was the woman to follow their wishes?). The researchers found that the reasoned action model was very successful in predicting later behavior. The correlation of these various attitudes with actual postbirth breast-feeding was .77, which is quite high. The model has also been used successfully to predict a variety of other behaviors (e.g., Vallerand, Deshaies, Cuerrier, Pelletier, & Mongeau, 1992). When intentions are stable, they predict behavior change; when intentions are weak or unstable, past behavior is the best predictor of current behavior (Sheeran, Orbell, & Trafimow, 1999).

Of course, no model is perfect. What are some of the difficulties with this one? As everyone knows, good intentions are not always enough. Sometimes we do not have the ability or the resources to do something we intend to do. As a result, it has been suggested that an additional variable—perceived control over outcomes—be added to the model (Ajzen & Madden, 1986; Madden, Ellen, & Ajzen, 1992). In support of this point, Schifter and Ajzen (1985) found that female students' intentions to lose weight were likely to result in genuine weight loss only among those who believed they could control their weight and could successfully lose weight if they tried. Attitudes about the desirability of weight loss had little effect on the behavior of those who felt helpless about their ability to lose weight. A review of this research (Madden et al., 1992) confirms that adding perceived control to the theory improves its ability to predict intentions and behavior; this is especially true when the behaviors present potential problems with respect to control (such as losing weight or stopping smoking). The revision of the model that includes perceived control over outcomes as an additional element is called the **theory of planned behavior.**

However, factors that are not included in the model, such as external constraints and opportunities, as well as perceived susceptibility and fear, may also be important. Boyd and Wandersman (1991) interviewed 190 college undergraduates about their intentions to use condoms during sexual intercourse. Three months after completing the initial questionnaire, participants were recontacted by phone and asked about the frequency of their condom use during the intervening period. Although behavioral intention was a strong predictor of reported condom use, perceived susceptibility to and fear of AIDS significantly predicted condom use as well. It is likely, too, that access to condoms and a willingness to purchase them also contributed to this behavior. Therefore, people might intend to use condoms yet not have access to them when they need them, or they might intend not to, yet end up using them if they are available and a partner insists.

Attitudes about the desirability of a behavior do not always control our actions. To some extent, people are simply creatures of habit. For example, how a woman fed her first child influences how she will feed her second, no matter what she and all her friends and family members think is right (Manstead et al., 1983). In a study that many readers may relate to, Ajzen and Madden (1986) found previous class attendance habits to be the single strongest predictor of college students' future class attendance, irrespective of any of the students' current attitudes toward attending class.

Finally, it is sometimes difficult to obtain measures of behavioral intention that are truly independent of attitudes toward the behavior, on the one hand, and actual behavior, on the other. Sometimes behavioral intention is not, as measured, very different from attitude toward the behavior. Asking a pregnant woman whether she intends to breast-feed her baby may be almost the same thing as asking her whether she thinks it is a good idea or not. Under such circumstances attitudes are more successful in predicting behavioral intentions than in predicting actual behavior (e.g., Ajzen & Madden, 1986). However, treating behavioral intention as a separate factor may not add very much to our understanding. With these reservations, the theory of planned behavior helps to clarify the role that attitudes play in determining behavior.

Summary

1. Attitudes have a cognitive (thought) component, an affective (feeling) component, and a behavioral component. Attitudes are usually cognitively complex but evaluatively simple.
2. The learning approach views attitudes as learned by association, reinforcement, and imitation. Cognitive consistency theories view people as attempting to maintain consistency among their attitudes and among the affective, cognitive, and behavioral components of a particular attitude. The expectancy-value approach views attitudes as cost-benefit calculations by the individual based on the pros and cons of the arguments.
3. Dissonance theory focuses on how behavior affects attitudes. Dissonance arises when decisions and behavioral acts are contrary to the individual's attitudes. Dissonance is typically resolved by changing attitudes. Postdecisional dissonance is greatest when people have free choice, remain committed to their decisions, and feel responsible for foreseeable consequences.
4. Dissonance resulting from attitude-discrepant behavior depends on barely sufficient incentives to commit the behavior, such as threats or promised rewards. The maximum dissonance occurs when incentives are low and clear personal responsibility for negative consequences of the behavior is high.
5. Alternative explanations for these dissonance effects have been generated by self-perception theory. When we have rather vague, undefined attitudes, behavioral acts may lead to new perceptions of our own attitudes, thus leading to attitude-behavior consistency through self-perception rather than dissonance reduction.
6. Cognitive response theory and the elaboration likelihood model distinguish between systematic processing, which involves close scrutiny of the arguments, and heuristic processing, which involves the use of peripheral cues that are irrelevant to message content.
7. A useful model of the persuasion situation classifies possible influences on the target in terms of communicator (or source), communication, and situational and target variables.
8. Credible, trustworthy, and liked sources are the most potent communicators, as are reference groups with which the target identifies. Source characteristics are often processed as peripheral cues. To avoid changing attitudes, people sometimes derogate the source.
9. An important aspect of a communication is its discrepancy from the target's initial attitude. Attitude change tends to increase with more discrepancy up to a point; then it starts to fall off again. With high source credibility and/or low commitment, this falloff point occurs at higher levels of discrepancy.
10. Communications can arouse emotional needs such as anger or fear and tend to be accepted if the position that is advocated reduces the need it has aroused. Very high levels of fear seem to arouse defensive reactions, however, and reduce the likelihood of attitude change.
11. The degree of commitment to an attitude (position involvement) is a critical determinant of persuasion. With high commitment, there is less persuasion.
12. Strong arguments are more effective than weak ones when the target can be induced to think about them, such as when the issue is personally relevant (high issue involvement).
13. Repetition of a message is important if attitude change is to be maintained. However, too much repetition leads to boredom and lessens support.
14. A person can become inoculated against persuasion by being exposed to weak versions of the forthcoming persuasive arguments and learning to combat them.
15. Forewarning of the position to be advocated increases resistance to change when the listener is highly committed to a very discrepant position.
16. Distraction can facilitate persuasion by reducing the listener's defenses against highly discrepant messages.
17. Sometimes behavior arises from attitudes and sometimes it does not. Attitude-behavior consistency is high when attitudes are strong, stable, salient, accessible, and clearly relevant to the behavior, and when there are few conflicting situational pressures.
18. The reasoned action model holds that behavior is controlled by behavioral intentions, which in turn are determined by attitudes toward the behavior and by subjective social norms.

Critical Thinking

1. Think through the principles of (a) the learning theory of attitudes, (b) cognitive consistency theories, (c) expectancy-value theories, and (d) cognitive response theories. Which of these four theoretical positions seems to you to have the broadest explanatory power, that is, the ability to explain much of what we know about attitudes?
2. Many factors influence whether we are persuaded by a communication, whether it comes from an advertiser, a politician, or some other intended persuader. What are some of the factors that increase the likelihood of persuasion? Think through the last time you were exposed to a persuasive message. Were you persuaded by it? Why or why not?
3. Much of the time our attitudes directly predict our behavior, but sometimes they do not. When are our attitudes and behavior least likely to go together? Why is this the case?

Key Terms

GLOSSARY

A

Actor-observer bias The tendency for observers to overestimate the importance of the actor's dispositions, and for the actor to overestimate the importance of the situation in explaining the actor's behavior.

Additive principle In impression formation, the idea that pieces of information about a person or attitude are processed in terms of their evaluative implications and are then added together to form an overall impression. Sometimes contrasted with the averaging principle.

Affective component That part of an attitude consisting of a person's feelings associated with beliefs about an attitude object; consists mainly of the evaluation of the object (like-dislike, pro-con).

Agenda setting The process in which the mass media focus public attention on certain issues and thus determine which issues the public is concerned about.

Aggression Any action intended to hurt another person.

Aggression anxiety Anxiety about expressing overt aggression, usually with respect to a particular target.

Altruism An act performed voluntarily to help another person when there is no expectation of receiving a reward in any form. See also *prosocial behavior*.

Ambivalence As applied to attitudes, ambivalence occurs when a person believes arguments on both sides of an issue. This person may express inconsistent opinions over time, depending on which arguments come to mind.

Ambivalent sexism A mixture of benevolent attitudes toward women (protecting women) and hostile attitudes (resenting women's efforts to achieve equal power).

Androgyny People who believe they possess both traditionally feminine and traditionally masculine characteristics are said to be androgynous. An androgynous person's self-concept includes both masculine, or instrumental, qualities (e.g., being independent and strong) and feminine, or expressive, qualities (e.g., being nurturant and gentle).

Anger Aggressive feelings.

Antisocial aggression Aggressive acts, such as murder, that violate commonly accepted social norms.

Archival research The analysis of data already collected for another purpose, such as census data or legal records of births, deaths, and marriages.

Assimilation In the study of attitude change, the tendency to perceive a communicator's position as closer or more similar to the individual's own position than it actually is.

Association A link in memory between different stimuli that occur together in time and place. Through pairing, reactions to one stimulus become associated with the other. This is one of the basic processes by which learning occurs.

Assumed-similarity effect In intergroup relations, the tendency for members of an in-group to assume that other in-group members share their attitudes and values.

Attachment The emotional bonds that form between people in a close relationship. During infancy, attachment is seen when a child responds positively to one special person, wants to be with that person, seeks the person out when frightened, and so on.

Attack advertising Political commercials that attack the opponent rather than advocating the strength of the favored candidate.

Attitude Enduring response disposition with an affective component, a behavioral component, and a cognitive component. We develop and hold attitudes toward persons, objects, and ideas.

Attitude-discrepant behavior Acts inconsistent with a person's attitudes. When an individual behaves in a way inconsistent with a belief, cognitive dissonance is produced, and there is a tendency for the attitude to change. See *cognitive dissonance theory*.

Attribution The process by which people use information to make inferences about the causes of behaviors or attitudes.

Attributional ambiguity Being uncertain as to the cause of some circumstance or event; as applied to potential discrimination, it creates a dilemma for people who are often subject to discrimination, because they do not know whether their failures are due to discrimination or to their own inadequate efforts.

Attribution theory The principles that determine how attributions are made and what effects these causal attributions have.

Authoritarian personality A personality type characterized by exaggerated submission to authority; extreme conformity to conventional standards; self-righteous hostility, especially toward deviants; and ethnocentrism.

Automatic processing Mental processes that look like reasoning, but that occur unconsciously, without intention or awareness.

Averaging principle In impression formation, the idea that pieces of information about a person or attitude are processed in terms of their evaluative implications and are then averaged together, to form an overall attitude. Sometimes contrasted with the additive principle.

Aversive racism Attitudes toward members of a racial group that combine both egalitarian social values and negative emotions, resulting in avoidance of that racial group.

B

Balance theory Heider proposed that we strive to maintain consistency among our sentiment and unit relations. We are motivated to like people we are connected to by physical proximity or other links, to like people we agree with, and to dislike those we disagree with.

Behavioral component That part of an attitude consisting of a person's tendencies to act toward the attitude object. A child's attitude toward a pet cat may include tendencies to feed and cuddle the animal.

Behavioral intention The conscious intention to carry out a specific act.

Behavioral self-blame Blaming one's own actions for a victimization that has befallen oneself.

Behaviorism The influential analysis of learning associated with J. B. Watson, Ivan Pavlov, and B. F. Skinner. It investigates only overt behavior, not subjective states such as thoughts or feelings. Behaviorism identifies association and reinforcement as the key determinants of learning.

Bicultural competence The development and possession of awareness and information about two cultures; knowledge, appreciation, and internalization of the basic beliefs of both cultures.

Biopsychosocial model The view that a person's state of health is jointly determined by biological factors (such as exposure to a virus), psychological factors (such as stress), and social factors (such as degree of social support).

Body language Information transmitted about attitudes, emotions, and so on by nonverbal bodily movements and features, such as posture, stance, or touch.

Bounded rationality Reasoning that is "good enough" to solve a particular problem even if it is not perfect.

Brainstorming A technique for coming up with new and creative solutions to problems. Members of a group discuss a problem and generate as many different solutions as they can, withholding criticism until all possibilities have been presented.

Bystander effect An effect that, when other people are present, makes it less likely that any one person will offer help to a stranger in distress. The diffusion of responsibility created by the presence of other people is one explanation for the bystander effect.

Bystander intervention The technical term for helping a stranger in distress.

C

Case history information Information about a particular person or event. This kind of information often has a more persuasive impact on people's judgments than objectively better but less vivid statistical information.

Categorization The process by which we perceive people or other stimuli in groups or categories rather than perceiving each person as a distinct individual.

Category-based processing Cognitive processing in which perceivers attend to individuals mainly in terms of which group or social category they are in.

Catharsis Sigmund Freud's idea that by expressing aggression, a person reduces his or her aggressive drive.

Central traits A trait is central to the extent that it is associated with many of the stimulus person's other characteristics. Traits such as being warm or cold are considered central because they are important in determining overall impressions.

Characterological self-blame Believing that one's enduring traits or personality is responsible for or causing a negative event in one's life.

Coerced compliant false confession A confession by a person who is pressured to confess to a crime but who continues privately to believe that he or she is innocent.

Coerced internalized false confession A confession by an innocent person who is pressured to confess to a crime and then comes privately to believe that he or she actually committed the crime.

Cognitive component That part of an attitude consisting of the person's beliefs, knowledge, and facts about the attitude object.

Cognitive consistency Tendency for people to seek consistency among their attitudes; regarded as a major determinant of attitude formation and change.

Cognitive dissonance theory Theory developed by Festinger according to which inconsistency (dissonance) between two cognitive elements produces pressure to make these elements consonant. The theory has been applied to a wide range of phenomena, including decision making, attitude-discrepant behavior, and interpersonal attraction.

Cognitive response theory The theory that attitude change following the receipt of communication depends on the cognitive responses it evokes. If the change produces negative thoughts, it will be rejected; if it evokes positive thoughts, it will be accepted. Counterarguing is a crucial mechanism for resisting persuasion, according to this theory.

Cohesiveness In group dynamics, the forces, both positive and negative, that cause members to remain in a group. Cohesiveness is a characteristic of a group as a whole, and results from the degree of commitment of each individual to the group.

Collective memory In political psychology, the memory of a political event shared by the people who experienced it;

tends to be strongest in people who experienced the event when they were young.

Collectivism The belief that the group's well-being is more important than that of the individual. Collectivist cultures emphasize loyalty to the family, adherence to group norms, and the preservation of harmony in social relations with members of one's own group.

Commitment to an attitude The perception that one's decision cannot be changed or revoked; a key determinant of cognitive dissonance.

Commitment to a relationship All the forces that act to keep a person in a relationship or group. Positive forces include interpersonal attraction and satisfaction with a relationship; negative forces include such barriers to ending a relationship as the lack of alternatives or having made large investments in the relationship.

Communal relationships In these relationships, each partner provides benefits to the other in order to show concern and to respond to the other's needs, with no expectation of receiving similar benefits in the near future. See also *exchange relationships*.

Companionate love A somewhat practical type of love that emphasizes trust, caring, and tolerance of the partner's flaws. Companionate love may develop slowly in a relationship as partners become more interdependent. Sometimes contrasted with passionate love.

Comparison level A standard we use to evaluate the quality of our social relationships. Our comparison level is the level of outcomes (benefits and costs) we expect or believe we deserve based on our experience in relationships.

Comparison level for alternatives A standard we use to evaluate the quality of our social relationships. Our comparison level for alternatives is our evaluation of one particular relationship against other relationships that are currently available to us.

Compliance Performance of an act at another's request.

Confirmatory hypothesis testing Selectively extracting from others information that preferentially confirms a hypothesis, instead of gathering information evenhandedly that both favors and opposes the hypothesis.

Conformity Voluntary performance of an act because others also do it. Conformity often results from a person's desire to be right (informational influence) and/or desire to be liked (normative influence).

Conjunction error An error that occurs when people believe more in the likelihood that several events will happen at the same time (because the events seem to go together) than in the likelihood that any one of the events will happen by itself.

Contact theory The theory that prejudice against a social group can be reduced by appropriate kinds of contact with individual members of that group.

Contingency model of leadership effectiveness Fiedler's model distinguishing between task-oriented and relationship-oriented leaders. When the group situation is either highly favorable or highly unfavorable to control by the leader, task-oriented leaders are more effective. In intermediate situations, where the leader has moderate control, relationship-oriented leaders are more successful.

Contrast In the study of attitude change, the tendency to perceive a communicator's position as being further away from the individual's own position than it actually is.

Control question test A method of polygraph testing in which a person's physiological responses to questions about a crime are compared with his or her physiological responses to questions about personal wrongdoings. An innocent person is expected to be more aroused when answering questions about personal wrongdoings, whereas a guilty person is expected to be more aroused when answering questions about the crime.

Cooperative interdependence Relationship in which the outcomes of two people or groups depend on each other, so that the rewards one gets increase the rewards the other gets. When members of a team work together to win, the success of one teammate benefits all members of the team.

Coping The process of managing internal or environmental demands that are appraised as taxing or exceeding one's resources. Coping may involve active problem-solving efforts and/or efforts at emotional control.

Correlational research Passively measuring two variables and determining whether they are associated. Studies relating smoking to lung cancer are correlational: They measure the amount of smoking each person has done and whether the person gets lung cancer, in order to determine if the two factors are related. The major problem with correlational designs is the difficulty in determining whether a correlation reflects cause and effect.

Correspondent inference theory A theory of attribution and person perception that details the conditions under which people assume that an individual's action is due to his or her enduring personal characteristics.

Counterarguing In attitude change, one mechanism for resisting influence by discrepant communications: The individual considers and actively rebuts the arguments made by the communicator.

Counterfactual reasoning Imagined alternative versions of actual events; people's "What if?" or "If only . . ." thoughts about past or present outcomes or circumstances.

Covariation Judgments of covariation involve determining how strongly two things are related, such as the time of day and the frequency of crime, or the ingestion of caffeine and alertness. When social perceivers expect two things to go together, they tend to overestimate the actual degree of covariation.

Credibility In attitude change, a communicator's credibility depends on his or her perceived expertise about the topic and how much he or she is trusted by the individual receiving the communication.

Crowding The subjective experience of feeling cramped or not having enough space.

Cultural stereotype Societal-level images of members of a social group such as those found in art, literature, religious teachings, and the mass media. For example, TV commercials may portray women as worried consumers and men as knowledgeable experts. See also personal stereotype.

Culture The shared beliefs, values, traditions, and behavior patterns of a particular group.

Cybernetic theory of self-regulation The process by which people compare their behavior to a standard, decide that it either matches the standard or does not, and continue adjusting and comparing until the standard is met or abandoned. Self-awareness is argued to be a precondition for this type of self-regulation.

D

Date rape (or acquaintance rape) Forced sexual activity that occurs between two people who are at least mildly acquainted and who may be dating.

Death qualification Refers to the process of jury selection in capital cases. Prospective jurors are asked to consider whether they can convict a defendant of a crime if they know that the defendant may receive the death penalty. Jurors who express reservations about conviction under these circumstances are "death-qualified" and excluded from the jury panel.

Debriefing An essential feature of ethical research, in which after the subjects' participation is over, the purposes and procedures of the research study are explained to the subjects, their questions are answered, and the scientific value of the research is discussed.

Decision-making theories According to decision-making theories, people calculate the costs and benefits of various actions and select the best alternative in a fairly logical way.

Decision rule A rule about how a group can reach a decision, such as majority-wins, two-thirds majority, or unanimity.

Dehumanization The process of taking away the personhood or human qualities of another person or group through one's actions or the ways one thinks about the person or group. Dehumanizing another person is thought to facilitate aggression against that person.

Deindividuation The process by which being part of a group leads people to do things they normally would not do if they were alone. Anonymity is the key factor in deindividuation. The behavioral consequences of deindividuation depend on the norms of the situation, which can be either antisocial or prosocial.

Demand characteristics Aspects of a study that make subjects more aware of their participation in research and thus bias their behavior. For example, subjects may try to avoid negative evaluations from the experimenter or may try to cooperate with the experimenter to verify the hypothesis.

Dependent variable In an experiment, the responses to the independent variable being manipulated or measured.

Desensitization Reaction to an overexposure to material that normally evokes strong emotions, such as violence or sexuality; the individual becomes insensitive to it.

Desire for individuation This (refers to) individual differences in a person's willingness to do things that publicly differentiate him or her from others or make him or her stand out.

Diffusion of responsibility A process by which the presence of other people makes each individual feel less responsible for causing events or solving problems. It may decrease the likelihood that a person will take action, for instance, to help a stranger in distress.

Discounting principle In making attributions, the tendency to reduce reliance on one particular cause to the extent that other plausible causes exist. If, for example, a judge gives the death penalty to a criminal, we might conclude that she is generally a tough judge, but we would be less likely to do so if we discover that the law requires the death penalty for this particular crime.

Discrepancy In the study of attitude change, the distance between the communicator's and the target's position on the issue discussed in the communication. For example, a communicator may argue that tuition should be doubled; that position will be highly discrepant to a student who believes it should not change, but only moderately discrepant to a student who thinks a modest increase is reasonable.

Discrimination The behavioral component of group antagonism. People discriminate against a disliked group by refusing its members access to desired jobs, educational opportunities, and so on.

Disinhibition As applied to aggression, a loosening of control over anger after it has been released under socially approved conditions; a person who has committed a socially approved aggressive act has fewer inhibitions about aggressing under other conditions.

Displaced aggression The expression of aggression against a target other than the source of attack or frustration, usually a safer target.

Dispositional attribution Perceiving the cause of a person's action as stemming from his or her disposition, such as personality, ability, or attitudes.

Dispositional optimism A generalized expectation, held by some people and not others, that positive outcomes will occur in one's life.

Dissonance The state of aversive arousal that results when a person simultaneously holds two beliefs that conflict with or contradict each other. See also *cognitive dissonance theory*.

Distraction In attitude change, a stimulus that draws attention away from a persuasive message. Distraction can increase attitude change by making it harder for people to defend a position against the arguments in the message.

Distraction-conflict model An explanation of social facilitation effects. The presence of others creates a conflict between two basic tendencies: (1) to pay attention to the audience and (2) to pay attention to the task. This conflict creates arousal, which may inhibit task performance.

Domestic violence Acts of violence committed by one family member against another family member or by one of several cohabiting individuals against another of them.

Door-in-the-face technique A technique for gaining compliance with a request by first asking for a much larger request. After the larger request is refused, the person is more likely to agree to the second, smaller request.

Downward social comparison Comparison of one's traits or abilities with those of someone who is perceived as worse off than oneself.

Dual-process model A model hypothesizing that people can process information in a careful, systematic fashion or in a more rapid, efficient, heuristic fashion. Aspects of the person or situation predict which mode of processing a person will use.

E

Ego involvement In attitude change, the subjective linking of an attitude to strong ego needs, thereby making the attitude more emotionally laden and more resistant to change.

Elaboration-likelihood model A theory of persuasion and attitude change in which the key variable is the amount of careful thought given to the arguments (elaboration likelihood): With more careful processing, attitude change depends more on the real strength of the arguments and less on peripheral cues.

Empathy Feelings of sympathy and caring for others, in particular, sharing vicariously or indirectly in the suffering of other people. Strong feelings of empathy can motivate a person to help someone in need.

Enemy image Strongly felt perceptions that a national enemy is evil and intends to act aggressively against one's own country.

Equity The principle that two people who make equal contributions to a task should receive equal rewards.

Equity theory An offshoot of social exchange theory that focuses on fairness in relationships. A relationship is equitable when the ratio of profits to contributions is the same for everyone. The theory postulates that when individuals perceive inequity, both underbenefited and overbenefited partners feel distress and take steps to restore equity.

Estimator variables Factors affecting eyewitness identification that are related to the witness or to the situation in which the event was witnessed. The witness's arousal level and the viewing conditions at the time of the event are examples of estimator variables.

Ethnic identity The part of an individual's self-knowledge that concerns his or her membership in a particular ethnic group, together with the value and emotional significance attached to that membership.

Ethnocentrism The belief that the in-group is the center of the social world and superior to out-groups.

Evaluation The most important basic dimension underlying impression formation and attitudes; the "goodness" or "badness" of another person, object, or concept. See also *affective component.*

Evaluation apprehension A person's concern about how others evaluate him or her; often a concern about making a good impression in public.

Evaluative priming technique A way to measure implicit stereotypes, based on the idea that the evaluation of a stereotype-consistent word (such as "gentle") is speedier after the presentation of a prime of the group (such as a picture of a woman).

Evolutionary social psychology An emerging specialty in social psychology that uses the principles of evolution and natural selection to understand human behavior and social life.

Evolved psychological mechanism Term used to describe human tendencies and preferences that are the result of natural selection. These tendencies are responses adapted to specific problems encountered by our distant ancestors.

Exchange relationships Relationships in which people give benefits with the expectation of receiving comparable benefits in return soon afterward. See also *communal relationships*.

Exemplar An example of a category that embodies the significant attributes of the category or the ideal of that category. For example, a robin is an exemplar of the category "bird."

Expectancy-value theory This theory states that decisions are based on the combination of two factors: (1) the value of the various possible outcomes of the decision and (2) the likelihood or probability that each outcome will actually occur.

Expectation states theory According to this theory, a person's status in a group may be affected by such diffuse state characteristics as age, ethnicity, and wealth.

Experiment Type of research in which the researcher randomly assigns people to two or more conditions, varies in a controlled manner the treatment each condition is given, and then measures the effects on the subjects' responses. Although experiments are often difficult to arrange, they have the advantage of yielding clear information about cause and effect. Any differences between groups in the outcome of the experiment must be due to the variables that were experimentally manipulated.

Experimenter bias A bias introduced into the results of a study, usually in the direction of falsely confirming the hypothesis, through unintentional actions of the researcher.

Expert testimony Testimony provided by qualified experts about pertinent research findings that help judges and jurors understand and evaluate the evidence in a particular legal case. Expert testimony serves to educate judges and jurors about issues that are not commonly understood.

Explicit stereotype A stereotype that we are conscious of holding. Explicit stereotypes are often measured with self-report techniques (e.g., rating women as strong or weak). We can control the expression of our explicit stereotypes.

External validity The extent to which the results of a study are generalizable to other populations and settings.

F

Faceism The tendency to emphasize men's faces and women's bodies, for instance, in advertisements and news photos.

False consensus effect Bias in perceptions of others so that one exaggerates how common one's own opinions or behaviors are.

False uniqueness Bias in perceptions of others that one exaggerates how uniquely positive one's own abilities are.

Field experiment A study in which variables are systematically manipulated and measured in a real-life, nonlaboratory setting.

Figure-ground principle In social perception, the basic principle that attention is drawn to stimuli that stand out against a background. Figural stimuli are those that stand out; the background is called the "ground." This principle has generated much of the research on salience in social perception.

Foot-in-the-door technique A technique for gaining compliance with a request by first persuading the person to comply with a small request. After agreeing to a small request, the person is more likely to comply with a larger request.

Forewarning In attitude change, informing recipients of the position to be taken in a persuasive communication, or of the communicator's intension to persuade them, prior to the receipt of the communication.

Framing The way in which the media describe a particular issue. For example, affirmative action can be framed as reverse discrimination against white people, or as helping to ensure equality for minorities.

Frustration The blocking or thwarting of goal-directed behavior. For example, a child is frustrated when a parent refuses to let him color the bathroom wallpaper with crayons or smear ice cream on the dining-room table.

Frustration-aggression hypothesis In its most absolute form, this hypothesis asserts that frustration always creates feelings of aggression, and that aggression is always caused by frustration.

Fundamental attribution error The tendency for observers to overestimate the causal importance of a person's dispositions and to underestimate the importance of the situation when they explain the person's actions.

G

Gender gap Differences between women and men in their attitudes or experiences.

Gender identity The self-knowledge that one is male or female. Gender identity is acquired early in life.

Gender self-concept The degree to which a person perceives that he or she possesses traditionally masculine or feminine characteristics. See also *androgyny*.

Gender stereotype Beliefs about the typical personal attributes of males and females. According to traditional gender stereotypes, women are have expressive or communal qualities, such as being nurturing and gentle, and men have instrumental qualities, such as being independent, assertive, and competent. See also *androgyny*.

Gender typing The process of labeling things, activities, and people as "masculine" or "feminine." For example, many people consider dolls, ruffles, and housecleaning feminine.

Gestalt psychology A theory, developed by Wolfgang Kohler, Kurt Koffka, Kurt Lewin, and others, that focuses on the way individuals perceive and understand objects, events, and people. The theory emphasizes the idea that people form coherent and meaningful perceptions based on the entire perceptual field, so that the whole is different from the sum of its parts.

Group A social aggregate in which members are interdependent (have mutual influence on each other) and have at least the potential for mutual interaction.

Group interest Group members' preference of outcomes that will benefit their group, whether those outcomes benefit them personally or not.

Group polarization The more extreme positions that people often come to support when a group discusses an issue. Polarization sometimes leads to a risky shift, and sometimes to a cautious shift, depending on the initial views of group members.

Group-serving biases The biases that members of an in-group tend to hold-favorable attributions for the performance of members of the in-group (internal attributions for success, external for failure) and unfavorable attributions for performance by members of the out-group.

Groupthink According to Janis, the impairment in decision making and sound judgment that can occur in groups. Group members ignore contradictory information, ostracize dissenters, and unify around their decision.

H

Habitual news reception The amount of the news that a person is customarily exposed to, day in and day out; usually indexed by measurement of the person's level of political information.

Halo effect The effect in which a liked person is assumed to have good qualities of many kinds, whether the observer has any information about those qualities or not.

Hardiness A personality variable consisting of a sense of commitment, a positive response to challenge, and an internal sense of control that seems to help people cope effectively with stress.

Health behavior An action undertaken by a person who is healthy to enhance or maintain good health.

Health belief An attitude about a particular health practice that influences willingness to adopt that practice; may include beliefs about personal susceptibility, the efficacy of the health practice, or the severity of the health risk.

Heuristic A shortcut for problem solving that reduces complex or ambiguous information to more simple judgmental operations.

Heuristic processing A way of processing information rapidly and efficiently that draws on cues, shortcuts, or rules of thumb to reduce complex problems to more manageable, simple ones.

I

Ideal self The personal attributes one would like to have.

Ideology An abstract, general belief system that encompasses consistent attitudes toward many different issues. Liberalism and conservatism are the most common ideologies in Western industrial countries.

Illusory correlation The belief that two things are related to each other because expectations dictate that they ought to go together, when in fact those things bear little or no relationship to each other.

Imitation See *modeling*.

Implicit cognition A judgment or decision that is under the control of automatically activated evaluation; it is the automatic effect of past experience on current feelings, thoughts, or actions that occurs without awareness.

Implicit association test A technique for measuring implicit stereotypes. Based on the idea that the response to stereotype-consistent pairs of words (e.g., Matilda and doddering) is speedier than to stereotype-inconsistent pairs (e.g., Hortense and sexy).

Implicit personality theory The ordinary person's theory about which personality traits go with other traits, such as "weak" going with "cowardly" and "calm" going with "decisive."

Implicit stereotypes Stereotypes that are expressed outside the person's awareness and are not under the person's control.

Impressionable years The theory that basic attitudes are susceptible to change in late adolescence and early adulthood, but not to much change thereafter.

Independent self The sense of oneself as bounded, unitary, and separate from the social context.

Independent variable The variable in a study that is interpreted as the cause of changes in the dependent variable. The independent variable may be systematically manipulated by the researcher in an experiment or passively measured in a correlational study.

Individualism Belief in the value of personal identity, uniqueness, and freedom. In an individualistic culture, personal goals come before group goals, and a person's sense of self is based largely on personal accomplishments rather than on group membership.

Informational influence One reason for conformity is the desire to be correct in our behavior or interpretation of an ambiguous situation. Informational influence occurs when we conform because the behavior of others provides useful information. See also normative influence.

Informed consent Consent given after research subjects are informed about the study, about the procedures that will be used, and about the costs and benefits of the research.

Ingratiation Flattering or doing favors for another person in order to persuade that person to like you.

In-group The group to which an individual belongs; membership in it forms part of his or her social identity. See also *out-group*.

In-group favoritism effect The tendency to give more favorable evaluations and greater rewards to members of one's in-group than to members of out-groups.

Inoculation defense In attitude change, McGuire's notion that people become more resistant to the effects of persuasive communications when they have been exposed to weak counterarguments.

Insufficient justification One type of experiment that tests predictions from cognitive dissonance theory; subjects perform a counterattitudinal behavior with inadequate reason or incentive for doing so and consequently come to develop more positive attitudes toward that behavior.

Interdependence The condition in which two or more people have some degree of mutual influence on each other's feelings, thoughts, or behaviors.

Interdependence theory The theory that because members of a couple or group are interdependent (i.e., the outcomes one person experiences depend on what others do and vice versa), individuals must coordinate their behavior to maximize their joint benefits. Interdependence theory is the most important social exchange perspective in social psychology.

Interdependent self The sense of self as flexible, variable, and connected to the social context.

Internal validity The extent to which cause-and-effect conclusions can be validly drawn from the research.

Issue public Those people who care most about a particular political issue and pay close attention to it.

J

Jealousy Emotion triggered when a person perceives a real or potential attraction between his or her partner and a rival. Jealousy is a reaction to a perceived threat by a rival to the continuity or quality of a valued relationship. Feelings of anger, anxiety, and depression commonly result.

Jury decision rule The decision standard required by law to reach a deliberated jury verdict. The decision rule can involve unanimity (requiring that jurors deliberate to reach a unanimous verdict) or majority rule (requiring that jurors arrive at a verdict supported by a majority of the jurors).

Jury size The exact number of individuals required for a jury, ranging from 6 or fewer to 12. Research suggests that the quality of jury deliberations is affected by the size of the jury deliberating a case.

L

Learning theory The central idea in learning theory is that a person's behavior is determined by prior learning. Current behavior is shaped by past experience. In any given situation, a person learns certain behaviors that over time, may become habits. When presented with the same situation, the person tends to behave in the same habitual way.

Legitimate authority In many situations, social norms permit those in authority to make requests. Illustrations of legitimate authority include the government's right to ask citizens to pay taxes, parents' right to ask their children to wash the dinner dishes, and an employer's right to assign duties to an employee.

Legitimizing myth An ideology that justifies the current social hierarchy, for example, the belief that success stems from hard work and great talent.

Lessons of history In political psychology, the "lessons" that political leaders believe they have learned from the past, often based on political events in their youth.

Lifelong openness The theory that basic attitudes are susceptible to change at all points in the life span.

Loneliness The psychological discomfort we feel when our social relations lack some essential feature. This deficit may be quantitative (too few relationships) or qualitative (unsatisfying relationships).

Low-ball technique A technique for gaining compliance in which the influencer obtains a commitment from the person before revealing hidden costs of the request.

M

Matching principle In dating and marriage, people tend to have partners who are similar to themselves in attitudes, values, ethnic background, religion, social class, education, and many other personal characteristics.

Mere exposure effect The effect by which simply being exposed frequently to a person or object tends to increase our liking for that person or object. Repeated exposure most often enhances liking when our initial reaction to the person is neutral or positive, when no conflict of interest exists, and when the exposure is not so great that it causes satiation.

Message learning The idea that attitude change depends on the individual's learning the content of the communication.

Meta-analysis A quantitative approach to summarizing and synthesizing the results of many empirical studies on a topic, such as sex differences in aggression. Statistics are used to estimate the overall size of the "effect," or sex difference, and also to test for the consistency (homogeneity) of a finding across studies.

Middle-range theories Theories that attempt to account for major categories of behavior but do not attempt to cover all human behavior in general. A middle-range theory might try to explain attitude change, attribution, or aggression, but not all three at once.

Minimal effects model The theory that mass communications mainly reinforce the recipient's prior attitudes rather than create widespread attitude change.

Minimal intergroup situation The basic research situation used to test social identity theory: People are arbitrarily classified into groups (e.g., the red and the blue teams) and then allowed to allocate rewards to each other.

Minimal risk A risk for the participants in a research project that is no greater than the risk encountered in daily life.

Minority influence Influence that members of a minority have over the majority in a group.

Mirror image The image held by members of two conflicting nations, so that each group believes that its own nation is peace-loving and that the other nation is hostile and threatening.

Modeling People often learn behaviors and social attitudes simply by observing the attitudes and behaviors of other people, known technically as "models." Modeling occurs when a person not only observes but actually copies the behavior of a model. Observational learning can occur without any external reinforcement. However, whether or not a person actually performs or models a behavior learned through observation is influenced by the consequences the action has for the person. Modeling is also known as "imitation" or "observational learning."

Mood-congruent memory The tendency for people to remember material whose valence fits their current mood state. For example, a person in a good mood is more likely to remember positive material.

N

Negative-state relief model According to this model of helping, people help in order to alleviate their own bad mood or personal distress at a victim's suffering.

Negativity effect Tendency for impressions to be influenced more by negative traits than by positive traits. Hence, positive impressions are more vulnerable to change than negative impressions.

Nonattitudes Expressed opinions that do not reflect a real and stable underlying attitude but are fleeting responses to a situation that calls for the expression of an attitude.

Nonverbal leakage The communication of true emotions through nonverbal channels even when the person's verbal communications attempt to conceal the emotions.

Normative influence One reason for conformity is the desire to be liked. Normative influence occurs when we conform to group norms or standards in order to gain social acceptance or avoid social rejection. See also *informational influence*.

Norm of reciprocity The social norm that we should reward those who reward us. For example, if someone helps us, we feel obligated to help them in return.

Norm of social justice A norm about fairness and the just distribution of resources. Norms of social justice, such as equity, may encourage prosocial behavior.

Norm of social responsibility A social norm dictating that we should help others who depend on us. This may contribute to prosocial behavior.

O

Observational learning Learning by watching what others do and doing the same; this learning also applies to forming attitudes by modeling those of others such as parents or teachers.

Old-fashioned racism Old-fashioned beliefs in white racial superiority, segregation, and formal discrimination.

Operational definition The specific procedure or operation that is used to measure or manipulate a variable in a research study.

Optimal distinctiveness A social identity in a group that is large enough to give the individual a sense of inclusion, but small enough to provide a sense of differentiation from others.

Ought self The personal attributes one believes one should possess, based on one's obligations and responsibilities or the expectations of others.

Out-group Any group other than the in-group.

Out-group homogeneity effect Perception that members of the out-group are more similar to each other than members of the in-group are to each other.

Overwriting hypothesis The hypothesis that information received by witnesses after seeing an event permanently replaces their original memories of the event.

Own-race bias A phenomenon in which eyewitnesses tend to be more accurate when identifying members of their own race than when identifying members of another race.

P

Paralanguage Information conveyed by variations in speech other than actual words and syntax, such as pitch, loudness, and hesitations.

Party identification A person's stable preference for one political party over its rivals.

Passionate love The emotionally charged type of love that sometimes characterizes the early stages of romantic relationships. Contrasted with companionate love.

Peripheral cues Aspects of the communication situation that are irrelevant to the content of the message (e.g., pleasant music, long or beautifully written messages), but that may influence attitude change when the individual is not engaged in systematic processing.

Persistence As used in political psychology, persistence is the long-time stability of sociopolitical attitudes throughout a person's life.

Personal distress An individual's reactions to the suffering of others, including horror, shock, helplessness, or concern. Since personal distress focuses on the self, it can motivate people to ignore or avoid the suffering of others, rather than to offer assistance.

Personal entitlement What a person believes that he or she deserves from a job or relationship.

Personal stereotypes An individual's own beliefs about the attributes of members of a particular group. Personal stereotypes may be similar to or different from cultural stereotypes.

Phantom-other technique A laboratory technique for studying interpersonal attraction, in which one person is provided information about another person (who, in reality, doesn't exist).

Pique technique A technique for gaining compliance by making an unusual request that will disrupt the target's refusal script and capture his or her attention.

Planning fallacy Consistently overestimating how quickly and easily one can achieve a goal and underestimating the amount of time, money, or effort required to reach that goal.

Pocketbook voting Voting choices that maximize the benefits to the voter's own financial situation.

Political socialization The process by which young people acquire political attitudes; it often (but not always) occurs in the preadult years and with parental influence.

Positive illusions Mildly but falsely positive self-enhancing perceptions of one's personal qualities.

Positivity bias A general tendency to express positive evaluations of people more often then negative evaluations. Also called the "leniency effect" or "person positivity bias."

Possible selves Schemas that people hold concerning what they may become in the future.

Prejudice The affective component of group antagonisms; disliking a group or the members of a group.

Primacy The tendency to use an initial impression to organize and interpret subsequent information.

Priming The tendency for recent thoughts about material to influence the interpretation of subsequent information.

Principle of least interest According to social exchange theory, the balance of power in a relationship is affected by the relative dependency of the two partners. The principle of least interest states that the partner who is less interested (less dependent) tends to have greater power.

Prisoner's dilemma A laboratory game widely used in studies of competition and cooperation. It poses the fundamental dilemma of whether to compete (with the hope of gaining large rewards at the expense of the other person) or to cooperate (with the hope of receiving lesser personal rewards but greater joint rewards).

Private self-consciousness A chronic tendency to focus on the private self. Privately self-conscious people try to analyze themselves, think about themselves a great deal, and are attentive to their inner feelings.

Prosocial aggression Aggressive acts that support commonly accepted social norms, such as a soldier shooting an enemy sniper during combat.

Prosocial behavior Behavior that helps or is intended to help others, regardless of the helper's motives. Prosocial behavior is a broader category than altruism.

Prototype A schema defined by the specific features of a particular type of person, social role, or situation, such as snob, librarian, or birthday party.

Psychoanalytic theory Freud's theory of human personality and behavior. It emphasizes instincts, unconscious motivation, and the psychological defenses used for protection against one's own irrational drives.

Psychodynamic theories Theories that analyze attitudes and behavior as resulting from deep motivational tensions and conflicts. Psychoanalytic theory is the best known of these.

Psychological control The belief that one can exert personal control over events, whether or not that control actually exists or is ever exercised.

Public self-consciousness A chronic tendency to be concerned with how one appears to others. Publicly self-conscious people are concerned about what others think of them, how they look, and how they appear to others. Contrasts with private self-consciousness.

Punishment An aversive stimulus that reduces the likelihood that the preceding response will occur again.

R

Racial ambivalence A form of racism that reflects conflict between egalitarian values and stereotypes that minorities do not work hard enough.

Rally-round-the-flag effect In political psychology, a surge in presidential approval in the general public after a highly publicized international incident involving the United States.

Random assignment Placement of subjects in experimental conditions in a manner that guarantees that assignment is made entirely by chance, such as by using a random numbers table. This is an essential characteristic of an experiment.

Random sample A group of people participating in a study who are selected from the broad population by a random process, and who therefore are representative of that broad population.

Rape Forced sexual activity without one partner's consent.

Rational choice theory A principal rival to political psychological theories, rational choice theory views people as motivated by self-interest and acting rationally within the limits of their information. This theory is derived from neoclassical economics.

Reactance theory Brehm's concept that people attempt to maintain their freedom of action. When this freedom is threatened, people do whatever they can to restore it, for instance, by refusing to comply with a request.

Realistic group conflict theory The theory that antagonism between groups arises from real conflicts of interest and the frustrations those conflicts produce.

Reasoned action model A model predicting an individual's overt behavior from conscious behavioral intentions, which, in turn, are based on calculations about the effects of his or her behavior and others' evaluations of it.

Reference group A group to which a person belongs or that a person uses as a basis of comparison. The group serves as a standard for the person's own behavior and attitudes. The group's norms can act as a persuasive force leading to attitude change, or they can prevent change by supporting the individual's position when it is attacked.

Reflected appraisal Self-evaluation based on the perceptions and evaluations of others.

Reinforcement The process by which a person or animal learns to exhibit a particular response by being rewarded when it is demonstrated.

Related-attributes similarity Similarity to another person not in a target attribute, but in attributes related to that target attribute, such as background or preparation.

Relative deprivation Feelings of personal or social discontent that arise from the belief that some persons or groups are faring more poorly than others, or more poorly than they have in the past.

Replication Because any single study is flawed, a hallmark of good research is replication. In its simplest form, replication means that researchers are able to reproduce the findings of others if they re-create the methods. It is also important to conduct conceptual replications, in which different research procedures are used to explore the same conceptual relationship.

Reverse-causality problem The problem that arises in correlational research when the presumed cause might in fact be the actual effect. Children who watch a great deal of television do less well in school than children who watch little television. However, is their television viewing causing their poor grades? Or does their poor school performance cause them to escape from schoolwork by watching TV?

Risky shift After taking part in a group discussion of an issue, people are sometimes willing to support riskier decisions than they were before the group discussion. This is part of a more general process of group polarization, which can lead to either riskier or more cautious decisions, depending on the initial views of group members.

S

Salience The quality that makes a particular stimulus stand out and be noticed. Bright, noisy, colorful, unusual, and novel stimuli are usually the most salient.

Sanctioned aggression Aggression that is permissible (though not necessarily encouraged) according to the norms of the individual's social group.

Schema An organized system or structure of cognitions about a stimulus, such as a person, a personality type, a group, a role, or an event.

Script A schema that describes the expected sequence of events in a well-known situation. For example, the script for going to a restaurant includes being seated, looking over the menu, ordering, eating, and paying the server.

Selective exposure The tendency to be exposed more to information (such as propaganda) favoring the individual's prior opinion than to information favoring the opposite position.

Self-affirmation People cope with specific threats to their self-worth by reaffirming unrelated aspects of themselves.

Self-awareness The state of experiencing oneself as an object of one's own attention.

Self-complexity The number of dimensions that people use to think about themselves. Some people think about themselves in many ways, whereas other people think of themselves primarily in one or two ways.

Self-concept The collection of beliefs we hold about ourselves.

Self-disclosure The sharing of intimate information or feelings about oneself with another person. Self-disclosure can be descriptive (revelations that describe things about oneself) or evaluative (the emphasis one gives to one's personal assessment of people and situations).

Self-discrepancy A discrepancy between how we perceive ourselves to be and how we would ideally like to be or believe others think we should be.

Self-efficacy Specific expectations that we hold about our abilities to accomplish certain tasks.

Self-enhancement The need to hold a positive view of oneself and to protect oneself from negative feedback.

Self-esteem The value one places on oneself.

Self-evaluation maintenance model Tesser's analysis of when people react to the success of others with pride (basking in reflected glory) or discontent (suffering by comparison). A key factor is whether the performance of the other is relevant to one's self-concept or not.

Self-fulfilling prophecy The tendency for people's expectations to influence their attitudes and behavior. Prejudice can serve as a self-fulfilling prophecy by influencing how the prejudiced person acts toward the target, which may, in turn, influence the target to act in a way that confirms the first person's prejudices.

Self-handicapping Engaging in actions that produce insurmountable obstacles to success, so that the inevitable failure can later be attributed to the obstacle rather than to one's own lack of ability.

Self-interest The idea that attitudes or behavior is motivated by what is best for the individual's short-term material well-being.

Self-monitoring In the study of self-presentation, the tendency to emphasize impression management to a great extent. Snyder and colleagues have developed a paper-and-pencil test to assess this personality disposition. On the Self-Monitoring Scale, high scorers are especially sensitive to situational cues about appropriate behavior. In health psychology, self-monitoring is observing and recording a target behavior (such as smoking) to highlight its frequency and the factors with which it co-occurs.

Self-perception theory The theory that people infer their attitudes from their overt behavior and from their perceptions of the external situation, rather than from their own internal state.

Self-presentation Deliberate efforts to act in ways that create a particular impression of the self, often a favorable impression.

Self-promotion Conveying positive information about oneself to others through one's actions or by saying positive things about oneself.

Self-regulation The ways people control and direct their own actions.

Self-schema A cognitive structure that represents how one thinks about oneself in a particular domain and how one organizes one's experience in that domain.

Self-serving attributional bias The tendency for people to see their positive behaviors as internally caused and their negative behaviors (such as failures) as caused by external circumstances.

Self-verification The process of seeking out and interpreting situations that confirm one's self-concept and avoiding or resisting situations and feedback that differ from one's self-concept.

Sense of group position The sense of members of a dominant group that they are superior, that their advantaged position is deserved, and that members of subordinate groups are threatening to take those privileges away.

Sequential lineup A police lineup in which potential perpetrators are shown one at a time. The witness must decide whether each person is the perpetrator before seeing the next person.

Sexual harassment Unwelcome sexual advances, requests for sexual favors, and other verbal or physical conduct of a sexual nature that are connected to employment or create an intimidating, hostile, or offensive environment at work or school.

Shift of meaning The tendency of the connotations of a trait to change when placed in a different context. This is the explanation for context effects by cognitive theories of impression formation.

Shock-competition technique Experimental procedure in which subjects compete in a reaction time game and the winner shocks the loser.

Shock-learning technique Experimental procedure in which a naive subject is a "teacher" and is supposed to shock the "learner" (who is a confederate) when the learner makes an error.

Show-up A police lineup in which a single suspect is presented to an eyewitness, who must determine whether that individual is the perpetrator.

Simultaneous lineup A lineup in which several potential suspects are shown next to each other and the witness is asked to select the perpetrator.

Situational attribution Perceiving the cause of a person's action as lying in situational forces acting on the person, such as social influence or economic incentives.

Sleeper effect Delayed attitude changes that are not apparent immediately after exposure to the communication.

Social cognition The study of how people form inferences and make judgments based on social information.

Social comparison The act of evaluating one's abilities, opinions, or emotions with those of another person or persons.

Social comparison theory Festinger proposed that people are driven to evaluate themselves. In the absence of objective nonsocial criteria, people evaluate themselves by comparison with other people. In an uncertain or ambiguous situation, people may want to affiliate with others in order to make social comparisons.

Social compensation A response that occurs when an individual expends great effort in a collective setting in order to compensate for others in the group who he or she believes are performing inadequately.

Social density The objective number of people in a given space, such as the number of people sharing a dormitory room or the number of people per square mile in a major city.

Social dilemma A situation in which the short-term choice that is most rewarding for an individual will ultimately lead to negative outcomes for all concerned. Social dilemmas pit the short-term interests of the individual against the long-term interests of the group (including the individual).

Social dominance theory The theory that all societies are organized in group hierarchies, which are sustained through discrimination, legitimizing myths, and the efforts of individuals with a high social dominance orientation.

Social exchange theory A theory that analyzes the interaction between people in terms of the outcomes (rewards minus costs) that the individuals exchange with each other.

Social facilitation The tendency for people (and other kinds of animals) to perform better on simple, well-learned tasks when others are present than when they are alone.

Social identity In the study of the self, that part of an individual's self-concept that derives from his or her membership in a social group or groups, together with the value and emotional significance attached to that membership.

Social impact theory A theory, according to Latané, in which the influence (either positive or negative) of an audience on a target individual depends on three factors: the number of observers, the strength of the audience (e.g., their importance), and the immediacy of the audience in time or space.

Social inhibition The impairment or inhibition of an individual's performance brought about by the presence of others.

Socialization The process by which a person acquires the rules, standards, and values of his or her family, group, and culture.

Social leadership Activities designed to promote group harmony and cohesiveness. The social leader focuses on the social and emotional aspects of interaction in order to keep a group running smoothly and happily. Sometimes contrasted with task leadership.

Social learning theory A modern offshoot of behaviorism that places primary emphasis on how people learn social behaviors from one another, especially through social reinforcement and modeling.

Social loafing Individuals sometimes work less hard as members of a group than they would if they worked alone. Individuals may feel that their own efforts will be less recognizable in a group, a belief that may lead to a diffusion of responsibility and diminished effort by individuals.

Social norms Rules and expectations about how members of a social group should think or behave. These standards determine whether an individual's specific actions, attitudes, or beliefs are approved or disapproved by the individual's social group. Also called "group norms."

Social penetration Altman and Taylor's theory about the process by which people gradually attain closeness and intimacy in a relationship. The theory emphasizes that as a relationship develops, self-disclosure increases in both breadth (range of topics) and depth (intimacy).

Social power One person's ability to influence deliberately the behavior, thoughts, or feelings of another person.

Social psychology The scientific study of how people think about, influence, and relate to others.

Social role A set of social norms (rules and understandings) about how a person in a particular social position (such as mother or professor) is expected to behave. Roles define the rights and responsibilities of members of couples, groups, and other social units.

Social status A person's rank or privilege in a group, based on such characteristics as age, gender, or position in a business.

Social support An interpersonal exchange characterized by emotional concern, instrumental aid, the provision of information to another, or help in self-appraisal. Social support is believed to buffer people against the adverse effects of stress and may promote physical health as well.

Sociotropic voting Voting choices motivated by perceptions of what is good for the nation rather than by perceptions of what is good for the self.

Source derogation In persuasive communication situations, reducing inconsistency by derogating the source of a discrepant communication rather than by changing one's attitudes.

Source-monitoring theory Source monitoring is the process of identifying the source of a piece of information stored in memory. According to source-monitoring theory, eyewitnesses sometimes include postevent information in their descriptions of an event because they do not correctly identify the source of that information.

Statistical information In social cognition, information based on a number of individuals or events, such as averages or totals. Such information tends to be less persuasive and to have less impact on judgments than inferior but more vivid case-history information.

Stereotype Beliefs about the typical characteristics of members of a group or social category. In the study of prejudice, stereotypes are the cognitive component of group antagonism.

Stereotype threat The threat that targets of stereotypes feel in situations in which the stereotype is salient. This threat can harm their performance in ways that are consistent with the stereotype.

Story model The most theoretically developed and empirically tested model of juror decision making in social psychology. The model assumes that jurors use the evidence presented at trial to form in their minds stories about the events in question, and that they then evaluate alternative story accounts on different criteria. According to the model, jurors then select the verdict that is the best possible match to that story account of the events.

Stress A process of appraising environmental events as harmful, threatening, or challenging and of responding to that appraisal with physiological, emotional, cognitive, and behavioral changes. Stress occurs when people perceive that their personal resources may not be sufficient to meet the demands of the environment.

Stressful life event An event in a person's life that requires him or her to make changes; negative, ambiguous, and uncontrollable events are most likely to be perceived as stressful. Stressful life events are believed to contribute to the risk of illness.

Subtyping Breaking down large categories of people such as women or the elderly into subcategories, such as homemakers, professional women, and grandmothers.

Superordinate categories Large and inclusive group categories, often created to defuse conflict between smaller groups.

Supportive defense In attitude change, positive arguments for an individual's own position, provided in advance of a persuasive attack to help protect that attitude.

Symbolic racism Antagonism toward a racial group based on prejudice and values rather than on self-interest.

Systematic processing Careful scrutiny of the arguments in a persuasive communication, which gives argument strength more weight, induces counterarguing, and makes attitude change more enduring; minimizes the role of peripheral cues.

System variables Factors affecting eyewitness identification that are under the direct control of the criminal justice or legal systems. Lineup construction and questioning techniques are examples of system variables.

T

Task leadership Activities designed to accomplish the goals of a group and to get the work of the group done successfully. The task leader directs and organizes the group in carrying out a specific task. Sometimes contrasted with social leadership.

That's-not-all technique A technique for gaining compliance in which the influencer first offers one deal and then, while the person is considering this possibility, improves the offer.

Theory of planned behavior A theory of the relation between attitudes and behavior based on how people consider and weigh the implications that a particular behavior may have as they form their intentions with respect to actions.

Third-variable problem A problem with interpreting correlational research. When two variables are correlated with each other, is one the cause of the other? Or is some third variable the cause of both?

Transfer of affect Changing attitude A by transferring to it the affect one already has toward object B.

Transsexuals Persons whose psychological gender identity differs from their biological sex, for example, someone who is anatomically a male but believe that he is really a female trapped in a male body.

Transtheoretical model of behavior change An analysis of the health behavior change process that draws on the stages and processes people go through in order to bring about successful long-term behavior change. Stages include precontemplation, contemplation, preparation, action, and maintenance. Successful attitude or behavior change at each stage depends on the appropriateness of the intervention. For example, attitude change materials help move people from precontemplation to contemplation, whereas relapse prevention techniques help move people from action to maintenance.

Typicality effect The tendency to behave toward an out-group member who is seen as most typical of that group in ways more consistent with one's stereotypes about the out-group.

U

Upward social comparison The comparison of one's traits or abilities with those of someone who is better off than the oneself.

V

Voir dire At the beginning of every trial, the judge may excuse from serving jurors who exhibit biases or who are unable to be open-minded about the case. This process is called "voir dire," from the Old French for "to tell the truth." The belief is that this process improves the quality of jury deliberations and verdicts.

Voluntary false confession A free and willing confession to a crime one did not commit.

W

Weapon focus effect A phenomenon in which eyewitnesses remember more information about the weapon used to commit a crime than about the criminal who was holding the weapon.

Working self-concept Those aspects of the self-concept that are salient in a particular situational context.